A Casual Observer's Notes on Nature

George Mitchell

To the memory of Mrs Flux

'Feeky'

She taught me how to think

I don't want to believe, I want to know

Carl Sagan (astrophysicist deceased)

Contents

PROLOGUE

You? Write a book about nature? Who are you kidding? What do you know about nature that experts on television programmes or other great authors cannot tell? Furthermore, what do you know about writing? It was hardly an encouraging start but the more I thought about it, the more I realised that I had nothing to lose. If no one reads these notes, then I don't care (I do really).

The first comment is not quite true. There are many things that anyone can observe that are not obvious about nature. There are many anomalies in everyday experience which, when pointed out to others, can be a fascinating surprise. They may go unnoticed by many. Some are difficult to explain but there are no explanations in this book. It is based purely on observation. Neither are there any opinions, although I apologise in advance if any personal leanings on emotive subjects shine through. There are definitely some maybes. You cannot observe without thinking 'why' but the maybes are just that, not opinions. No one should be able to take me to task for inaccuracies as I have just written down what I have seen or experienced in my lifetime. However, it's guaranteed there are many who will tell me not to believe what I see. Also, I have to be careful not to exaggerate and that is easy to do to prove a point. A flock of fifty five geese can easily turn into *around a hundred*. As my mum used to say to others, 'I've told him a million times not to exaggerate. I don't know who he gets it from.'

Nature is a huge subject. It covers absolutely everything. There is no such thing as an expert in nature as a whole, but there are experts whom I admire in its many spheres. I state categorically that I am not even close to being an expert, just an interested bystander, one *Homo sapiens vulgaris* with a tale to tell. Many of my observations requiring explanation may be answered by these experts but it is difficult, sometimes, to get their attention. There is a subservient feeling in approaching a university professor with an anomalous subject, often generating a condescending answer such as, 'oh well it's probably just . . .' Although not all encompassing, it happens throughout the

1

hierarchy of academia and industry. 'I am the boss, so you can't tell me. I tell you.' Friends will tell me something which a person in an influential position has stated, or that they have read, about the natural world and I often have to challenge that view as I have seen something that proves it is not true. They don't like it. 'How would you know better?' Why wouldn't I? My sight is as good as theirs. This is my inspiration for these notes and throughout you will find many such examples.

This book, although touching on other spheres of nature, is mostly about wildlife and what I find fascinating about its many aspects. It is very much my personal journey. It is written in the anticipation that the notes equally fascinate other like-minded people and, also hopefully, some with just a passing interest in wildlife. Some subjects may be common knowledge and a reader may already know about them but they surely are still of interest. They are not meant to be read and torn apart by 'experts'. I sincerely hope that they shall not and, indeed, hope that they cannot be contradicted. Explanations and enlightenments though will be gratefully received.

Part 1

INTRODUCTION

Children are swayed by the advice given by their parents and for very good reason. Throughout human history this was advice on how to survive by someone who had until, at least, more than reproductive age. Don't eat this fruit, beware of that danger, keep away from this, don't do that. Today we still need that advice but it is complicated by much more. Keep to society's rules, follow this religion, vote for this political party, etc, etc. These subjects are not really to do with survival. I have noticed that most people I have met in life (and more) vote as their parents did, they believe the same religious doctrines (or indeed none) and generally follow the same lifestyles including the same ideals of bettering their status financially. It is by no means all encompassing. There are many rebels, including me, but the early indoctrination had to be shaken off.

There were two pieces of advice given to me by my father in my childhood. 'Listen carefully to what is being said' and 'look and learn.' The former always posed a problem. That's why he said it. I was too impetuous, too eager to please, always getting the wrong end of the stick by not taking time and analysing. Outwith my small home geographical area I struggled to communicate, being constrained by a bastard dialect, talking far too fast and having an accent like gravel being thrown at a corrugated iron roof. I still struggle. 'Look and learn' though was different and appealing. It gave time to think and analyse: to work out all the reasons and possibilities and come up with enlightenment. It is what I did and have done all my life. The result of that mindset was to contradict much of the other indoctrination because it did not make sense, except of course the survival advice. I am still a primitive being.

My dad meant well. I would come home from school and recount what I had learned that day, possibly looking for a little help in understanding it. On some occasions he would contradict the teaching. 'The teacher is definitely wrong there.' He was not an academic but was self-taught. You could not fault his survival tactics that he handed down but his science knowledge, especially, was suspect although he was hugely interested. Nine out of ten times, the teacher was proved correct but what stuck in my mind was the one time out of ten she was wrong. This led me to question everything to the point of the teachers saying, 'Why can't you just accept it and let the class move on?' A teacher was asking me to accept a statement that, as far as I knew, may be untrue. My report card stated 'slow to accept new ideas' reflecting this. It was correct but once the new idea was finally accepted it stuck forever. I loved to be enlightened. There must surely be millions like me.

My father had a hard upbringing in a huge family, brought up through the great recession, living in a tiny cottage. Much of his early life had, of necessity, to be spent outdoors which led to his closeness to nature. This affinity was passed on to me. Always a keen gardener, due to a need to provide produce for the table, my early plant knowledge was gleaned from him. His garden was the image of his mother's not least because the plants were divisions of the specimens in her garden. Mostly they were herbaceous plants, named by him as he was taught. As my interest in biology and taxonomy grew in teen years, I saw mistakes. His Canterbury bells turned out to be *Dicentra exima*, a cultivated variety of the weed fumitory. Shakespeare described it as 'rank fumitory', being the first plant to colonise uncultivated ground before the invasion of the introduced non-native menace, rosebay Willowherb. His *Spiraea* turned out to be *Astilbe*, not a shrub but an herbaceous lookalike with its similar leaf shape and flowers resembling *Spiraea triumphans* and similar cultivars. This anomaly is still a mistake made regularly by amateur gardeners today. Trees he loved to identify. 'That's an oak' which was correct but he failed to say which one out of the hundreds of species, sub species and varieties that exist. 'You can tell the difference between a sycamore [*Acer*] and a plane tree [*Platanus*] by the leaf veins.' Comparing the two picked leaf specimens he would point out that the sycamore had red veins and the plane, pale. The confusion is easy as a sycamore bears the Latin name *Acer pseudoplatanus*, meaning 'false plane'. What he held in his hand was indeed a sycamore leaf but the other a Norway maple (*Acer platanoides*). That Latin name also hints at a similarity with *Platanus*. The bark of some maples is also similar to the plane to add to the confusion but if he had compared the fruits he would have seen that the two species are not even closely related. There are no plane trees in this region.

I have to modify that statement. I do not KNOW for certain that there are no plane trees growing at this latitude in Scotland. I have learned to watch out for these statements by others. What I should have written is 'to the best of my knowledge' or 'as far as I know.' The more scientific way to play safe would be '*Platanus* is not indigenous to these parts.' The reason for the correction is that, perhaps in some sheltered area of some botanic garden or old estate, there may be a specimen or specimens.

I wrestled with telling him he was mistaken on these points and did slip it in occasionally but didn't push it. I think he eventually bowed to that particular area of greater acquired knowledge. What I couldn't pull him up on though was his superior gardening skills. He was a great grower and producer. I pause again, just to push the previously made point: I am not an expert in any field of nature. Merely an observer as I was taught. These notes are a result of that: my lifelong philosophy of 'Look and Learn'.

I was city born and bred. Living in a simple, post war scheme on the banks of a river with a derelict, previously lordly, estate on the doorstep I was always fascinated by nature. Wild animals, birds, fish, insects and plants were my complete interests and many other kids were the same. My collection of different species of slug was of neighbourhood renown but they had to go as their slime trails up my arm caused warts in line with the trail. The reason may be out there but I haven't found it yet. For my eighth birthday present, after pleas, I got white mice which lived in either an orange box or my jacket pocket. They went to school with me, much to the horror of one paranoid female teacher. Rabbits by the dozen (literally) were bred for showing by my father. Tin baths full of frogs and toads. Sammy the duck lived under the gooseberry bush. One bantam cock was a short lived pet. The neighbours weren't chuffed with his serenade at four in the morning. He was swapped for a pair of fantail pigeons who were in their turn swapped for two racers but that's another story. There were many more creatures lugged home including hedgehogs, bats, a rook and a jackdaw who I taught to talk (well,

I knew what it was saying). All this in a post war prefab rear garden. Things changed. Development ruined my wilderness so when, in early adult life, I saw a chance to move to the countryside, albeit on the outskirts of the city, I jumped at the chance. I could enjoy nature every day of my life without interference. I did for many years but it's not the same anymore. In my lifetime, the countryside around me has changed. It is no longer managed by traditional methods. Intensive farming has taken over. No more partridge, lapwing, skylark, reed or corn bunting. No mistle thrush and only the odd song thrush which relies on my 'lawn' (it wouldn't sound so pretentious if you saw it). Not even oyster catcher or curlew now around here. Very little brown hare either. Small streams teemed with brook trout. Not anymore. All were very common species when I arrived. It's not all encompassing as there are areas not so badly affected but they are still affected.

These changes have been recorded before and predicted. They're not new but are part of my observations which corroborate these predictions. It cannot be denied, that is how it is now.

Nature must inevitably adapt in response to changing environment but these changes are exclusively man made to the detriment of wildlife. If we change their environment then it is predicted that there will be changes to ours and they won't all be as good as one may think for we are all part of nature, surely, all just carbon based life forms linked by our DNA. If I am to write about wildlife I had better know what that means. I know what the *wild* bit means but *life*? What does it mean to be alive? So I have always wondered and will start with my quest for the answer to the biggest question of all, just as everyone else must have wondered, 'What exactly is life?'

1

LIFE

The words, *'What is life?'* have been the subject of many books or chapters of books by many eminent scientists so you won't find the answer in these humble notes. However, you won't find the answer in any of theirs either but it doesn't stop them, or myself, or you, contemplating it.

On the face of it, it seems an arrogant belief that we, *Homo sapiens*, are special and that all plants and animals are put on earth for our benefit and for us to use as we wish. Thank goodness we are now enlightened by heavily scrutinised evidence. That comes in many forms but the DNA revolution has put the final nail in the coffin of these old beliefs. Unfortunately not everyone wants to know. When I look around I don't need DNA evidence to see that life is just life, whatever its form. Plants are just as alive as you or I. There is a tree in my garden, an ordinary tree, *Ulmus glabra*, (wych elm). Ordinary it may look but as I sit looking out the window and contemplate its life, I am fascinated. It belies its age. It's not a big tree, so it doesn't look old. There are actually six mature trees in the garden but this one faces the elements more than the rest. It grows at an elevation of 560 feet above sea level in the North East Scotland and that's exposed. Its knurled and twisted branches strive to put on annual growth against the prevailing sou' westerlies. A study of the first Ordinance Survey maps of the early 1800s shows these very trees marked as individual specimens. That means that this diminutive tree was of a size big enough then to be individually recorded, so how old is it? I can only surmise that it must then have been at least fifty years old at that time, possibly a lot older as elms are not fast growers. It could have been in my garden when Bonnie Prince Charlie was getting thrashed at Culloden. It could easily be 300 years old or more. Every year it comes into season and reproduces sexually just like we humans. It struggles to put on growth so that it can carry out that function. It's easy to see how, but why? It cannot think as it doesn't have a brain, a heart or a nervous system. It is not even aware of its existence, so what's the point. Well maybe that **IS** the point, there may be no point. That may be just how it is and therein lays the enigma for *intelligent* humans. They need to see a reason for life: a meaning. If I take a cutting of new growth, I can grow a new elm tree, but it's not a new tree, it's the same tree: a clone. I can take a section of the root system and do the same, so where is the centre of life? In fact with micro propagation the tree can be recreated from tissue cultures of a few cells. Life, it seems, has to be at the sub cellular level. There my observation has to stop. It's too micro for me to see. Many scientific books can try to explain it further but I am sure they were born out of these same observations.

Propagation raises another question. If successive cuttings are taken from clones ad infinitum you have, in essence, eternal life. *Populus tremula* (aspen) rarely sets seed. Apparently, in Scotland, seedlings have never been germinated in the last 10,000 years. I would question that on the premise that you would have to identify by DNA every single specimen to come up with that statement. However, it still may be true. It spreads by sending out roots which sprout new growth which can grow into magnificent trees. Analysis has shown that specimens are some of the oldest living organisms on the planet. My own country's 'Fortingall Yew' in a Perthshire churchyard is between 2,000 and 5,000 years old. The bristlecone pine 'Methuselah' in the Great Basin in Nevada is reputed to be over 5,000 years old. Giant sequoias such as 'General Sherman' and 'The President', tall though they are, are a mere 3,000 years old. None of these examples are old, competition wise. The American version of our aspen is *Populus tremulosa*. An individual named 'Pando' in Utah is **80,000** years old. Not only that but at an estimated 6,500 tons, is the heaviest organism discovered on earth. New information, still to be confirmed, is that another clone in Utah could be as much as **one million** years old: one organism. My native Scotland is the home of such organisms, albeit in much reduced numbers due to human activity. Aspen woodlands were a great resource of timber in human prehistory.

When does death come to these organisms? Does it ever? It will when Earth follows Mars' history or when the sun's hydrogen runs out, but in human timescale, it's as near as dammit to immortality. Can that be justified?

If life is perceived not as the organism but much simpler, then all life has the ability to be immortal. DNA science has shown that I pass on my genes to my children, so when I die, part of me lives on. Therefore all my ancestors can say the same. So there **IS** such a thing as everlasting life. I am not going to die without a trace, biologically, so I have that going for me. I hope to live forever.

This next story was related to me by my zoology teacher whom I mention later.

Many years ago a small village hidden in the dales of Yorkshire had a peculiar affliction. Many of the inhabitants were not normal. Zombies would be a good modern word to describe them. In fact it was probably this story which inspired the creation of that word and the science fiction horror film 'Village of the Damned'. Having no character or all the go ahead attributes of normal, healthy human beings they spent their miserable lives shuffling around. Inbreeding was said to be the cause and they were shunned, as such practice was a cardinal sin in those godly times. They spawned the name 'cretins' that is still used today to describe such behaviour. This anomalous society came to the attention of evolving medical science and researchers wondered if the cause could be environmental. It came to light that they had no contact with the sea or any food from it. This provided an inkling as to the true cause. Soil, plant and domesticated food animals were sampled and it was found that there was no recording of one particular trace element essential to human and animal health: **iodine**. When iodine was administered over a period, I believe from seaweed extract, they made a 100% recovery and went on to lead normal lives. It was hailed as a miracle back then of course. No it wasn't. It was a chemical.

9

What's going on here? Any first year medical student knows the answer that a small amount of iodine is essential for the functioning of the thyroid gland. The thyroxine it produces controls many bodily functions. The ocean and its inhabitants are rich in iodine, as are soils that have been associated with the sea in antiquity. The soil in the Yorkshire village had no such contact and the inhabitants were starved of it. Iodine can be deposited by precipitation but in areas of high rainfall leaching carries this mineral away. Elevated inland areas are particularly prone and incidences were found in Alpine countries as well. This dependence has a history. According to DNA and fossil records, for a large part of our evolutionary existence, our distant ancestors lived and evolved in the oceans and iodine was part of their evolutionary make up. When they finally ventured out onto dry land a dependency on it came with them. My zoology teacher may have made the story more interesting but then I was only fifteen and all zoology was interesting. How influential was that way of teaching, telling a story leading up to a revelation? Her influence is reflected in my notes in this book as you will see. There is nothing like a story to make a point more interesting. It's how I have always enjoyed being enlightened. Eventually her story on that subject was to catch my attention even more.

Medical research into the affliction didn't start with the cretins. Normal people could get these symptoms to a lesser degree from abnormalities of the thyroid gland which, in humans, is in the neck area. Goitre is one where the gland swells up. An underactive one causes lethargy and other symptoms, whilst one that is overactive causes the opposite effect, coupled with bulging eyes and many other afflictions. It was research into these quite common conditions which led physicians and scientists to put two and two together and link them with the Yorkshire cases. Further research led to other conclusions. As people age, the gland, in common with other glands in the body, begins to become less efficient. Blood tests will reveal the level of thyroxine in the blood and a balancing dose, derived from the same gland in domestic animals, can work wonders. It was also discovered that there was a genetic predisposition to premature under functioning of this gland and that's where I come in. As my mum aged it affected her and other family members on her side. It should come as no surprise then that I was affected. Up until then it would be hard to find a more active person. Tried everything, wanted more . . . It was commented, on more than one occasion, that I lived three lives in one. I had to make the most of my limited lifetime.

'My, it's cold today' I shivered. 'No its not, what the hell's wrong with you?' These conversations became more and more common. My skin felt dry and flaky as a result of stopping sweating. Appetite waned as did normal bodily functions and general virility. Worst of all I couldn't be bothered doing anything anymore but it didn't bother me in the slightest. As symptoms progressed, if someone spoke to me, I would gear myself up to reply but the words just didn't come. I had become a zombie. If someone is sick, they see a physician but I couldn't be bothered. You can visualise the Yorkshire cretins feeling the same. It didn't bother them that they were the way they were. I was forced into an appointment and after ten seconds, diagnosis was complete, to be confirmed by a blood test. The level of thyroxine was found to be zero. I couldn't care less. Six months later the course of treatment worked wonders. All back to normal and I had my three lives back. Only then did I realise the seriousness of the condition I had suffered. Well, it runs in the family and my mum and her kin suffered to a much lesser degree. It's all part of the ageing process. There was one slight difference in my case. I was thirty-four.

It is very unusual for the thyroid gland to fail altogether in an otherwise healthy young man and I am eternally grateful to medical science. I will be all my life and I am not in the slightest inconvenienced by daily ingesting some slaughtered cow extract to keep me being me. That's the scariest bit of the lot and why this experience fits into this chapter. People think they are in charge of their personalities, but they are not. **Personality is chemical**.

This discovery of medical science coincides in history with another author's storyline of the effects of a chemical on personality. Robert Louis Stevenson may have used that very inspiration in his 'Dr Jekyll and Mr Hyde'.

As a further point of interest, how much of this magic substance, iodine, does a human body require for good health? Answer:

11

One ten thousandth of a gram per day. Now that we know the cause and effect, with the World Health Organisation's existence, the world should not be affected today but it is. As mentioned, inland areas and areas of high leaching are prone and the country worst affected is China where an estimated seven million are still affected, 200,000 of these being cretins of the highest order with stunted growth, bulging tongues and dysfunctional brains. All are easily treatable. The Chinese government is implementing a programme of introducing supplementary iodine in normal table salt but in these desperately poor country areas they are being hampered by the cheap supply of the normal commodity in a black market.

Life forms may look complicated but they are, in essence, simple. The whole experience of hypothyroidism brought home to me that life is made of many tiny parts, all doing their own thing, depending on one another to function as a whole. Just like a computer. This magical piece of modern life is simple in its make-up. Basically just a lot of little switches responding to electrical signals. Of course, a computer is not alive. It's as dead as a lump of wood. Well, actually that depends on how old the lump of wood is. A newly cut log goes on functioning as it did when it formed part of the tree. Only when sustenance stops with drought does it die. It is also infinitely more intricate than a computer at cellular and especially subcellular level. A plantation of trees was planted near me in parkland and despite my advice that the wrong species was being planted for the wet conditions, I was ignored. Not an unusual occurrence. To save money, they had a brilliant idea to make support stakes from a large pile of felled *dead* wild scrub trees from the thinnings of another area. Suitable lengths were trimmed and pointed and the planting carried out. Nowadays they congratulate themselves on their work, seeing it reach maturity. The only problem, not admitted, is that there are none of the originally planted trees existing. The stakes though are now a beautiful copse of rowan, willow and alder. It's not exactly life after death as the wood hadn't died in the first place. It was just trying to survive and the environment was more conducive to its survival than the unsuitable healthy ones. The complexity of life seems unfathomable but, like the computer, it is basically made up of simplicity built up to function as a whole. In my electrical engineering youth, I was in charge of

12

the running of a highly complex system. Whole rooms, pre computer days, filled with rack upon rack of wires and seemingly endless frames of electromechanical switches. In reality, it was the forerunner of what we now know as a computer. It was a pre-digital age computer - same principles, same outcome, just somewhat slower, massively larger and very much more cumbersome. The whole caboodle buzzed, whirred and interacted perfectly. An outsider commented, 'How can you know where all these wires go?' My reply was that I didn't, and I didn't have to. All I knew was what the outcome should be and if it went wrong, the skill was to work out which little event was wrong. Once that was established, fault finding was confined to a simple area of circuitry and 99.9% of the system was irrelevant. No different from the doctor treating a sore knee. Kidney function is irrelevant. The whole scheme only looked complicated.

We cannot really know life at all, as in Joni Mitchell's song, but science is getting close. What they are coming up with is complexity built up from simplicity. I can accept that. A new and exciting research into life's origins is being investigated. Science is looking deeper than cells and DNA for life's origins. The stuff that makes up the universe is full of energy and all of that is at subatomic level. It seems that if we are to crack the difference between rocks, reproducing bacteria and me (all made of the same atoms) then particle physics may hold the answer. It's beyond me but I await further research with baited breath.

Ultimately though, life on earth at organism level leads to the inevitable.

If the average man in the street was asked what the prerequisites were for his, or any other life form's, existence on this planet the answers would surely vary. Some may say the existence of water, others oxygen (practically the same thing), many some miracle of one god or another. Notwithstanding whether any of these are correct, my question was about **their** existence and not how life got started in the first place. The answer has to be death. For life to flourish for any length of time, death is an essential element. Without it, life would have strangled itself out of existence long before complexity of species began. Even if humans started with an Adam and Eve, the scenario is oblivion for that particular species. It's not opinion, its mathematics. Countless trillions would have swamped the planet. We die for a reason as does every other life form. We make way for future generations. It is the ultimate sacrifice for our offspring. Jesus is not unique, as the story goes in the Christian bible. 'He died so that we may live.' So will I and everyone else. I'll tell my kids to mention their gratefulness at my funeral service. So why do we fear death so much? Nobody wants to die because of the inherent will to live, especially when young. Survival is paramount. Both are written into the scheme of things, metaphorically speaking of course. It's all part of nature. This instinct to survive is evident in all life forms. Even plants take steps to survive. The difference with humans is that we are the only forms that have developed intelligence sufficiently to know death is coming and to fear it. It has been taken past the instinctive stage. We worry about what comes next and clutch at a myriad of straws thought up by a myriad of influential idealists. As my mum said, at ninety-two when she saw her body wasting away, 'I'm tired of living but afraid of dying.' A last vestige of animalistic survival instinct.

The religion of Bhuddism is surely closest to the truth. They believe all life forms are interconnected. What affects one affects others in a chain reaction. Modern science thinks that anyway and they don't call it a faith. It's a proven fact. What makes Bhuddism a religion is the next step: a leap of faith. They believe we are reincarnated into another animal life form (If there is a choice, I'll choose a rabbit for they seem to have the greatest promiscuous fun). There is absolutely no evidence to support this view which spoils an otherwise beautiful doctrine. But wait, maybe there is something in it after all. It depends on the definition of life. All forms of life contribute to its continuation. Everything is recycled: sometimes quickly by scavengers and blowfly maggots but often slowly, by fungi and micro-organisms. Every bit of me will disappear. If I happen to be covered in sediment then it may take hundreds of thousands of years to break me down and if I am very, very lucky, I will leave a rare trace of my existence in the form of my fossilised bones even further into the future. But it won't be bones. It will in effect be a model, a plaster cast of bone, hardened into sandstone. Contrary to the expression, nobody has dug up a dinosaur bone. My genes and every other organic molecule will have long since been recycled, either by my descendants, or by other life forms, including rabbits.

The way ahead seems clear for wise humans: live life to the full. Enjoy every waking minute whatever your fortunes in health and mind. There is no point in worrying about an inevitability. Then on your deathbed you can say with a smile, 'I gave it my best shot, bye.' But I don't want to die. It looks like I am not a wise human. Every one of us is governed by many instincts outwith our control. Both life and death are just part of nature, as is every other living entity. We can all agree on that but there is another side to consider.

2

SUPERNATURE

Yesterday upon the stair,
I met a man who wasn't there,
He wasn't there again today,
I wish that he would go away.

W Hugh Mearns, 'Antigonish'

I took my eight year old grandson to see an eminent astrophysicist giving a talk and slide show of the solar system and the observable universe. It was part of science week in the city and this was in the university lecture theatre giving it the feel of a real lecture. Now you may think that it was a bit advanced for an eight year old. Not a bit of it. You see, he wants to be an astrophysicist. We had arrived early and the scientist was just chatting among the audience. Intrigued by his age, he spoke to my grandson. 'Do you know much about the universe?' he asked. 'As much as you do' was the reply, to my complete embarrassment. 'Perhaps one day' kindly replied the scientist. The lecture started accompanied by an excellent slide show and throughout questions thrown at the (mostly adult) audience resulted in a small hand continually being raised next to me, beating all others.

'Does anyone recognize this?' 'It's the great red spot on Jupiter.'

'Which planet is this?' 'Venus.' Etc, etc, . . .

It got so bad that the great man started to very subtly involve the rest of the audience. But when it came to 'Can anyone tell me what this heavenly object is?' no other hand went up except his. 'Sedna, the farthest known orbiting body in our solar system' was the wee man's reply. Which brought the response, 'Oh my god, he really does know as much as me.'

It then was the audience's turn to ask questions. Many sensible ones were asked and answered until he had to acknowledge the permanently ceiling pointing hand of the red haired kid. 'What is there after the end of the universe?' Eight years old remember. 'You may have asked a bigger question than you think' the scientist replied, 'we just don't know.' The kid went on, 'Perhaps there is another universe, and then another?' Where is his mind going at that age? 'You know something? There may well be' the scientist acknowledged. End of lecture. And isn't it intriguing that this is the exact postulation science is sitting on today. Who knows, sometime in the future, one red haired scientist may crack that very question. That would make me proud but he had better grow up fast as my time is running out.

Of course he didn't know as much as the scientist. It's not unusual for young kids to apply themselves in this manner. They just have to like what they read and read he did, endlessly engrossed in his subject. A word from me brought him back to earth when I pointed out that these science books he had read were written by this very man and others. He may of course turn out to be a joiner or ditch digger. There's nothing wrong with that, but I have a mind that he is set on astrophysics and if he has the mental capacity, then he will. One thing is sure, he doesn't take after me. Feet firmly on the ground my grandson: he lives in the real world of physics and facts.

So I am driving him home afterwards, a bit late since he has school next day. It's a really dark moonless night. I am surprised when he asks, 'Can ghosts see in the dark?' 'There's no such thing as ghosts, son.' 'Yes there is' came the indignant reply, 'Caitlin's got TWO.' There is no way I can continue the conversation, not knowing the full story, but I am disappointed that this little realist has gone off track. When I asked his dad on our return, who I thought was also a realist, he admits, 'Yes, that's correct, they are the ghosts of a mother and daughter and they are seen regularly by Caitlin's family. They live in an old cottage on an old estate.' 'Goodness me' I replied, 'the lucky devils, they are sitting on a fortune.' I diverge slightly to explain.

Perhaps you can remember Uri Geller? He was an Israeli who appeared on television claiming that he could use the power of

17

thought to bend spoons. Millions saw him defy the laws of physics and bend the spoons and practically the same number of people believed he had done just that. Derren Brown does just as good nowadays. You can watch him levitate something above ground or do fantastic mind things with numbers. In America, David Blaine is amazing. In front of a crowd in New York's Central Park, he picked a caterpillar from a bush, put it in his mouth and closed it. When he opened it, a butterfly flew out. Entomologists may have picked out that the butterfly didn't match the caterpillar species. I wouldn't know but it looked good. The new UK one is Dynamo: remarkable illusions including walking on water on the River Thames.

All this is just 'magic', isn't it? There is a big difference here. The latter three go by the name magicians which everyone knows means that they perform sleight of hand, mind and eye tricks. It may be impressive but these are tricks and we all know it. Don't we all? The laws of physics changed with Derren Brown. The laws of nature short circuited in Central Park. Archimedes' Eureka moment in the bath a waste of brainpower: a body floating in water (in this case Dynamo's) apparently does not displace its own weight of water. Furthermore, they themselves admit that they are only damned good illusionists. Not so Uri Geller with the spoons. He would have us believe that he really could manipulate the laws of physics and that he really had special powers and a huge amount of people believed him.

Enter James Randi. He is an American 'magician' turned charlatan hunter. You have to be in the trade to expose how tricks are done. Now, he is not going to tell how Derren Brown, David Blaine and Dynamo perform their 'miracles' as that goes under the heading of entertainment. No, he is after the cheats and conmen/women. He promptly exposes Geller and shows the world how he did it. In fact many students in Tel Aviv were doing it but the world didn't listen. Many people still believe it was supernatural powers and to this day, Geller is a celebrity.

Randi made a lot of money as a top magician in his lifetime and so he has put his money where his mouth is. He has offered a million dollars to anyone who can prove the supernatural exists.

Doris Stokes was a medium, celebrated as the best. She drew huge audiences and made a fortune communicating with the dead and showing uncanny knowledge of victims' sorry, peoples' lives. Case by case, Randi again showed the world how she did it. Audiences continued to flock until the penny finally dropped. She had been a fraud all along. James then started turning up in the audiences of other famous mediums who were also drawing huge crowds (and making wads of money). 'The show is cancelled due to illness' was common, along with a variety of other excuses. Of what were they afraid? If they were not con merchants then they made a mint **and** the bonus of Randi's extra million.

Good news for little Caitlin's parents as well, eh? *Money for old rope* and so I passed on his details. Guess what? They didn't bother. A million *smackeroos* for the taking and they didn't want it.

Do you believe Uri Geller? Do you believe that mediums can contact the dead? Have you seen a ghost that can be regularly seen? If you are sure, then don't hesitate, the money's yours. Here are the details:

Million Dollar Challenge
James Randi Educational Foundation
2941 Fairview Park Drive, Suite 105
Falls Church
VA 22042 USA

Check out the website at *http://www.randi.org*

But I must caution you. Have the proof and don't waste his time or Banachek's, the mentalist who supervises claims. He was the only magician to sway scientists into thinking there may be something in supernatural powers. He, of course, knew there wasn't. The million dollar challenge has been running for many years now and it has yet to be won. A modest thousand claims have been made since 1996 with no success at getting past even the preliminary stage. How strange.

So is there no such thing as the supernatural? I certainly

wouldn't state that, as I am not qualified to judge. I am stating only that I, personally, have seen no corroborating proof up until now. If it were possible to throw a switch and start the world again from scratch, belief wise, I suspect that it would not be long before the supernatural got a foothold again. Life is such a mystery and it's an easy way to explain the mysteries of nature. This doesn't seem to apply to animals, only humans. There doesn't seem to be ghosts in a dog's or a chimp's (or a worm's or bacterium's) world as far as they are concerned. Any pets I have owned were not afraid of the dark. There exists in human experience many strange occurrences which can't on the face of it be explained by conventional wisdom. It doesn't naturally follow though that any 'supernature' is involved. It's difficult to approach any such scenario with an open mind because we have all heard the stories or seen the films. In early life that is a huge influence and I am no exception.

Santa Claus is one thing: harmless, childhood fun. Grimm's fairy tales though, in my experience sows the seeds of unreal scenarios. Hansel and Gretel may stick in a child's mind. Cannibalism of children isn't a fairy story, it's a horror one. Why it was never pounced on by Hammer Films is a mystery. There is a 2013 fantasy production apparently. Tales of 'ghosties' around the camp fire at scout camp and sayings such as 'the bogie mannie will get ye' may be brushed off by some kids but not by others. In my own young life, all these seeds germinated when at fifteen, a big, tough guy, teddy boy me snuck into an 18 rated 'X' film with my equally big, tough guy, mates. It was much easier then. It may have been against the law but nobody gave a toss. Revenue was revenue. The experience gave me recurring nightmares: me, who was convinced that there was no such thing as the 'supernatural'. There wasn't in my waking hours but night-time was a horror. I kept dreaming about poor beautiful Lucy in her nightdress when she smiled in the woods to reveal her incisor dentistry, confirming she had joined the ranks of the undead. The film *Dracula* featured Christopher Lee and Peter Cushing. There is a reason for the '18' label and apparently, according to parent talk, the other 'tough guys' were equally affected. No wonder then, that such a thing as the 'supernatural' gets a footing. If there was no exposure, and life was based on only real facts, perhaps there would be no belief problems in the world but it's never going to happen. Listening to humans talk universally rules out my Utopia.

Gods must come under the 'supernature' category as well as there is no earthly evidence of their existence, but which one to choose? There are so many, thousands in fact. Some cultures have more than one and some, such as Hinduism, have many. Christians believe there is only one: theirs. Many have come and gone over the centuries, going out of fashion as cultures changed. Their legacy lives on in the names they gave to calendar months and days and still used by us today. Children don't normally have to choose which god to believe in as this choice is often made for them by their parents at an impressionable age.

It would appear obvious to me that faith is a highly personal thing and a human right to believe in whatever one likes. Many people find solace in that faith. It must be wrong to interfere with that right because it differs with another's personal belief. It is totally abhorrent to me and most people that some are prepared to kill others because of that difference. Throughout the course of history it's no secret that differences in godly beliefs have caused untold suffering and death. The Crusades' Christian soldiers, 'marching as to war' was a long time ago. In modern times the march goes on, on many fronts. It has always NOT been a personal belief. Some religions mutilate both male and female genitals of innocent children with no thought to why their god would give them these parts in the first place. It may be true that a god or gods exist. How would I know and I would never challenge another's belief, but as an observer I can only say, once again, I see no evidence for their existence.

A vast number of people follow the unsubstantiated daily dose of astrology. They share their predicted twenty-four hour experiences with another 500,000,000 people worldwide depending on the position of heavenly bodies. I couldn't make it up but someone did and believers don't scrutinize the evidence.

Many other beliefs don't make any sense. The unlucky ones eg walking under ladders, breaking mirrors, standing on cracks in pavements, and many more are surely nonsense but avoided by a great many. Row 13 in an aeroplane is avoided by some, somehow thinking their chances in a plane crash may be better in row 14. Black, it's just a colour but it seems to come across as an evil colour: probably born out of the fear of darkness as crimes are easier to commit under cover of darkness. It extends as a prejudice in everyday life: 'the dark side' is a common expression, black cats crossing your path are unlucky, crows and other corvids can be associated with witchcraft and evil. In the garden, they are shooed away from bird tables, denied the feast that other birds enjoy, despite being just as hungry. Kids (and adults) are fascinated by some beetles. Oh yes, they will let them crawl over their hands and girls will even tolerate them being in their hair: that is if they are of a nice colour, preferably red with black spots ie a ladybird. If you are a beetle which happens to be black you are often exterminated quickly underfoot. Black is bad. Surely, it is purely an extension of indoctrinated superstition and thankfully, nowadays, education is enlightening children to the fallacy of superstitious views on nature's creatures. That is, of course, if other superstitious beliefs don't overpower that obvious fallacy.

This next subject sits on the fence of being included in this chapter. For many it is just New Age traveller hocus pokus. If it falls under the 'supernature' heading then there cannot be any proven evidence. At this moment in history science holds it in contempt, simply and correctly, because scientists who have looked into it have failed to be convinced by testing it under laboratory conditions of double blind tests. As regards myself, as indicated, I have to be shown the proof of anything albeit in the personal laboratory of a rational brain. It is spiritually called water divining but more commonly known as 'dowsing'.

At an early age I was introduced to this supposed phenomenon by friends who were from traveller families in the community. Their old ways were unsustainable due to mechanisation in the countryside and they were forced to settle in the post war council schemes. Many of their superstitious beliefs were bantered around, along with fortune telling tea leaves, tarot cards and crystal balls. Non traveller adults still treated all this with caution, fearing tinker's curses and the like, but kids are kids and integrated freely. One friend professed to be able to dowse with a forked willow twig and it certainly performed although we couldn't prove its success. I had a go over the same area with not a twitch. I couldn't tell if the movement of the twig was due to his manipulation or if it was genuine. I plumped for the former, as I thought it must be impossible for one individual to differ from another in that respect. These people were masters of trickery and kids enjoyed that. This was just another of these sleights.

My early working life was in the city and my workplace window overlooked a historic cobbled street. One day my attention was drawn to an individual pacing the street with a pair of bent wires. He occasionally paused and drew yellow chalk marks on the ground. I couldn't let this one pass and went out to ask the obvious question. He was employed by the utility companies to locate old gas and water pipes for upgrading. Indiscriminate digging could lead to disruption and danger of explosion and there were no location maps, as in modern times. Further, he marked the different services separately, including sewer pipes. When excavations started I never got much work done being glued to the window. He was incredibly accurate. What struck me most was that the workmen never questioned his ability and accepted it as matter of fact. There was no sense of wonder at the phenomenon.

When I moved out of the city, I had occasion to install a septic tank and soak away. Field drains and water pipes were somewhere within the new pipe route and an individual in the village charged me £10 for locating them perfectly with his bent rods. Sometime later a newly acquired piece of land presented similar problems. I hired a driver and excavator to carry out drainage work. The bent rods were carried in his cab for the purpose of locating existing old drains. He not only found these but could tell which carried water and which were dry. He also located the further routing of my water supply pipe and the old well, abandoned in the early nineteenth century and long since ploughed over, confirmed later by old map inspection. Of course I was intrigued. Once again, how could he do it when I couldn't? 'But you can.'

He explained that with his help I could. I held the wires as

23

instructed and with his hand on my shoulder we walked. It worked alright. The rods crossed with some force when I crossed the line of the water pipe and the force disappeared when I moved away. I marched back and forth, crossing and re crossing the pipe line with the same results. He then stated that I would still be able to do it without his hand on my shoulder but the reaction would not be so great and after a few further tries it would disappear altogether. That was exactly what followed. I add that his hand on my shoulder was on my thick winter clothes. There was no skin contact. Quite an amazing experience for me and yet these individuals do it daily, accepting it as the norm. No big deal.

The local golf course had a common problem. When this relatively new course was constructed the land was bulldozed into desired contours and although new drains were laid the old agricultural drains, laid late 1700's, were completely ignored, storing up inevitable trouble in the future. During one wet summer, the water in the broken drains bubbled to the surface creating havoc. A dowser was employed to find these so they could be repaired. The three inch fired clay drains which revolutionised agriculture and road improvement in the past were laid half a chain apart. A chain is twenty-two yards, so expect to find one every eleven yards. Despite probably having that knowledge, he was incredibly accurate once again, this time with a forked twig.

Very recently a dry summer meant that the golf course's water feature ponds, used for irrigation, nearly ran dry. It was decided to sink a borehole to prevent future problems but where, if anywhere, to drill? A dowser with a reputation for success was employed. His fee was £150 payable only on success and the result of his survey . . . drill here. He also gave an indication of how many litres per hour to expect. The only way to determine his success was to drill and install a downhole pump and large storage tank. Cost to the club, £75,000. That's an awful lot of members' subscriptions to gamble on a charlatan, if he was one. Suffice to say he collected his £150.

It's not only individuals who make a living from this gift. Companies (the photograph on the following page shows one

such company) are run which can find not only water but other things as well, although their main business is borehole or underground spring water.

They have more than one of these vehicles costing a lot of money to run. Companies of course are expected to supply the goods to the customers' satisfaction, in this case successful results, and if they don't they fail.

This company's latest find was a wartime Spitfire in an Orkney Isles swamp. There was a legendary memory of this crash and they were employed to find it. It takes a lot of money, time and effort to go to Orkney.

So what am I to make of all these experiences? I look to science to find the answer and don't find it. In fact it is nearly ignored. I was intrigued that a documentary was to be screened where a double blind experiment was to be carried out by eminent scientists. A few supposedly gifted dowsers were chosen to be tested. I may say that they looked like they were straight out of a New Age traveller's camp and the appearance fee may have been an incentive but no matter. The experiment consisted of plastic bottles buried in boxes of sand, some containing water and some not. In true scientific fashion, neither the scientists nor the dowsers knew which was which. The results were revealed to be no more successful than what would be expected by chance. There we have it, mumbo jumbo.

Wait a minute. Are they telling me that I should now dismiss what I have experienced and seen as nonsense? I can hardly do that.

'If you had seen what I ha'e seen, you wouldna' be sae swanky oh.'

If I had asked any of my subjects to find bottles in sand they would have laughed and refused. That's not what it is about. Any experiment involving them, they say, would have to be done in the field: literally. One pointer may lean towards the earth's magnetic field, so they say, but that means that they would have to 'feel' magnetism: impossible? There are one or two other observations to mention.

Recent experiments into bird, fish and animal migration point to an ability to sense the earth's magnetic field. I will return to that in dedicated future chapters but the inference is that these creatures can do it.

An electrician colleague of mine had the uncanny ability to test whether a 240 volt electrical circuit was live by licking his fingers and putting them across the terminals, an action that could be fatal to normal people so he obviously wasn't normal. He used to grasp the live conductor and touch an unsuspecting colleague's neck or arm with the other hand (mine included) sending them across the room. Touching the glass of an avometer and running his finger up the glass would see the needle following his finger and staying up the scale when he removed the finger. The needle would stay there indefinitely until someone else touched the glass, whereupon it would immediately return to normal. He also could tell if an insulated wire among a bed of wires was carrying a current by lightly holding his hand over it without touching. This phenomenon we tested by running an extension cable to a distant room and switching it on and off at random. He responded by shouting on, off, on, off in perfect response. It was an open circuit ie there was no appliance attached. To reiterate, there was no contact with the cable. This was obviously an abnormal person and I would have loved to have known if he could 'dowse'. To add to the oddness of Jimmy: he could put his hand in a pot of hot wax, used for sealing underground cable ends, without a burn whereas my fingertip contact caused severe pain. He played tennis in Spanish midday heat and never sweated. His diet included copious amounts of salt that he ate by the handful.

I subsequently knew another person who could do the cable experiment and she too didn't sweat at all. They both had abnormally dry skin.

Suffice then to say that there are people who can do strange things with electricity and magnetism and here's another weird experience. In the 1960s, in the heyday of the Mini car, I owned a Mini van that refused to pass a certain stretch of road. I am not talking once or twice but dozens of times as it became almost a party trick and it never did pass that point without incident. The first time it happened was in the dark and could have been a nasty experience. The engine cut out, all lights went out and there was a smell of burning. I steered blindly, guessing the road contour and suddenly the engine started and the lights came back on. A steep bank on the right could have claimed me so I had a lucky escape. The Mini van battery was in the open behind the driver's seat and a petrol can in the back became the suspect for shorting the battery. This was removed. Next day I drove to work by the same route with no incident but on the way back it happened again. Still suspecting some electrical fault, I didn't notice the geographical similarity. No further incident until returning home again over the same route. This time the penny dropped. It was at the same location. I turned the van and headed back up the hill to test again. Sure enough everything cut out again. The length of the cut was 100 metres or so before restoring to normal. I tried again and again with the same results. This now became a topic of conversation between friends and they all wanted to experience this to find the problem. Piled in the back, which was the norm then, the route was tried and tested with not a single trip being incident free. Different drivers made no difference. Same 100 metres, always at exactly the same point AND ONLY IN ONE DIRECTION. Creepy theories from friends fell on deaf ears. I am not a fool (that's an opinion, sorry) and suspected that the natural laws of physics were at work. It so happens that an 11 kv electricity line runs parallel to the road about fifty metres away for just those 100 metres and so fell suspect. I rang the electricity company and arranged a meeting. They asked if I had been drinking, which I admitted I had, but that was irrelevant. I was at a friend's birthday bash and he goaded me into phoning there and then as a result of all the speculation at the party about the phenomenon. A meeting was arranged for the following morning and the subject demonstrated to a hugely sceptical and very busy electricity board expert who didn't take kindly to time wasting as he sternly pointed out. With both of us in the van it happened on cue. He searched around the vehicle and me, looking for how I had done it. 'Ok then, you drive.' I was now just as stern. He did, again and again, and my little green van, unerringly, never let me down. He had a detector for some interference registering purpose which came up with nothing both in my vehicle and his, which of course, never suffered the experience. Leads were trailed on the ground and the power line minutely inspected. He would have engineers carry out further tests and I would be advised of the results. I received a letter. No faults found and a suggestion, 'Use a different route.'

I kid you not: so much for scientific investigation. It often doesn't depend on the subject but on the attitude of the investigator so you have to look deeply into results of experiments to find true enlightenment and proof. I tell this story because it may come under the heading of unknown electro/magnetic anomaly.

I traded in that van for another similar and no other problems were experienced on that, or any other stretch of road. Be it man or van, every individual is different.

So where are we with the dowsing? Science still scoffs so I have a challenge, perhaps for some physics student but not to exclude eminent professors. Let's forget the water thing. Pick any field you like, hold the rods of your own choosing, and walk with old Arthur, the JCB driver's hand on your shoulder. When the rods move as they surely will with some force, you only have to explain the origins of that force.

In this book then, I have to discount the supernatural and stick to observations of a worldly kind but I have to be careful. There are pitfalls as this next experience shows.

3

A YOUNG SCIENTIST

When I was a lad, a tiny wee lad,
My mother said to me,
Come see the Northern Lights my boy,
They're bright as they can be.

Mary Webb, 'The Northern Lights of Old Aberdeen'

That is exactly what she said to me at two in the morning, one clear December night. I was eight years old. Her bedroom in the tiny post war prefab faced north. She woke me up to see the spectacle: the *Aurora borealis.* 'Aren't they beautiful?' They sure were. 'But what are they mum?' She didn't know. That bugged me. Parents are supposed to know everything.

A few years later, I was at the fairground we called *The Carnies* (carnival). Prizes at that time were often goldfish and I was a crack shot at the pistol shooting, having worked out and allowed for the deliberately off centred sights. My poor acquisition was chased around an overcrowded tank with a net, fished out into in a plastic bag of water and taken home. The bathroom sink sufficed until a bowl was procured and it sat on top of the sideboard, christened Billy. The next Christmas in my stocking from Santa, along with the orange, apple and chocolate watch, was a torch. Simple presents then. The beam seemed to light up the heavens with the new batteries. Keeping an eye on Billy one night with the house lights out, I shone the torch on his bowl. Startled, he panicked and broke the surface with his thrashing. On the ceiling were revealed the 'northern lights'. They waved back and forth, just like the real thing, so the secret of the aurora was revealed to me. Like the torch on the water, in northern latitudes the sun at night on the other side of the world is just at the right angle in winter to shine on the ocean waves and project the spectrum (as in a rainbow) onto the black canvas of the clear night sky. The waving motion of the aurora is the magnification of

29

the light through the ocean waves. If you have seen an aurora, that is what it looks like. Problem solved, and that's how it was in my convinced mind until teenage education in science proposed a different theory. How dare they, the cause was so obvious. There was just a little flaw in my observations. The colours didn't match the whole spectrum. I had considered it but imagined that wavelengths of some colours wouldn't carry that distance. Eventually, greater minds than mine convinced me that it was due to the interaction between solar particles and the earth's magnetic field. As Einstein did to show that mass bends light and proving it during a solar eclipse, scientists predicted a solar flare would cause the northern lights phenomenon on a certain period and it happened on schedule. Reluctantly, I ate humble pie, not to appease anyone else but myself. I was wrong: some scientist, me. I expressed my stupidity to my science teacher. Instead of scoffing, she was impressed, 'You have seen a phenomenon and put forward a theory to be tested, albeit in your own mind. That's how science works and that's how we have come to know what we know. You didn't seek an unnatural explanation. No space ships or godly wrath. Your explanation was plausible but wrong. Famous men in science did exactly as you have done.' How good a teacher was that and how good did she make me feel?

So I can console myself with the fact that very many eminent scientists and mathematicians felt as I did in the past and no doubt many will do in the future.

Many an elegant proof is destroyed by one ugly fact.

Mind you, if anything goes wrong with their proof of the aurora in future, I have an alternative. It won't because it is a proven fact and you have to respect facts.

You cannot argue with a fact. You can try to disprove it or contend it but if it is a fact it is to no avail. A fact, is a fact, is a fact, period. The trouble is, how do you know it is a fact? There are many pseudo facts. The modern term is a factoid. *'A factoid is something that looks like a fact, could be a fact but is in fact, not a fact'.* An example would be 'the sun rises in the east'. The world is full of factoids but when a proof to a theory arises, the factoid should be forgotten, however unpalatable it seems. Yet I spoke to someone recently who believes in that particular ancient factoid (the sun does rise in the east): one who still believes that the earth is the centre of the universe (she had been drawn into some obscure North American cult). She also believed that dinosaur fossils were a red herring, laid down by her god to test one's faith. You may not be able to argue with a fact but equally, you cannot argue with an indoctrinated zombie. There are many who just will not accept obvious evidence supporting a fact and that **is** a fact.

Life is full of pitfalls if you are to determine fact from non-fact but a good way to start is to see with your own eyes. 'Look and learn'. Eyes are not infallible as there are many illusions, such as the sun rising in the east, but back observation up with reason and other evidence and you must end up not far off the mark. The aurora is still a lesson in my mind but I love looking for evidence in everything I see in nature. I just don't jump to conclusions anymore.

That science teacher was a zoologist and, like all good teachers, she left a lasting impression for which I am very grateful. Her teaching methods were down to earth and she didn't mince her words. My class consisted of twenty-seven girls and three boys of which I was the only one to finish the course and that was bound to cause both sexes embarrassment in some subject matter, me especially because I had no males to snigger with. Human anatomy discussions in those far off days of teenage embarrassment caused undertones which she couldn't stand. Annie was a big girl, not big and fat, I mean just big built. She sat at the back of the class and her presence dominated it. During a lecture covering the digestive system we had got as far as fluid in the bladder and Annie was asked what happens next. All eyes turned to Annie. The round face lit up like a lantern and she clammed up, purely because of my presence. 'Come on girl, you're not all bunged up are you?' The face got even redder to the delight of the rest of the class. The teacher didn't like the hilarity and came down on us like a ton of bricks. 'If you are going to study zoology, then forget all this stupid embarrassment or leave the class right now, especially as the next lecture is on the reproductive system.' For effect, she flung the door open. No one left and a new academic aura prevailed in the classroom.

In my first science year, this teacher endeared herself to me by asking the class if anyone knew where she could get frogs for dissecting. She would pay SIXPENCE per frog. Next day I delivered a dried milk tin full to the brim. The strange thing was that I was the only one to bring in frogs. Either the others didn't know where to find them or they didn't need the money. Both scenarios didn't apply to me and I knew of many other places. I had my mind set on becoming a millionaire but, after the third tin, she politely said that she had enough for now and that she would let me know when she needed more. She never did. I realised also that my childhood leisure time was spent differently from the rest of the pupils in the class. Well, they were GIRLS. In third year, she asked if anyone was interested in joining her on a week-long trip to wildest Perthshire for the Easter holiday week to study highland wildlife. Between ours and her other classes, she got only ten takers including me, of course. This was done in her own time. Such dedication to teaching is rare. The trip was wonderful: up before dawn to see blackcock on the 'lek'. How many people have ever seen a Greenland or gyrfalcon?

All teachers have nicknames. This one was no exception. With her frogs, ox eyes, worms and other grizzly dissection subjects requiring preservation, she was continually messing about with methylated spirits, ether and the like. Kids had a name for these liquids, born out of the habits of the unfortunate residents of the city's model lodging house for down and outs. Some of them drank the stuff. They were the 'feeky' drinkers. The term is possibly from the Romany language I had grown up to hear often. 'Peeve' was normal alcoholic drink and 'feek' was this stuff. This teacher's name was Mrs Flux. I don't know if her husband was a plumber to suit his name but it lent itself to the alliteration 'Feeky Flux' which perfectly described her. It soon was shortened to the affectionate 'Feeky' and was not in any way derogatory, although she may have judged it differently. If she is still alive today, then 'Feeky', I salute you. You were my inspiration. I treated her like a second mum and she was the first port of call for scientific questions. Some of them crop up later.

Feeky advocated reason to come up with enlightenment, as with the northern lights story. 'Everyone can be a scientist' she said, 'all you have to do is observe and reason why.' Sometimes, though, reason doesn't come up with an answer. A perfect example of the same mind-set as she taught is exemplified in this next conundrum. It is no wonder that humans opt for theological answers.

Holidaying on a tropical beach, lying on a deckchair in the warmth with cool ocean breezes tempering the sun's heat seems idyllic but after a couple of hours reading a book, with not so young eyes getting weary and starting to see double, the novelty wears off. The warmth is fine: it's the doing nothing bit. The mind wanders and takes in the natural world around me, so different from home. Then I realize it's not so different. Nature is doing what nature does, albeit different species. Looking up you cannot miss the ripening fruits of the coconut palm and contemplation begins. There are many wonderful things in nature that seem to be the result of a designer: the bee's honeycomb, a peacock's tail, etc, the complex eye being one of my favourites. All are the result of simple rules but very many people cannot accept that and not surprisingly. One of my own favourites must be that humble coconut palm.

This organism, on the face of it, seems to display remarkable foresight, planning, and execution to propagate its kind. The palm tree (above) is typical on tropical holiday brochures.

That's not a bad position from the tree's point of view. Out there somewhere across the oceans there may be new lands to be colonized, possibly thousands of miles away. In fact coconut palms start the stabilization of new ocean sand spits preventing their washing away and make new lands. How to get its seeds there?

There is no point casting ordinary seeds out as the ravages of wind, waves, and salt would soon destroy them. I apologise for using the term 'ordinary seeds' as all seeds are equally complex and suited to their environment. The coconut palm equips them well with a hard, tough, waterproof coat and an inner mat of coir which traps air to make them incredibly buoyant. In the centre safely sits the nut, the next generation. It is equipped with food and moisture in the way of a white lining and rich milk to give it a good start. The whole thing has a shape ideal for rolling down the beach into the water and up the beach at the other end when cast up by the waves, if indeed there is another beach. A round shape would be no good as it would roll about too much and never settle, but it is circular shaped just enough. It also needs to have an extended surface to maximize the wave motion and the three sided shape doubles for both purposes (see above).

It seems an awful lot of trouble to go to on an off chance. There is no feedback to prove success in order to improve design.

Christopher Columbus didn't know if there was land out there but the coconut palm seems pretty sure. The hunch must have been right for the coconut palm has spread around the globe in the tropics from its initial base, apparently in the South Pacific islands. There is another big problem for the castaway riding the ocean currents, when to germinate? Too early and it will surely perish. It has to 'know' when it hits land.

As a youngster, as you yourself have probably done, I visited the fairground and tried the coconut shy. In those frugal times, winning one was like winning the lottery. My mum told me to shake the nut to hear the milk sloshing around before accepting it. This meant it was healthy and not cracked and empty. Note the sloshing. It's not full to the brim for a reason. If the coconut is on the ocean the milk is in perpetual motion, so *'don't germinate'*. If and when it is cast up on a beach, after a time lag to ensure it isn't just a temporary stop, *'germinate'*. Then the still, settled liquid acts as a spirit level. The root grows down from the surface and the shoot upwards. The rich liquid feeds the growing seedling until it can sustain itself. A new tree is born and a new island, or even continent, is colonized: surely a wonderful achievement for a mere tree? Of course coconuts can be planted as a crop away from beaches anywhere in the tropics. They can also drop, germinate and try to spread inland on larger land masses but they are constrained by competition from tropical forests or salt water swamps, the domain of the mangrove. Their niche is the sandy beaches and the whole design of their fruit is purely and simply for the ocean voyage.

Palm trees cannot think, let alone think ahead. They cannot design and build. Coconuts cannot 'feel' motion or non-motion. In my wildest dreams I cannot see how this came about naturally but it surely did. It also shares a human trait. To see its offspring do well in the future. That's the wonder of nature and only one example of millions.

I also cannot help considering how life got us to the point that we humans are the only entities that can lie on a beach and contemplate all this in the first place. Both the coconut palm and my calculating brain are the products of evolution which is the subject of the next chapter. I must point out that the following notes are recorded purely from my experience, not anyone else's.

4

EVOLUTION

If evolution is true, how come mothers only have two hands?

Milton Berle

At twelve years old, freshly initiated into secondary school, a child is easily influenced. They have their heroes. I have already mentioned mine: Feeky, my zoology teacher. She was a SCIENTIST. She introduced me to the Central Library in the city. If she had read it, I read it, and so it was that I read 'The Origin of Species'. It was difficult, not the 'Treasure Island' that I had been used to but it got my attention. At thirteen, I took the book out again. The sheer simplicity of the theme led me to surmise, *'Why didn't I think of that?'* Thinking of all my experiences with nature previously, it was so obvious. I wasn't the first to think that way as I subsequently found out. Thomas Huxley became known as Darwin's bulldog for championing his cause and that statement became synonymous with his name in history. He was no small-time naturalist himself, following on from Darwin's evolutionary landslide, and his theory that present day birds are the descendants of the dinosaurs is now virtually taken as fact. It was easier for me to think that way than in Huxley's day. Such heresy did not go down well in those superstitious times but those pioneers of the truth about the natural world led down-to-earth naturalists to accept the obvious.

So how do we know it's true, or in these notes, how do I know it's true? Science produces so much evidence that it just has to be, especially as there is no evidence to the contrary. Many science books go into great detail explaining that evidence but how can I, or you, see evolution happening? We don't live long enough to see separate species evolving in relation to their environment. That takes millions of years but we can see the evolution of variety within a species which is the starting process and it can be amazingly rapid. As Darwin concluded, species are not fixed and unchanging and everyone surely perceives that they aren't. How did it take so long to see it?

Humans, for a start, have long exploited that fact for their own ends and I am one of them. My racing pigeons were bred to secure the best traits of muscle, wing and homing ability. The number of human-engineered pigeon varieties is many: some so bizarre that they could not possibly survive in the wild. All thoroughbred breeding does the same, surely proving Darwin's point.

One of his famous observations, widely known, was the subtle differences in finches in geographically separate Galapagos Islands to suit different environments. I don't have to travel that far to concur with that: Darwin told me what to look for. The St Kilda wren is isolated from the mainland common *Troglodytes* and differs to the point of being a sub species. Further afield, I have tracked down the St Lucia parrot and the Mauritius kestrel. All these are markedly different from the common species but there are very subtle differences in many geographically isolated species if you look close enough. The Caribbean grackle is endemic throughout the Caribbean. You can share your breakfast with them. On every Island it is obviously the same bird. It looks like a cross between a blackbird and a starling. On the tiny Grenadine of Bequia I noticed that the females were larger and browner. Their beaks were stouter and longer but one of my silly sounding observations is that they have a more evil look about them, probably because their eyes were more oval than on other islands. Throughout the Leeward Islands variance varies between both ends of the spectrum. There is no variance within a single island population so I have to conclude that variation came about through isolation. Darwin probably would have described it better had he visited Bequia.

Dogs are typical with new breeds being registered all the time. Mine was a crossbreed, not quite a Heinz (57 varieties) but crossed with a purpose in mind. His sire was a greyhound x deerhound and his dam a greyhound x deerhound x collie: a typical lurcher. They make the best pets in the world but their breeding was for poaching: combining speed and stamina with toughness, intelligence and herding instinct. All man selected traits in the past. It's so easy that you can breed to order. All you have to do is 'play god' to select the desirables and reject the others. We could do it with humans too but surely it will never come to that. It has been tried and speculated in the past. Adolf tried it and failed. Modern racism flies the same flag. Aldous Huxley (Thomas's nephew) wrote about a future where that doctrine succeeded in his book 'Brave New World', no doubt inspired by his uncle's enthusiasm. Humans were bred for a specific purpose. He even short circuited the need for intimate sex. It may be possible but that must be the biggest non-starter.

Manipulating the higher animals may be contentious but no such stigma exists with plants. We can experiment with and select or reject at will, the principle is the same. Gardeners have produced tens of thousands of variants to suit themselves.

I used to sow and grow many bedding plants for the garden centre market. One year the anti-frost heating broke down and ruined many hours of work. The greenhouse thermometer registered -4°C during the night of 4th May. The frosted seedlings were abandoned in seed trays outside to make way for new ones. As the weather improved I noticed one or two French marigolds growing in the trays. They had survived. I grew them on and cross pollinated them as an experiment. The resultant seeds were germinated the following spring in early April, outside. There were many seedlings which survived, although the majority perished. There is no conclusion to this experiment unfortunately as circumstances changed. No time to twiddle around in business. Had I continued, however, could I have bred hardy French marigolds? Certainly if I could have kept it up for thousands of years, it would surely happen. In nature, if climate changes slowly, plants will perish or survive depending on variance. Animals can migrate but plants are left to live or die and they have just as many strategies for the survival of their offspring. Some pines produce a percentage of seeds which only germinate at the temperatures of forest fires and there are very many more, even in my limited experience.

Daphne mezereum is a choice garden shrub. Despite the documented best conditions for it to flourish, it often doesn't conform for a variety of reasons not immediately obvious. It can fail in these supposed ideal conditions and thrive in non-ideal ones. This makes it a challenge to connoisseur gardeners.

Couple that with its slow growth and it means a specimen attracts a good selling price in my horticultural trade. I decided to bulk up, copying my counterparts in the Netherlands who are the real specialists. One advantage of this plant is that it breeds reasonably true, human pleasing wise, from seed. You can be lucky and get a winning variation of colour. Not quite so simple. There is the small problem of dormancy. Dormancy is well known in nursery circles. In many plants, seed is produced to cope with unfavourable seasons. Not just your average poor summer but seasons millions of years ago when volcanic eruptions or other natural disasters could wipe a species out and many have indeed perished. Best to produce seed set with an alarm clock. Some seeds are indeed programmed. 'Don't germinate for two years, or three years, etc.' Nurserymen cannot wait that long for germination and so have learned to trick the alarm to go off sooner. *Acer palmatum* (Japanese maple) seeds require experience of a minimum of two summers and two winters before germination can take place. The seeds are collected in autumn, mixed with compost in plastic bags, put in a fridge for a period then put in the airing cupboard. Repeat the process and then sow in spring to get good percentage germination. Back to the daphne: try that with their seed and the results are poor, certainly not commercially viable. The reason is that the germination is staged over many years. I sowed 1,000 seeds in a cold frame. The first summer around fifty germinated. The second year about the same and each year for five years the seedlings were harvested until the count went down. The cold frame was replanted with a different crop but even ten years later, daphne seedlings continued to appear. How long that would have continued is speculation. That's a mere decade so, is a century out of the question, or even longer? However, it is surely a remarkable survival strategy for a 'mere' plant. You can't underestimate plants.

The French Pyrenees area is a magical place to visit. You can park the car at a lakeside car park where the waters are a beautiful verdant green from the bloom of glacier erosion high above. If you climb from there in the month of May, in the shadow of the magnificent snow clad Pic du Midi, you pass through forests of *Fagus sylvatica* (beech) in full leaf. The higher you climb the less green they become as they have only partially broken out of bud. Higher still, the less the foliage has developed and the smaller the trees are, until right up to the snow line just short of the glacier's edge, where the plants are only a few feet high and have yet to break bud. The growing season is much shorter the higher the altitude. These are of the same stock, surely, as the ones lower down. They receive the same, if not more daylight which is a commonly quoted trigger for spring growth but obviously there must be many other factors. If one was transplanted to lower down, would it grow bigger and come into leaf sooner? I haven't tried but perhaps mutations have occurred to favour lower temperatures and late snow cover. I relate this because my own beech hedge shows the same variation. Some plants are green in late April whilst the latest do not fully foliate until mid-June. These late ones would be at an advantage at higher altitudes. My hedge consists of seedlings and at most times of year they are undistinguishable from one another. In actual fact they are as different as you and I. That difference is of no consequence to their survival in my garden but in the high Pyrenees . . . evolution in brilliant action.

If you have ever bought plants from a garden centre, you may have unknowingly gone home with a free one. You would quickly know about it as it will have spread all over your garden. *Cardamine hirsuta*, aka hairy bitter cress, very quickly flowers and sets seed. These explode and cascade all around. They germinate just as quickly, especially under glass or polythene. It would appear that this weed has latched on to the garden centre trade to spread around the country. Many plant disease pathogens have done the same. Fire blight prone plants require a plant passport to be sold in the trade. Garden centres rarely grow their own plants. They import from growers around the country along with the cress. It is just as much a nuisance in the growing nurseries and mine was no exception. Practically every pot had some, requiring huge amounts of labour to weed. I decided to wage war with a goal to eradicate it. Every morning, staff would survey the whole nursery for an hour and every seedling was uprooted. There was no way any seedling could survive. It seemed to be working but close inspection revealed an evasive strategy by way of tiny versions of the plant. In fact the more we weeded these out, the tinier they got, to the point of being almost microscopic. We had artificially changed the

41

environment to favour small plants and evolution duly responded. It wasn't permanent though, as immediately we slackened our efforts, the size slowly increased again, but surely if we had kept this up long enough, it could be achieved. Nature has plenty time to do this.

Eventually, given enough time, a new species comes into being and the fossil records show this beautifully. What makes a species a species is that a living entity has diverged far enough from a common ancestor that they cannot interbreed. That can't be strictly true as it depends on the interpretation of interbreeding. Separate closely related species can try and often do copulate and produce an offspring, the most commonly known being between the horse and the ass. The resulting mule though, in lineage terms, is a dead end. It is sterile. There is not a mule species. Ignoring the abhorrence angle, it should be perfectly viable to produce a 'mule' hybrid between a human and a chimpanzee for they are as closely related as the horse and ass. There is no doubt it has been thought of in 'in vitro' terms to prove the point and may have already been done, at least up to embryo stage, but why should we try? It would be unbelievably cruel to produce a freak to be ogled at. Furthermore a surrogate womb would be hard to find. In the plant world, no such stigma exists and it is regularly done. Some of them were my bread and butter. One you definitely would have heard of is a cross between two normally geographically separate but closely related species of tree.

Cupressus macrocarpa is an indigenous Californian species of cypress. With plenty of moisture from Pacific frontal systems confronting the Rocky Mountains and a reasonably warm climate tree species here are vigorous, giving rise to some of the tallest trees in the world. Although nothing like the tallest, *Macrocarpa* can grow in excess of 100 feet: hardly a choice garden plant.

Chamaecyparis nootkatensis is a conifer, closely related to *Cupressus* but adapted to life in the arctic in Alaska. Hardiness is the key feature.

These two species never meet in the wild, being separated by thousands of miles and totally different climates. Man's ingenuity has brought them together. Although difficult to cross pollinate it

42

has been achieved producing, as you would expect, a vigorous growing but hardy, sterile hybrid. There are only a few successful pollinations. As the cross cannot produce offspring itself, as in the case of the horse/ass scenario, the only way to propagate it is to clone it: a copy. A cutting by human hand is the only way it will multiply and millions of clones were produced for profit. This 'mule' has the botanical name x *Cupressocyparis leylandii*. As the name spells out, 'x' for crossbreed and then *Cupressocyparis* ie a mix of the two parents *Cupressus* and *Chamaecyparis*, followed by the place of breeding, Leyland. It's common or garden name, Leyland cypress: in short, the hated or loved hedging plant, *Leylandii*.

Personally, I have propagated and sold tens of thousands of clones, contributing to my income in life. In its heyday it was a huge seller as builders of modern new housing estates maximised the available land by building closer together. Residents wanted privacy and quick and *Leylandii* provided the perfect solution if kept in check by regular pruning. Miss a year at your peril. These can grow to 100 feet if unchecked and it has now required an act of parliament to control their heights. To appease my conscience, I did warn my customers at point of sale.

The Scottish mountain of Morven is in the Eastern Cairngorms National Park. It's in full view from my home. At an altitude of 871 metres (2,858 feet), it falls short of the 3,000 feet Munro status, being classified as a Corbett. It is one of those mountains that seems a slog to climb. You never see the top until you are at the top. Every ridge seems to offer hope of being the last one but more keep coming. The top is a plateau. There are still heathers and blueberries at this height although rather stunted. Windswept it certainly is as the rounded shape seems to accelerate the air up the slopes. No surprise then that there are no trees. Apparently, there used to be but it may have been a warmer spell between the last ice age and the present day. You would assume back then it would have been colonised by conifers such as Scots pine with their fine needles to cope with the wind, just like the low growing heathers. No trees today though. But look a little closer. If you get on your hands and knees, under the heather shelter, there are many dwarf willows bearing catkins in the spring. These are the 'least willow' (*Salix herbaceae*) and its habit is fully adapted to living below heather height. There is another surprise, perfectly formed specimens of the everyday trees sycamore, rowan and oak.

They all exist beneath the heather cover as it would be suicide to grow any taller. Rowan seeds could have been excreted by birds but it is a long way for a sycamore winged seed to blow. As for an acorn, the mind boggles, but they are all there in miniature. It seems a natural bonsai situation of restricted growth. It would be an interesting experiment to dig one up and see if it remained dwarf in better conditions. Even better would be to see if any seed would reproduce normal specimens. If they remained dwarf, then evolution would have run its course on the way to producing a new sub species. That's how it happened to other familiar windswept species.

The wild heather, 'ling' (*Calluna vulgaris*), is only one of the species colonising the highlands and islands of Scotland. *Erica tetralix* and *Erica cinerea* are common but it is the ling, turning the mountains purple in autumn which is synonymous with these wild areas and you don't get any more wild, windswept and remote than the Islands of the St. Kilda archipelago. Out in the Atlantic, only Rockall is further west in the British Isles. The heather clad hills have more than just the wind to endure. The winds are salt laden keeping the swathe very low and dwarf. Life was extremely tough for the past human inhabitants, evacuated at their own request in 1930, and it was just as tough for the plants marooned there. Once again, people can move but the plants can't. They have to adapt or die. Some of the dwarf specimens were translocated to the mainland by plant collectors, eager for something unusual. Even under new ideal conditions, they remained dwarf. Not only that, but their seed produced true dwarfs. A sub species born out of isolation, and that is the nearest I have got to evolution in action. Heathers throw sports easily and any slight variation in colour was propagated, or bred from, forcing further evolution to give a wide range of specimens for the horticulture market. You can buy St. Kilda heathers today.

After all that humans are surely under the same influences, and a myriad of evidence shows that we are. I seem indeed to be under the same evolutionary pressures as the Morven oaks, the

St Kilda heathers, coconut palms and my garden elm.

That elm tree captures my attention in many other ways without even stepping outside the house.

5

ULMUS GLABRA

A man who sits under a tree and dreams makes more journey than a man who goes around the world without dreaming.

Mehmet Murat ildan

My garden wych elm (below) doesn't just fascinate with its life story. Many other species enjoy its existence. Great, coal and  blue tits are continually flitting up and down its branches in summer, picking off moth eggs, caterpillars and pupae. The moths love this tree, as do predatory spiders, which are also food for the tits. There are many more insect species using it as well. All these depend on it for food and overwinter in the craggy bark crevices. They are all part of the food chain but that chain starts at a much more basic level.

I cannot see where it starts but microbes through nematodes to, eventually, perceivable species is the story. If a tablespoon of soil contains as much species as to outnumber all the people on earth, then this old tree is probably just as rich. It has been mooted that if all the substance of the tree was removed, leaving only nematode worms in situ, then you would still recognise it as a tree. The tree itself is part of this ecosystem. It relies on the balance. If you removed all the insect eaters, then the insect life would pare it to the bone.

Tits are the most obvious insect eaters but it also sustains wrens, dunnocks, robins, and more in season including, tree creepers, willow warblers, blackcaps and whitethroats. At the top of this particular chain seems to be the sparrowhawk. So the hawk is dependent on the microbes, the nematodes and the tree as much as any other species. Upset one and they all suffer.

A hole in the trunk where a bough has been blown off in antiquity and rotted into the bole is used by jackdaws each year. A shortage of nest sites locally means there is huge competition for that coveted hole. Squabbling goes on year round and it is protected energetically by the superior pair. Wood pigeons also always have a nest as do chaffinches and higher up, greenfinches. Blue tits nest in the nest box. It's a popular tree for birds. In winter, a female pheasant scrambles up the trunk to find night time refuge from the resident patrolling fox, its tracks obvious in the snow in the morning.

This wych elm has another peculiar attraction for wildlife. Its seeds mature in late June/early July. That's far earlier than most broadleaves such as oak and beech and at that time of year it is a place of pilgrimage for jays. I have no idea where they come from, only that they arrive at this time. Jays have, in my lifetime, been rare in the north east of Scotland but have become increasing more prevalent for reasons unknown. Suffice to say they are uncommon but a count of five this year is probably a family group and nice to see. Wood pigeons of course gorge themselves on the fallen seeds.

It's not just the birds. The unseasonal harvest attracts red squirrels. They have to cross open country of half a mile from a mixed plantation of beech and pine to get here. There are six this year which is up on last year. They never arrive together, so how do I know there are six? They have different shades of coat. They range from very pale (blondie) to chocolate brown (darkie). This is not a year round identification as they shed their coats and grow different colours in winter when they come and ransack the peanut feeders. They are a delight to watch.

Pipistrelle bats take over the jackdaw hole in summer to raise a family. On more than one occasion they have used one of my nest boxes. My bat detector clicks furiously as they scoop up the emerging moths at night around the branches.

The tree produces a lot of seed. I have tried to estimate the amount and come up with a figure of 50,000 annually. Given it has been doing this for at least 250 years, that's a total of 12,500,000. It beats my grandmother hands down with her meagre seventeen births, with only nine reaching adulthood. But it doesn't. With that amount of seed, the countryside should be thick with wych elm. It may once have been but not today. Of all that seed, most are going to be eaten. The biggest culprits are the bank voles which live in a warren of passages among the roots. It is estimated that one can consume 1,000 seeds in a single day. In such a bountiful environment, their population should rocket but no, it is stable because the seed bonanza coincides with another bird's need to feed its new family. The young birds sit screeching on the branches as the mother makes a kill. Tawny owls: I curse them at 2 am as I need my sleep but would rather have them than not. An argument about that owl's 'song' is blamed on William Shakespeare.

In his poem *Winter* (from *Love's Labour Lost* which we learned in the literature class) he wrote, '*Then nightly sings the staring owl, Tu-whoo, tu-whit tu-whoo, a merry note, while greasy Joan doth keel the pot.*'

It wouldn't have taken purists long to jump on to that one. There are two owls involved, one with tu-whit and the other tu-whoo. Feeky explained that very phenomenon to me. A bird does not make these two 'notes' consecutively. Now, it has been stated to me as a common belief that the tu-whit (outside my window, just feet away, it sounds more like a high pitched keewik) is made by the female and answered by the male with 'tu-whoo'. Unable to sleep through this, I have plenty of time to observe. In the 'simmer dim' of a northern summer night, an adult flies into the elm with a loud tu-whit, followed by two fledglings. I cannot tell the sex of the adult. The female is a bit bigger than the male but I never see them together to compare. The purists could tell. At this point there is never any answering 'tu-whoo'. The adult has made a kill and is calling on her offspring to feed them. My observation seems to be that the sharp, higher pitched 'tu-whit' is used as short distance communication. I have watched this behaviour every summer and after a while, the SAME bird settles down to a recurring 'tu-whoo'. This is answered by more than one 'tu-whoo' from afar, in a long distance low pitched communication, possibly territorial. I have continually checked that it is the same 'tu whit' bird in the tree. I don't know if both sexes make the 'tu-whit', but both certainly make the 'tu-whoo'.

Just another observation of nature bucking the textbook: there are many more still to come. So Shakespeare was wrong (imagine, humble me challenging the great bard). An 'S' was misplaced. If only he had taken the 'S' from the end of 'sings' and added it to the end of 'owl', he would have been spot on. *'Then nightly sing the staring owls'.* Feeky got it right.

Any of the elm seeds that fall on my lawn trying to germinate are doomed, being mown down before they get going. The ones that blow into the shrubberies and cultivated areas are hoed out with the weeds. If a north wind blows it is curtains as well. South of the parent tree lies extensive, intensively managed farmland and its ritual dousing of broadleaved weed killer. Maybe though, just maybe one or two will find their way into a little niche under the beech hedge or into a thicket of gorse where they can slowly grow, waiting for a future as a mature tree. There's no hurry. They can wait. So this tree, in its lifetime, with all its profusion of seeds will only probably equal my grandmother's issue to carry its genes into the future. It may sound callous but in my grandmother's time, wastage was allowed for, just like my elm. All these observations on wildlife and I have got no further than looking out of my window.

Both plants and wildlife throw up many other strange facets for me to contemplate. All animal behaviour is always of great interest, some amazing, some just fascinating and some weird. You just have to 'look and learn'. I have my favourites, not usually reported.

6

STRANGE BEHAVIOUR

Mystery creates wonder and wonder is the basis of man's desire to understand.

Neil Armstrong, astronaut

Driving through farmland in springtime I spot something out of the ordinary, six greater black backed gulls in a grass field containing a dozen sheep. They are not feeding, just standing like sentinels. Oddly, not any lesser black backs, common or herring gulls. Whilst it is not uncommon to see these species of gull inland in the springtime, in this instance fifteen miles, it is usually the latter species following the plough or walking newly sown fields in search of invertebrates. Driving home at tea time they are still there, and the next day, and the next. On the fourth day it all becomes clear. There is an addition to the inhabitants, a new born lamb. It was the afterbirth they were waiting for. They stayed until the last ewe had delivered and then they were off. If there had, unfortunately, been a still born lamb they would have had the eyeballs. Then they would have been blamed by the farmer for the death, an all too common misconception. Not in this instance however. Now the mystery is this. How did they know in the first instance that the ewes were pregnant? I didn't know until I saw the lamb on the fourth day. Is this an acquired skill, learned from their ilk or is it inbred (genetic)? This species has obviously evolved for life on the ocean with its webbed feet and wings made for riding the ocean winds. No doubt coastal land came into their feeding range and with agriculture and human waste available this would attract them further inland. But these six came inland on a mission, seemingly involving forethought and patience.

It's not the only gull enigma. Herring gulls regularly pitter-patter their feet on short cropped grassland. Feet evolutionary webbed for swimming. The purpose supposedly, is to imitate a rain

50

shower and entice earthworms to the surface. I am not sure about that. Earthworms respond to rain in the mating season, which is a warm summer night. They mate above ground. Feeky explained it erotically, 'Two worms come together on a warm damp night.' That's nice for the worms but they have another lucky sexual bonus: they are hermaphroditic, having both male and female organs so they can enjoy the best of both worlds **at the same time**. The gulls do their pitter-pattering year round, not just in summer. Surely they wouldn't waste their time for nine months of the year. They may be just puddling the ground to see what life floats to the surface. They peck away at any a-risings. I have watched closely and most times it is small invertebrates with no sign of worms. Of course there are sometimes worms which were near the surface but rain should mean nothing to them out of season. The question, notwithstanding, is did they learn to do this or, again, is it hardwired? Is it universal or confined to areas? If it is a local phenomenon, then this would point to learned skills. If it is universal then maybe it is genetic. It is only herring gulls which do this but often other gulls hang around to share the spoils after the perpetrator moves on. Why don't they copy them and do it themselves. Experts may have the answers but it strikes me as very advanced behaviour, in both cases, from mere seagulls.

If you look a little deeper into the history of greater black backed gulls though, there may be a clue: seal colonies. They have been the black backed's bread and butter since time immemorial. Afterbirth and stillborns as food are part of the gull's history. The seals pup in colonies rather than as individuals and the gulls know when that time is, the same as orcas in the southern oceans, and there is not much difference really in food value between a seal colony and a sheep 'colony'. Notwithstanding, it still portrays intelligence to venture inland in search of pregnant sheep.

Whilst many species are on the brink of extinction in the UK, wood pigeons are doing ok. The changes in the countryside decimate some species and favour others. 'It's an ill wind . . .' What any bird species needs for survival is food and places to nest. The wood pigeon has both in abundance, courtesy of man. Although they eat seeds, as in other pigeon species, a large part of their diet is greenery such as shoots of trees in spring (ash especially) and wild (and cultivated) brassicas. Winter crops are new to farming. The old rotation system is history. Selective breeding of crop species has led to increased hardiness, basically by artificially manipulating evolution and crops can now be sown in autumn to quickly ripen in spring, giving an early yield. Crops like oil seed rape are the caviar on the wood pigeon menu. Couple that with the proliferation of ideal nesting cover by way of commercial conifer plantations in the countryside and mature, man-made gardens and parkland in towns and suburbs and we have pigeon Nirvana. So much so that they can now breed practically all year round and not as other birds do, to time with harvests. Look to the sky during daylight hours in my part of the world and you invariably see wood pigeons going hither and tither.

Wood pigeons have a curious habit which fits into this chapter. Stand and watch them flying overhead, look up and point at them, or move about and they are unwavering. Point a stick at them though, or more to the 'point' a gun, and they immediately take a defensive tumble. This is my curious point. Again, is this response learned or is it genetic? They all seemingly do it, so have they all had the gun experience? Surely not? Could it be genetic? How long has man been shooting them with guns, shotguns at that? It is nigh impossible to shoot them with a bullet or with bow and arrow or spear. This is a fast flying species. This is a very recent threat to them. This habit bucks the theories.

I have a large garden. Youth thinks big but now it is wearing towards being a rod for my back. The neat and tidy shrubs, hedge and trees of thirty years ago don't stop growing at a particular height for my convenience. They have to be pruned. Each year produces more a-risings and I apologize for contributing to carbon in the atmosphere by setting light to the ever increasing pile. Here is another odd event requiring explanation. As the smoke billowed northwards two buzzards and a kestrel appeared, perching on alternate fence posts and totally engulfed in the smoke path. At first I thought this may be a ploy to rid themselves of parasites but quickly ruled that out. That would have been just as fascinating, but they were all intent on staring at the ground. It seems obvious that they were expecting an exodus of rodents from the fire. There wasn't any, of course, as I had just piled it up and set fire to it. Are you with my thinking? From where does the expectation come? Experience I have to rule out. Forest fires would have been a big harvest for these rodent eaters in prehistory but how many forest fires have these individuals experienced, or even garden fires? That leaves genetics. Over millennia did mutations lead to adaptations for species to take advantage of these forest fires which existed alongside their evolution? It sounds far-fetched. I can only watch and wonder. It seems the only feasible answer.

In the countryside, mice are everywhere, *'Wee cou'erin' timorous beasties'*. Turn over a stone or log, dig over a piece of ground, disturb logs in the woodshed and nests are found. They are prolific breeders and eat practically anything. The 100 kilos of natural crocus bulbs I planted ten years ago are reduced to a sprinkle. What was once a dazzling display of orange in early springtime is no more. After each winter the tell-tale scrapes are everywhere. Thank goodness for the snowdrops, aconites and daffodils. They don't like them. This abundance of mice is good news for predators. Foxes, badgers and crows all take their share as although the birth rate is high, so too is the death rate. Only living for around two years, there are plenty of dead or infirm ones to be scavenged. Live ones are kept in check by buzzards, kestrels, sparrowhawks, owls, stoats, weasels and the like. In late October, when the grain harvest is finished and the weather turns colder, there is a great attraction to centrally heated houses. Outhouses also give cover and both are impossible to mouse-proof. If it weren't for the damage, there would be no problem but damaging precious things is what they are good at. Making snug nests for the winter, it seems they habitually chew anything including electric cable insulation, both in houses and vehicles, causing dangerous short circuits. Everyone living in the countryside has the same problem and the only answer is control. Sentinel mouse traps are the most humane way. Anyone who has tried poison will know the smell of rotting mouse bodies lasts a long time. Also, poison is a cruel death and can move up the food chain. The traps in my wooden outhouse produce a steady stream, despite efforts to keep them out. In the morning, any bodies are thrown over the fence to feed the local buzzard who always seems to be around. Lately, though, two crows have latched on to his supply chain. When I look out on a winter's morning, there is a pair sitting on the fence waiting for the scramble if indeed any are available. The buzzard is bombed out. Immediately after my check if they see that there is no issue, they fly away to return to try their luck next morning. The buzzard hangs about all day fruitlessly checking and rechecking but the crows don't waste their time. Clever birds crows.

These particular ones are carrion crows but there are hooded crows around and also a mixture of the two. They are virtually the same species but would prefer to mate with their ilk. If not available, they will readily interbreed with the true carrion variety. This adaptation of grey colouring is prevalent in the far north of the globe, obviously to facilitate camouflage in snowier places as with the difference in mountain and brown hares, but I live in the crossover latitude with both species existing side by side. Again, it is this very evidence that Charles Darwin surmised. Species are not fixed and unchanging.

Another 'miracle' of behaviour is co-ordination between individuals and the speed of their reactions. There were many games we played at school which contributed to an understanding of the world.

Hands-on experimentation beats any theory. Someone holds a ruler out horizontally and you have to hold your hand above it. The person in his own time drops the ruler and you have to catch it before it hits the ground. It's not easy. Most fail but I had a good record. I'm that type of 'on edge' person. Not much of an evolutionary advantage in modern life except for catching falling rulers. Speed of reaction differs in individuals. So what if your life depended on catching a ruler? I'm in.

It would certainly increase your focus but you would still be constrained by how you are made up by way of your genes. In this situation I would have the edge on my classmates in life and so might my children.

An advert appeared in a safety magazine. The picture was of a safety hat worn by a workman while climbing a ladder. A six inch nail had penetrated the hat to a depth of just clear of his skull. The picture showed the helmet and embedded nail. The article explained that it saved his life as without the hat, his brain would have been penetrated instead of the hat. It conveyed a pretty dramatic message.

No-one could argue against the message that a safety helmet should be worn but that very scenario happened to me minus the hat. The result was a nasty cut but no brain penetration. The upward movement was turned into a downward one so fast that a blink is an eternity. When it comes to life threatening situations, the brain and nervous system show remarkable speed.

Wildlife survival has more than equalled that speed and it is spectacular. A shoal of sardines or any other predated species moves as one. A swarm of bees does not have individuals bumping into one another. A flock of starlings 30,000 strong seem to change direction as one unit. In the Scottish highland capital of Inverness, at dusk in winter, they swoop in en masse to roost on the buildings seeking the warmth of one another and benefit from the couple of degrees of difference between town and countryside.

All these occurrences appear as one movement but on close inspection there is a wave motion. In the sardine's case it is hardly discernible but a slow motion camera can portray this wave's elegance. How does it work? The last individual cannot possibly know the intentions of the first to change direction, so how do these creatures do it? There is a simple rule. You only have to react to what your nearest neighbour does. What the rest of the numbers do is irrelevant. A highly speeded up Mexican wave: it's exactly the same principle. This is akin to the nail in the head scenario. Reactions are lightning fast. One may think surely that they can't be as fast as to encompass that vast number by individual reactions.

There was another classroom experiment that Feeky carried out. No-one got bored in her class. She had her thirty pupils hold hands in a broken circle. She holds a stop watch and times the experiment. She taps the shoulder of the first individual who, on that signal, then squeezes the hand of his/her neighbour. Their brain has detected the squeeze and sent a signal to the other hand to act. The neighbour, on receiving the squeeze, does the same and so on round the circle. The last individual, on getting the squeeze, raises his hand and the watch is stopped.

In case the kids are unprepared, the exercise is done three times. What time is recorded on the stopwatch? The result is under two seconds, most of that taken up by the time taken to raise the last hand and to press the stop watch. If you haven't done it, try it and be amazed. That's just a bit of fun but what if your life depended on it? Throw in a few million years of any sluggard being predated and an organism develops the skill to the finest degree. It's no wonder we marvel at the spectacle.

Vespula vulgaris: out of all the creatures that strike fear into the heart of humans, the common wasp figures high on the list. Tables and chairs are overturned in restaurants in a mass hysterical rush to escape the company of a small insect. Companies make a living out of eradicating them from house lofts and outbuildings. It's a con. Well, they do what they say they do but it is totally unnecessary: a waste of money.

A potential customer spots wasps in June/July entering a crevice in the house structure. Modern houses with tiled roofs offer great crevices between the 'bell cast' bottom row of tiles and the fascia board. It would be a surprise to learn of a modern bungalow without a wasp nest having been previously built in this space. The vast majority go unnoticed and with no problems. If, however, one year the tenant notices that creates panic and immediate action. The pest control officer with protective suit puffs in poison to kill the satanic insects. The wasps out foraging at the time arrive home and they are not too chuffed. Look-out, they may sting you in retaliation. So would you in defence of your progeny. What do you expect? Now if you had let them be, this would not have happened.

I have a great respect for wasps. I don't wish to be stung. It has happened and, although it is not pleasant, it's no big deal to me. I have suffered a lot worse. Wasps attract yet another misconception.

At the year of writing there are three obvious wasp 'bikes' around my home but there will be more. One is under the fascia board above the back door, one is in the garden shed and another in the garage, the latter two the size of a small football. The largest is surely the one above the back door, although the nest cannot be seen. A constant stream flows in and out just above head height and the 'postie' is not too chuffed delivering the mail, despite my reassurances. I demonstrate the lack of threat by putting my hand over the entrance hole and the creatures buzz around, landing on my hand and enter through the cracks in my fingers. They are totally engrossed in their task and my hand is of no consequence.

Now, supposing I swat one and kill it. The others go into attack mode, stimulated by a scent emitted, apparently evolved as a response to an ant invasion. They will now sting any living entity nearby in defence of the colony, quite understandably.

A typical nest can contain between 5,000 and 10,000 wasps. Nesting wasps are no threat if left alone. A basic observation of their life cycle sheds light on the reason for their bad publicity. The nest building started later than usual this particular year because of the cold spring. It was June before I became aware of their activities. The overwintered, previously fertilised, queen starts the paper nest and it steadily grows. She lays the first eggs and when they hatch they quickly metamorphose into adults. They contribute to the nest building, chewing wood into pulp and enlarging the nest. This allows the queen to lay more and more eggs. The workers, to feed the larvae, turn to hunting insects and the greenfly in the beech hedge are prime targets. The cotoneaster's tiny flowers are a particular attraction for bees and wasps alike so they are also pollinators at this time of year. The adults have mandibles for pulverising insects but they cannot eat solid food themselves. They feed them to the larvae and in turn, they secrete a sugary syrup to feed their slaves.

When enough grubs have metamorphosed, the job's done. The nest is abandoned forever and the wasps disappear, apparently for the drones to mate with new queens. They don't swarm like bees and I have never found out where they go but it is certainly nowhere near the old nest. The workers, sterile females, are left to roam the countryside in search of sustenance. It is autumn and over ripe fruit abounds, soft fruit in the first instance and then apples, etc. It is a futile exercise of instinctive self-preservation because they are all going to die. All animals share that fate. A wasp cannot tell the difference between sweet fruit, coca cola, barbecue beer or toffee apple and that's when they can be a problem. They are not out to sting anyone, but caught in a woman's hair, swallowed with a mouthful of beer or being sat upon brings on the obvious response. You have to be careful at that time of year but it has nothing to do with the wasps nesting in your loft. They are harmless if left alone. They will not return to that nest.

Here's another strange thing. There is a co-ordination between nests. This year all three nests were emptied the second week in August, unusually early. It is often well into September. I can guess that, at last, a better summer contributed to the raising of progeny to the required numbers due to the abundance of food. Apparently, the reason for the precise timing of leaving is so that genetic diversity can be achieved by interbreeding between colonies. After all, the drones and new queens in a nest all have the same mother. How they communicate between colonies is just another of nature's amazing mysteries.

Wasps are fascinating creatures and good for pest control and pollination. Forget the paranoia.

Bees, on the other hand, are still feared but more tolerated. Insecticides have drastically reduced numbers nationally but there are apparently other reasons. The honey bee pollination of our food crops is cited as vitally important. That may be so commercially, as in fruit orchards, where there is a lot to pollinate.

A slight misconception is that the honey bee is the chief pollinator, followed by the bumble bee. I have healthy apple trees with good pollination but absolutely no honey bees. There used to be, but no more, so how can that bee (sorry). A youthful activity was to raid a wild honeybee nest and the prize honeycomb was shared on the way home whilst picking the stings out of the skin. It is many years since I have seen a wild honeybee nest. The bumble bees have a quick look at the apple blossoms and certainly contribute but have better preferences. They have a huge choice as there are more than 170 varieties of flowering shrubs in the garden to choose from (an indulgence on my part).The ginger common carder bee is the most prevalent bee species. This is the one we kids used to call 'the doctor' in the mistaken belief that they healed sick bumble bees. Bumble bees would rather harvest the dandelions along the roadside verge, the dwarf rhododendron collection and then move on en masse to the large *Cotoneaster horizontalis* growing against the house wall at the back door. Its tiny insignificant pink flowers must produce the goods as bees and wasps love it. Wasp numbers are not high enough for the apple blossom in May but swelled enough by late May/June to feast on this rich treasure. With the northern, nearly 24 hour daylight, midsummer the bush hums round the clock with hundreds of pairs of tiny wings, again much to the consternation of the postman in the morning.

So what does pollinate the fruit trees and bushes? I concentrated on one apple tree, a James Grieve, planted by me and cordoned on the south facing fence. It produces easily 300 big apples in a good year, enough for me, the blackbirds and fieldfares, the slugs and the wasps: this despite the unfavourable northern location. Close observation revealed tiny midge like insects floating around in and out of the flowers which go almost unnoticed. They cannot carry nearly as much pollen as on a bee's body but they can still carry pollen and there are many of them. Common house flies, awakening from goodness knows where, have a go as well. Finer days bring butterflies and many moths feed at night, harvested in turn by the local pipistrelles (where do they come from all of a sudden?). It turned out that the biggest pollinator by far was the humble hoverfly and more than one species at that. Entomology is not my passion but apparently there are around 250 varieties in the UK alone. They constantly patrol the flowers, almost unnoticed, and do the job admirably.

Their season stretches well into October when the bees have gone. How they have survived the adjacent chemical onslaught is a mystery. I would like to think my little wildlife oasis has helped. In the wider countryside it has been suggested by research that 80% of our native wild flowers are no more, so my collection of shrub varieties are a big attraction. Perhaps I should purchase a hive. That said, it is not true that honey bees are required for pollination in the countryside as in the national publicity but it still would be a great loss to commerce and nature if they succumbed to man's activities as they seem to be doing.

In this northern location, as previously stated, it is not

commercially viable to grow apples, pears and plums. At first impressions, the lack of heat in September makes for poor ripening. This should not be a problem as they can be ripened in storage, but it is more apparent that the real reason is the uncertainty of good pollination. There are plenty of insects about and the honey bee introduction in a hive would give ample pollinators for an enterprise but we have 'The Garb o' May' to contend with: the second and third weeks of May often sees the last fling of winter. It can bring snow flurries and sub-zero temperatures but normally the *nor' easter* brings cold rain and wind. Insects take cover and sit it out. It usually lasts around a week or so but that is the crucial time that most commercial varieties are fertile, especially *Prunus* species like plums. A year without the Garb, or a less severe one, produces fantastic crops but that is no good for an ongoing business, so no big orchards around here.

Contemplating strange behaviour, it doesn't come more mysterious than the next two chapters: probably my favourite wildlife mystery.

7

A BIRD'S EYE VIEW

There is much here that does not meet the eye, that is obvious.

from 'The Pink Panther – A Shot in the Dark'

Perhaps the chapter's title should read: *A View on Birds' Eyes*

It seemed to me to be a serious enough question to ask. In 1960 a panel of experts was to speak on the subject of birds in the city's prestigious Music Hall and it attracted a large audience, including myself of course. I wouldn't miss that. After the three presentation speeches, the floor was thrown open for the audience to ask questions and this was mine, 'Do all birds have bifocal vision?' It really didn't deserve the reaction it got. The panel was in stitches as was everyone else in the audience. After the hilarity cooled down, my sixteen year old red face didn't. What had I said to cause myself such embarrassment? What was this ignorant kid doing dabbling in such thoughts? Well, it was at a time that bifocal glasses were a brand new concept and the question had evoked connotations of birds with glasses. At least I think that was what it was. This was a revelation to me that the majority of the general population didn't think the way I did on many aspects of nature. Where on earth did that idea come from? The panel composed themselves somewhat and with one voice commented that birds' vision has nothing to do with bifocals and that they have binocular vision, the same as we humans. They have to judge perspective and distance as, for example when flying to a perch, they have to be precise to land accurately. For this they need both eyes to work together in binocular vision. That was the answer given. Now, at sixteen, I have not got the confidence to refer them back to my original question but I would ask the reader to refer to it. On hindsight I would have loved to have asked, 'on to which perch does an ostrich fly?' All birds are different and the differences have evolved to suit their individual niches. Where did this subject spring from in my young mind and was I talking nonsense?

I knew about binocular vision first hand, or rather the lack of it. After the Second World War, with my side being classed as the victors, there were many kids' comic books on the battle theme depicting the soldier's life as macho bravado which it certainly was not. There was often a depiction of a view through a commando's binoculars surveying the enemy. It appeared as two merged circles. I couldn't understand that as, when I looked through binoculars, I only saw one circle. As I grew into teenage years there was a new concept in motion pictures: 3D. The first film was called '13 Ghosts' and as I said before, although X-rated, this was never enforced if you were anything near the legal age. Special glasses were issued with red and green lenses. If you looked at the screen without them you only saw mush but with them on the reality and depth brought the action to amazing reality, apparently. The rest of the audience were oohing and aahing and some were screaming. Me, I saw mush. I had to walk out and demand my money back. That wasn't nice language to use on a kid but then I wasn't supposed to be a kid watching an X-rated movie.

It turned out that I had a genetic defect in my left eye. The muscle doesn't work and I am practically blind in that eye. Glasses cannot correct muscle dysfunction so I am saddled with that for life. No 3D television in my home as it requires binocular vision. Having the use of only one eye should apparently be a big problem to me for judging distance and spatial awareness. Surely that cannot be correct? I have lived my life with no such problems and, according to ophthalmologists, my brain has learned at an early stage to compensate for the deformity. I can judge the distance to my perch perfectly. Then if I only have one eye, I must have monocular vision. Binocular vision is said to be vastly superior to monocular vision. Then, if a bird has the advantage of binocular vision, a pigeon or other preyed upon species would use this to focus on a bird of prey in the sky to judge the peril. It should train both eyes on the danger, but it doesn't. At the first sign of a predator the bird turns its head sideways and focuses ONE EYE on the hawk. This is an easily observed action in prey species. Approach a skein of wild geese in a field and they are on guard the moment they are aware of your presence. The heads come up and they all stand side on to you and watch your every movement with one eye.

Bird eyes differ in many ways from human eyes. One difference is that the eyes are fixed in the sockets. It cannot glance sideways. It has to turn its head. If you hold a pigeon's beak and look at its eyes, there is very little of the pupils you can see from the front. If you move your head to the side just a little, you cannot see the far pupil, meaning that binocular vision is confined to a very narrow angle. This is all that is required for judging the distance to a perch or similar action but for surveying the land and sky all around for danger it is very inefficient. To use that binocular vision for that purpose, it would have to continually turn its head to face and focus on what it wants to see, leaving it exposed to danger from another direction. The solution is to have very good monocular vision as well as binocular and that is why the bird focuses one eye on a predator but there's more, much more. Whilst it has a beady eye on that hawk, danger could still come from the other direction. Well, it has monocular vision in the other eye to cover that, and that is what humans cannot do. I count myself out, obviously, but humans with two good eyes cannot focus on two things at once. Try it and agree. They may be aware of two objects on either side but they cannot focus on both of them. For that they have to either close one eye and concentrate on one object, or face one object and use their binocular vision. A pigeon can see both clearly, meaning that it can focus on two things at the same time with different eyes: 'bifocality'. Some birds have bifocal vision but do they all? As for my simple question: I wasn't enamoured with the 'expert' tag of those speakers. This fact about bird vision was explained to me by that zoology teacher, Feeky, when I asked her about the 'one eye' behaviour I had seen in pigeons, blackbirds and thrushes (we were dissecting animal eyes at the time). A blackbird, she said, turned its head sideways to focus on the worm, whilst the other eye could look out for danger. A pigeon can feed and be aware of its surroundings to 300° without turning its head, the other 60° covered with only a slight head movement. However, it became obvious to me that there was a flaw in this 'all birds' statement. Feeky never got it all her own way and she encouraged argument. She got plenty of that from me and relished it, unlike other teachers. Owls, I observed, had eyes facing the front. They still are fixed in the sockets but they can cover practically 360º, as everyone knows, by having an extremely versatile neck. If they spot danger whilst roosting during the day they confront it head on with binocular vision which, as we all know, is acute. They also hunt that way as well so it would appear that owls don't have bifocal vision. That anomaly was the reason for my original question.

It so happened that very recently this subject reared its head again. Another talk by a famous author on her experiences with birds. Her theme was very different from mine in this book, although some subjects were similar in addressing observations. Not wanting to be embarrassed, as I was nearly half a century ago, the three anomalies I noticed in her talk I left for the after talk chat as she mingled and signed books. I squeezed in the question. In her talk on the subject of the blackbird, she had said it was a fallacy that the blackbird on the lawn turned its head to see the worm. It does it to HEAR the worm. I cannot prove that it doesn't but I also cannot accept that the high calibre eye now facing the worm is not used. I was also taught that birds of the air, in general, do not have an acute sense of hearing (owls and some birds of prey excepted). When I mentioned it may involve the bifocal ability, she was unmoved. There was another subject I questioned. Homing pigeons, she had said, had an area in the upper beak containing iron crystals which were used to detect the earth's magnetic field giving them their homing ability. This is typical. A famous person in an influential position makes a statement that her listeners take as gospel. I had to point out that I had read, in scientific literature, that this was disproved categorically. The crystals were used for a different function. There was more about homing pigeons. If they are transported to the release point in total darkness, they cannot navigate home. They have to see the sky and then memorize the route to follow home. It is a fact that if you are going to tell me anything about homing pigeons, then you had better be a successful racing pigeon fancier and she was not. I politely told her this is not true. She sipped her tea and turned to talk to someone else.

If you are a successful pigeon breeder and racer, then you are a good observer of your subjects, the same as all other thoroughbred breeders. You have to know each one down to the finest detail and train them to perfection for the chosen task ahead. Training flights are common. Birds are basketed and driven to a release point. Mine were transported in the boot of the car and you don't get darker than that. Let's take one example to disprove both points. I had to go on business to Braemar, seventy miles west. I then drove south and east over the mountains and down the River Tay valley to Tayport. The reason for this particular point is that it trains young birds to cross water, in this case the wide Tay estuary. It is also to familiarize them with the lie of the land on the last leg of a race as was believed. Tayport is seventy miles from home. The basket is set on the ground on the south side of the car for twenty minutes. This is important on two counts. First, it settles them after the journey and lets them see the sky. Second, they are to be released singly so that they learn to navigate on their own. I don't want them seeing to the north and the route of the previous bird. Another plus to this release point is that you can follow them with binoculars all the way across the estuary. The first bird is picked out and released. After a few circles it veers north, not in a straight line but zig zag, with head turning either way as if it knows when it is going wrong rather than when it is right. It seems obvious that it is the eyes that are being used here. Remember, these young birds are only four months old and have never been here before. Whatever those eyes may see, it is something we cannot. By the time it has crossed the estuary, it is on a bullet straight line for home. The rest are released in the same manner when the first one disappears.

Just to recap: transported in pitch black in a triangular route and straight line home in an hour and a half. Not only that, but race birds were in my day transported to the race point in closed railway goods vans overnight: comments by the speaker on homing necessities . . . nonsense. Of course I put it in a nicer way towards the end of the book signing. The facial expression said it all.

She may be correct in one aspect. Evidence seems to suggest that pigeons navigate using the earth's magnetic field, although nothing to do with iron crystals, and there are other factors. Science has done much work on this by studying the European robin in Sweden. We have European robins her in the UK as well but there is a difference. The Swedish ones migrate as far as North Africa. Ours stay and sit on spade handles in the garden to make lovely pictures for Christmas cards. With experiments at migration time in captivity, birds line themselves up with artificially induced magnetic fields and fly south, wherever the artificial south happens to be. At the moment all that can be deduced is that they, apparently, know the position of the poles. In the wild they can detect the nearest one, north, and fly in the opposite direction. The location of the magneto receptors in birds is still a mystery but latest research seems to point to the eye. Recent scientific observations on nesting turtles suggest a geomagnetic connection to find their home beach and, although not mentioned, I wouldn't be surprised if the eye was involved as well.

It is being suggested that electric charge is involved and that takes the subject to a more basic level of atomic and even sub atomic activity: into the weird world of particle physics where one particle can be in two places at once. Can birds' eyes really tap into quantum entanglement and tunneling electrons? One thing is for sure. Up until now we can only speculate.

Pigeon fanciers will know what a smash is. It is a pigeon race that results in massive losses due to disorientation in fine weather conditions for no apparent reason. One such smash was blamed on the sonic boom of Concorde. Research into this phenomenon led to a discovery that massive solar flare activity coincided with the disasters, leaning further towards the magnetic field theory being involved.

Another factor regarding the eyes of racing pigeons: fanciers regard 'eye sign' as vitally important in selecting breeding birds. This is the irregular area around the pupil which can vary in depth and colour. Humans don't have it. There are even 'eye sign' classes at winter shows. The Holy Grail is the 'violet'. Many long distance champions possess it and the evidence is that they can pass on faithfully their champion homing ability genes to the next generation. Sums of up to £100,000 have been paid for a potential champion breeder.

If any part of a migrating or homing animal is worthy of research into navigation this mysterious area would be a contender, surely. So as far as animal eyes are concerned, there really is much more to them than meets the eye.

It would be a good guess to say that the same geomagnetism is involved in general bird and animal migration, although certainly not exclusively.

Animal orientation is the most fascinating of all subjects to me and I dedicate the next chapter to it.

8

MIGRATION

Before migration was studied, some people thought swallows simply spent the winter asleep in mud.

attributed to Aristotle

In 1952 a Manx shearwater was taken from its nest in a burrow on an island off the coast of Wales, UK. It was flown across the Atlantic and released in Boston, Massachusetts, USA. Three weeks later it was back on its nest. By all standards this is an astonishing feat by a bird the size of a pigeon. The time factor and the navigation are the astonishing bits, not the distance. These birds migrate to waters off the southern coast of South America. That's around 8,000 miles. Couple that with their longevity, regularly more than fifty years and that's an awful lot of miles. Add on their long oceanic voyages for food and it has been estimated that one bird can easily top 10,000,000 miles in a lifetime. The fascinating thing about this experiment is that it did not concern traditional migration routes. It was an unknown release point with 4,000 miles of pure ocean to negotiate. Latitude can be calculated by many observable signs, not least being the position and height of the sun. Mariners have never had much problem with that. Longitude, though, was their dilemma and it took a big shipwreck off the Isles of Scilly in 1707 to force the then scientific community into action. This led to the well-known story of John Harrison, a Yorkshire carpenter turned clockmaker, and his invention of a reliable chronometer resulting in his eventually winning the Royal Society's prize for cracking the problem. It seems though, that the Manx shearwater had conquered that problem as a species a long time before. Quite amazing and we still haven't the foggiest how it can do it without the chronometer.

They are not the only birds to clock up a huge mileage. Arctic terns nest in the Arctic and winter in the Antarctic, the longest

68

migration on the planet. Their adaptations to long hours on the wing are self-evident but how do they navigate? It has long been a fascination to me since I kept those homing pigeons as a boy. Pigeons cannot make these fantastic journeys, being land birds but the navigational skills are the same. Migration routes of our summer visitors seem preprogrammed into their brains but take them away from these routes and can they correct their bearings to get home? The answer is obviously yes, as in the case of the shearwater and my pigeons. Racing pigeons are taken on a specific direction each week during the summer to race home. The longest races are a mere 700 miles: a cinch for the shearwater but a fair slog for a pigeon. So what happens if route direction is suddenly switched? Well, in my experiments, no difference. You can take them many miles in any direction and the time taken per mile is the same, wind and weather dependent of course. Sometimes this isn't a direct route. Training flights were necessary for fitness and obliging lorry driver friends would willingly take them for release and that was dependent on their destinations. The one who regularly took mine went to Thurso (120 miles north) and Fort William (120 miles west). The northerly released birds, as the crow (or pigeon) flies have the huge expanse of the Moray Firth to cross, followed by the Cairngorm massif. The westerly released birds are immediately confronted with Ben Nevis and the Nevis range, some well over 4,000 feet followed by the Monadhliath mountains. I just cannot see them flying over all these obstacles considering that 'the mist covered mountains' is the norm. That means they have to navigate around them, using the glens, and they don't run in straight lines. There are some losses but considering the terrain and the attraction of a 'kit' of pigeons to a peregrine falcon in its natural environment, it's not surprising. When you think about it though, don't all flying birds have to possess the same ability? Most birds have to search for food and prevailing strong winds can lift and displace them, calling on this 'homing instinct' to get back to nest. They can obviously use familiar landmarks to do this over reasonably short distances. We land bound humans do it all the time otherwise we wouldn't get home. In old sailing ship days before GPS, lighthouses, and all other navigational aids, a ship fishing in the middle of the North sea could plainly sail east and hit the shores of its native land but to find the exact harbour out of many, landmarks were extremely important. In my native city they had theirs:

There are two landmarks from the sea Clochnaben and Bennachie

These promontories are well known to the natives of this area. Clochnaben is a huge rocky outcrop like a pimple on the side of a hill and the Mither Tap of the Bennachie range is synonymous with the area: so, steer your ship between the two and you will sail into Aberdeen harbour.

This can't be used over hundreds of miles though, so there must be a lot more to it. It has been suggested that some migrating species navigate by the stars. In experiments with American robins, when faced with an artificial ceiling of the celestial sphere, they aligned themselves in their migratory direction according to the night sky. That's some feat for a small brain. What about during the day on migration or when intentionally or accidentally misplaced? It is suggested birds can calculate their latitude by the position of the sun. It's still only a suggestion but the seasons have a big influence obviously in the timing of migrations. It doesn't take much mental agility for me to work out the time of year by the position of the sun and my life doesn't depend on it like the swallows, wildebeest, caribou, etc. The 'Mither Tap' to me means equinox. On 21st June and 21st September, the sun sets exactly behind the peak. At the end of the sunless winter in Baffin Island they celebrate the return of the sun on a precise date. People even in this country, living in the shadow of a mountain, have barbecue parties to hail the same precise return of the sun above the horizon at the end of January. It would appear feasible then, to expect that migratory species time the big event with the sun's position as a trigger.

People have many different notions of the signs of spring eg buds opening on trees, the first swallow, woodpeckers drumming, song birds singing, or the cuckoo. Mine would be the song of the willow warbler, always welcome. I normally hear that locally before the first swallow appears to nest again, but many swallows arrive before the willow warbler. They do not immediately return to their nest sites. Lochs and rivers are their first visit to gather sustenance after their long journey from

South Africa. This observation is backed up by records. First, last and transitional sightings are well documented by amateur ornithologists, me included. If you happen to be there at the right time, you will see that they have one or two quick reconnaissance trips in early April to the nest site, to check things are just so, but they don't linger. The insect life in the general countryside has not reawakened yet so they are reliant on the aquatic flies, which have started hatching on rivers and lakes. By the first week in May, however, they are back for the summer. Their primary food source seems to be greenfly. These hatch and spread to new growth. In this latitude, trees such as my elm, oak, beech, ash and their favourite, the lime, do not foliate until late May and into June, so no point relocating before that. Nest building begins in May, so when the nestlings eventually hatch, they are born when the glut of insects is at a peak, their life cycles played out in the short northern summer. The farther north you go the shorter that summer but crucially, the more insects there are. Two or three broods have all the food they need. These observations of course may be different elsewhere as seasons are a little different in more southern parts. All this drew me into an unintentional argument.

The following article appeared in the local paper one year on 14th August.

Foggit weather:

Amateur weather forecaster Bill Foggitt is predicting that an Indian summer is on its way - because the swallows are still here and the midges are flying high. So far this year the weathermen, with all their maps, knick knacks and high technology resources have failed to come up with the sunshine. After a cold, damp July, North East folk have certainly had enough of the rain and mist and if Bill's swallows and midges bode well for a sunny autumn, who are we to argue?

Me, for a start: it seems we have to blame the weather on the forecasters. The Foggitt statement is even worse. This Yorkshire amateur long range weather forecaster, known for his accuracy, had predicted an Indian summer 'because the swallows are still here'. Eh? 14th August? I just had to reply. My letter appeared in the letter column to put him straight. It was entitled 'Foggitt's

Folly' (the editor's words). Apart from pointing out that many swallows are still here for as much as another two months, it was not unusual for some still to be here in November. I also suggested that he may have been confusing them with swifts but even they go at the **end** of August. In any case, someone so conversant with nature would surely know the difference as the two are not even closely related: their vague similarity due to convergent evolution with their similar lifestyles. Swallows and martins belong to the family *Hirundidae*, while the swifts, along with nightjars, are *Apodidae*.

That would give Foggitt a bloody nose. Obviously some disagreed and wrote in to say so.

Hard story to swallow:

Reference the letter of August 22nd and the associated departure of swallows. The assertion is that the swallows are normally here until October and occasionally stay a bit longer. This I cannot accept as the general behaviour pattern. Swallows do tend to gather in large numbers in late August with the great majority heading south around the end of the month. There is nothing unusual in swallows gracing our skies in September but only very seldom are there more than just a few in October. I have always regarded a late departure of swallows as signatory of an open winter - this fact very often proving to be the case. I feel that swallows possess an instinctive time sense that is subject to weather conditions ahead, otherwise their main departure would not vary from year to year. Here's to many more November swallows.

I did reply to politely say that expert documented observations on a wider scale told a different story.

The misconception here is that if swallows leave their nest, they go straight to Africa. Who could argue that they possess an instinctive time sense? That much is obvious but detecting future weather which is brewing in the Caribbean or mid Atlantic is surely confined to my 'supernature' label. It goes with the rowan berry observation frequently quoted. 'The rowans are thick with berries this autumn, sign of a bad winter to come.' Not only do these trees apparently 'see' weather patterns six months ahead but a whole year ahead as the viability of fruit depends on the

72

successful pollination of the flowers the previous spring. The correspondent's note on early or late departures of swallows goes against the facts. Swallows and other migratory species leave pretty much on cue every year. That's what observation shows. The writer's mistake is in confusing the departure from his locality with migration times. The nest departure varies. My own swallows always raise two broods. In an Indian summer they often raise a third and so accounts for the nest leaving variation. This is **as a result** of good weather and consequently good food supply, not a harbinger of it. There are other factors determining the raising of a third brood. One is how early they start nesting in springtime. If the weather is good in May (without a bad Garb) they will nest earlier and consequently have more time to have a third nesting in the autumn. Another reason is the loss of a nest due to predation or, more usually, human disturbance. This can lead to unusually late attempts and my latest recording was one pair feeding youngsters in the nest on Armistice Sunday, 11th November with deep snow on the ground. Whether they ever made it to Africa I don't know. In general though, they leave the nest sites in early September and the skies can be thick with them. Insects are preparing for winter by mating and laying eggs, swarming in nuptial dances around tree copses. The grain harvest in these parts historically stirs up a myriad, although not so much nowadays with insecticides. In mid-September, skies are crowded with swallows if only you look up. Crane flies and other insects, whose grubs spent the summer in the soil, are breaking out to complete their life cycle. This late flush is harvested, not only by swallows and martins but by unlikely birds such as starlings. They fly up vertically to snatch a share of the bonanza. Eventually, the insects either settle to lay their eggs and die or find crevices in tree bark or buildings to overwinter, depending on species. That becomes the winter larder for tits, wrens, etc. Another point of interest from observation: swallows are not insect eaters exclusively, as some may think. They are partial to a bit of arachnid. It matters not if their prey has wings or the amount of legs it has. Spiders are just as nutritious but if they cannot fly, how then can they be swallow food? In autumn, cobweb spiders spread across the countryside to find new habitat. They spin silk and use this as a parachute to be lifted and carried by the wind to new locations. On a still

September morning the countryside can be covered in dewy silk. The swallows lap them up. They may not be very big but there seems to be millions of them (that's my non exaggerated estimation). Then, as in their springtime foraging, it is the lochs, ponds and rivers around which they spend time. As the countryside insect bonanza dries up, aquatic insects are still on the go. The birds build up their strength and the youngsters mature. They roost in the reed beds. In fact, instead of flying south, many fly north to traditional water areas where they know food will be available. Birds from my area were recorded, by ring identification, feeding in autumn forty miles north at one of their favourite lochs.

I have no idea when the first swallows leave or if any leave in August. Broods are seen on wires then but that is because the second broods are now old enough to fly around and they are fed by their parents whilst sitting on rooftops and wires. Seeing them like this in August seems to suggest they are getting ready to migrate but these young birds have a bit of growing up to do first. It doesn't mean they are preparing to leave for South Africa. I would have to observe on the south coast of England to corroborate any August departures and I haven't done so. There is certainly a big migration of swallows recorded in September, but whether they are southern English birds or my swallows, again, I wouldn't know. It could be that the life cycle of insects in the north lags behind the south. Grain harvest here is September. My plum tree fruits are only just ripening mid-month whereas in the south of England, all that is history. Habits vary geographically within a single species. Remember the European robin. I only know that every year without fail, all swallows I have recorded at nest sites around here in the north east of Scotland are either feeding fledglings or still nesting in early September, and that's despite the weather, so that's a lot of swallows that have yet to fledge and/or strengthen to make the trip.

You have to observe the broader countryside and record data before you can draw any conclusions. I try to do that. In my diary on **22nd October** last, I recorded two successive flocks, of around 300 swallows in each, flying southwards very low. I also recorded the weather. Rain and mist with strong wind from the south east. That's the reason they were flying low. Hardly an odd few and hardly good migrating weather. I was surprised at this myself. This may be an effort to avoid predators. This observation was only in my small 100 metre snapshot part of the broader countryside as visibility was poor. I can only guess that this was a migration flight because I cannot prove it, but the date surely puts all such arguments to rest. For interest, the last recorded swallows over a ten year period were all in November except one on 1st December. Acknowledging these observations from experts, I must add that these were the LAST recorded. Late September/October migration fits in with the cooling of Mediterranean temperatures and subsequent increased insect activity there in preparation for their, albeit milder, winter. Swallows arrive at the olive groves and scrublands at this time along with many other migrants. It is an important stopover before crossing the Sahara. It would be foolhardy to arrive too early.

There is another weird and wonderful observation about swallow migration which may give a clue to migration in general. I had two large outbuildings which had at least four swallow nests each year. In the late 1990s they were converted into dwellings (above).

During construction, they would go to great lengths to access the building. Every time a door opened, they flew in. To relieve the situation, I opened the window of a garden shed and a pair immediately used that. Birds have been using it ever since. They have to protect it though, as every year, the others try to take over. Fifteen years later, many still return, most with no nest site and if anyone in the converted houses leaves a garage door open in summer, they come home at night to find swallows in it. They buzz around all summer, trying all the time to find an access. So why don't they move somewhere else after all this time? A quarter of a mile away, there is a derelict house. It has its own resident birds. One pair of mine has managed to squeeze in to nest there. How do I know it's my swallows? Because after every fledging, the whole family moves back over here and mix with mine (as in the photograph on the previous page.

This is not a migration gathering: it happens two or three times a year, every year. Successive families roost on the ridge of their ancestral home along with the ones still denied a nest site. All the way from South Africa and they want to be precisely here, not anywhere else. It is like an invisible force that keeps them here. They can't help it. As an observer, I would conclude that this is significant in understanding the phenomenon, because the average lifespan of a swallow is TWO YEARS. In fact, the oldest documented swallow life was recorded in 1936 at eleven years, one month, and eleven days: a real swallow Methuselah. So these are not the original birds. A few generations on and they are still bound to this place, even though they cannot nest here.

So swallows returning each spring seem to have a specific destination in mind. Nest sites are always at a premium and food sources are just as important for feeding growing families. My ones settle here but swallows are distributed all over the country. To some, the rugged west coast of Scotland is home. Midges are never in short supply there. Under the swing bridge over the Caledonian Canal on the 'road to the isles', a pair happily breed, completely unperturbed by the constantly moving position of their nest. Some though push further west, across the stormy Minch to the Inner and then Outer Hebrides. It seems a bold step, but it must be worth it. The Machair, coastal wildflower pasture, on the outer isles has an abundance of insects to sustain them but you can't help thinking it must be easier for them to stop on the mainland with less stormy winds. Not so, and there is an even stranger journey for some. The isolated archipelago of St Kilda lies another fifty miles west of the Butt of Lewis into the wild Atlantic. After their South Africa to UK journey, they head off onto an amazing last leg. You have to wonder why? Most of the islands' adapted flora, across a surprisingly wide habitat range, requires pollination by insects and swallows need insects. It turns out that there are plenty. The removal of the human population at their own request left derelict houses, leaving a fascinating snapshot of a rugged human lifestyle. It is now a world heritage site and it is good news for swallows. The empty buildings have increased their availability of nesting sites from odd outbuildings to whole rows of houses. Last year's youngsters don't have to compete for nest sites and can raise their own families. Swallows are a true wonder of nature.

In my turbulent mind the jury is still out on zoos. On the one hand animals never go hungry, no predators and no parasites. It seems idyllic until you come across a lion or tiger pacing back and forth in a seemingly endless bored manoeuvre. The wild is where they belong. It is akin to me working on an oil rig or being in prison. Some can become institutionalized but not for me. I'll stay on terra firma and try to obey the law. Safari parks are the nearest thing to the wild and a vast improvement on cages for big cats and other mammals. Singapore Zoo is probably one of the best for birds. You can feed the bee eaters by throwing up a whole handful of mealworms and not one falls to the ground. There is no substitute though for natural environment. The penguin enclosure is very popular with children. Their natural home in the South Atlantic Ocean is substituted with a faeces polluted puddle. However happy they look, they don't have a choice and if they were sad you couldn't tell the difference. No familiar human facial expressions on a penguin. To see an Emperor penguin in a zoo makes me think of the waste of navigational skills given by nature. It lives in the vast expanse of southern oceans around the Antarctic continent. To breed, they return to their nest sites each year in the depths of winter. The reason is that when the young are ready to fend for themselves, conditions are better in summer. There would be no point nesting on the ice shelf near the water as this would melt before the young were old enough to swim, so they nest far from the liquid ocean. They trek 'inland' as much as fifty miles, despite being poor movers on solid surfaces. That's a long way to waddle and slither on your belly. The conundrum is this. Depending on the extent and shape of the sea ice, the 'coast' is not a constant, so they have to leave the water at different places each year. They then find their way to the colony nest site in loose groups, but a solitary penguin can still do the trip unerringly. Picture the scene: Antarctic midwinter and a blizzard raging, you cannot even see the beak in front of you, a classic white out for fifty miles and yet they seem to know where they are going. Captain Scott's ill-fated party did not have GPS then, but they did have a compass. The penguin has neither.

How about other animals' migratory skills? Whales obviously can migrate huge distances yearly and many more species do the same: reindeer, turtles and even lobsters all seem to know where they are going in environments totally hostile to us. My interest when young was the Atlantic salmon. They leave my local rivers as smolts to feed around Greenland, then return to breed when mature. There are plenty of theories, as usual, as to how they do it but are there any proven facts? David Attenborough presented a programme on that very subject, albeit Pacific salmon. He categorically stated that they navigate to the headwaters of their birth tributary by sense of smell, identifying the *'signature'* smell of the tributary, and then running up to the headwaters to spawn. Viewers were convinced, it seems, but is this correct? Has he seen the evidence or is he stating it from script as a presenter? Has research shown this to be a fact? There happens to have been some research on that very river. Returning Pacific salmon in a tributary of the Fraser River were taken downstream to below a fork where they had to choose one way or the other. Apparently they invariably chose the correct one. Fish were returned with their noses blocked up and they became confused as to which way to go. Conclusion: they smell the correct tributary. Case closed. Depriving an animal of a sense and drawing an obvious conclusion is not clear cut. Apart from the obvious trauma this would cause the fish, a game we played at Boy Scouts was to put a peg on the nose, blindfold the eyes and then identify a foodstuff by taste. Being

78

told the object was an apple you happily bit and chewed it. It was an onion. Senses work together and the sudden loss of one affects the others. Perhaps it is taste that identifies the tributary or even another unidentified sense, as in birds. All senses work together. A dog salivates at the sight or smell of food. A pickled onion on a fork has a remarkable ability to make me similarly salivate to the extreme. I do this even at the sight of a jar. Amazingly, the very THOUGHT of a jar has the same effect: a combination of senses providing an involuntary response. However, let's go with what has been suggested, that salmon can detect the tributary's signature smell. Stating water has a signature, if not defined, is as useful as stating there is life after death. We are now getting into the airy fairy theories of homeopathy and water having a 'memory'. Close to me, adjacent tributaries are draining rainwater off the same hill and sometimes, at the watershed, draining the same rain shower to different river systems. Which does a salmon choose? *Signature?* It sounds scientific. Another of my local rivers had tagging experiments. A fish trap in a well populated tributary caught and tagged some females and they were taken in a tank to the headwaters of a less populated tributary ten miles **upstream.** There was a Royal sporting reason for doing this. These tributaries are fed from a watershed literally metres apart. Next day they were back in the fish trap up the tributary **downstream.** Some sense of smell that. These ones at least were not having any other tributary. So it surely cannot be true that they navigate by sense of smell, at least not wholly. What I am being asked to accept is that a tiny young salmon parr leaves its birth tributary with that 'smell' imprinted in its brain and remembered for three years, ready for its return to breed. Not only that but it has to negotiate with that sensitive nose from the icy waters around Greenland through a thousand miles of open ocean to get even to its home river estuary. We know that fish have an acute sense of smell for hunting. Sharks can detect minute amounts of blood from afar, but that's specific foreign particles in the water. There would be no such known particles in this case. In my youth, my local river was heavily polluted by effluent from many paper and textile mills. The last few miles to the sea ran white with bleach, pulp and dyes: if we humans could smell it, how about the salmon? They ran up in their thousands, unlike today as noted in another chapter, so how can the statement be justified? It seems impossible to be able to smell 'something' in the water from a distant tributary through that soup. It is obvious that the statement is incomplete and that surely other factors are involved, but that is what the man said. Going on previously mentioned observations and research, this navigation must surely have some things in common with other species migration and magneto reception is a good contender.

'Then the salmon swim as far upstream as possible, to highly oxygenated waters free of predatory smaller fish. They then pair up and spawn.' Don't they?

Some more observations . . . since the more environmentally aware campaigns have led us to clean up our rivers it is most encouraging to see rivers previously devoid of salmonoid life being recolonized. Where did these salmon come from? Some rivers were stocked with fertilized eggs from other rivers but there is no way of proving the resultant hatchlings returned. You cannot tag an egg but the research method of tagging fish led to other sources. Salmon from other river systems were turning up in these new clean ones. In the south of England many French tagged fish were being recorded in their rivers. So it is not true that they return of necessity to their home rivers.

Consider the statement that they swim as far as possible upstream to spawn? In a local shorter river, salmon regularly spawn only a few miles upstream from tidal waters with many miles of the main river existing upstream. It is possible that a muddier banked river has a shortage of gravel beds and any gravel bed in fresh water is at a premium but it is a fact that they do this. Expert observation reports salmon spawning throughout the entire freshwater length of even the longer, gravelly rivers, So it is certainly not true that salmon always swim to the farthest reaches to spawn, and not even in a tributary. Of course it is advantageous for the offspring to hatch far up the river system where predators are less in number but you can't tell that to a randy salmon who has been waiting weeks for higher water to swim upstream. It also seems not to be true that they pair up in the spawning grounds. I have seen males seemingly protecting a female from other male advances only a few miles from the sea. Perhaps they mate when they first hit fresh water and they run up together, the female being fiercely guarded all the way. This would account for the fact that, although they do not eat while in fresh water, they snap at anything that comes close, such as angling lures. They just become subjected to the influence of testosterone or oestrogen with associated aggression and mood swings, just like we humans. The end result of all this observation and speculation is that we still do not know for sure how it's done.

Another of my observations on salmon: it is revered as 'Salar the Leaper' and I include it on my cover photo. Salmon leap to negotiate rapids and waterfalls. Everyone knows that. Tourists congregate at falls to see the spectacle. Would you argue if my observations suggested a different scenario? That thrashing tail in mid-air is to no avail. No propulsion there. The tail propels in water. Taking a run at the falls, it is easy for them to make a mistake and leave the water. It is not intentional. Watch over a period and you will see that the ones leaping are dashed down to start again. Put on the Polaroids and look into the water at the fast flowing glide at the top of the falls and you will witness the fish running over the top, not one of them have leapt into mid-air. There's more. You would think that the fish that have made that great effort to breach the falls would be happy to rest in the pool beyond, but they don't. They then drop back to the fast flowing glide, to just before the water tumbles over, and they stay there, amazingly, effortlessly for a period before moving on. Just like an athlete, breathless after a race they have to get their breath back. Athletes have air all around them allowing them to breathe deeply but a fish has no lungs. Needing to extract oxygen from the water, resting there in the fast flow accelerates the water over their gills making breathing easier than in the calmer waters of the pool above the falls. That's what is obvious if you look closely.

When marine biologists first started exploring life in the wider oceans, they trawled up an intriguing glass like creature (next page). Completely transparent this entity seemed out of place in the mid-Atlantic. It was hailed and recorded as a new species hitherto unknown to science. This was not unusual. After all it is estimated that, still today, the vast majority of marine life has yet to be discovered and many species regularly are. It was named

81

Leptocephalus (Latin for flat head). Many years later, researchers kept live specimens to look deeper into their life cycle in more detail. To the surprise of the scientific world they metamorphosed into . . . eels.

Now it was already known that the European eel migrated to spawn in the Sargasso Sea, a huge weedy morass in the Atlantic off the Gulf of Mexico. It was assumed that young eels just hatched and rode the ocean currents to reach our shores as elvers. This stage was then unknown, understandably, as they didn't have the benefit of DNA knowledge. The science world acknowledged their mistake and accepted the new discovery. That's the beauty of science. Mistakes are rectified and acknowledged and knowledge moves on.

I loved that story, related as an exciting science story by Feeky at my influential age of thirteen to show that science sometimes gets it wrong.

It was more than just the story. I had had plenty of experience with eels in my local river. The elvers arrived in July and, in their teeming thousands, lined the muddy banks feeding on algae and micro life. They actually arrive in the estuaries in spring as glass eels but my observation further upriver coincided with the school summer holidays. As kids we collected them in jam jars, fascinated by their wriggling antics. We marvelled at their ability to cross land to get around obstacles, climbing the riverbank by sheer weight of numbers and moving to the upper location. My observation worth noting is this, today there are virtually no elvers in the river. Lack of fish in the North Sea is one thing. That was inevitable, but eels? Although they were harvested in small numbers to a limited market no wholesale slaughter, as was the case with other fish, was taking place. There seems to be no reason for it. Rivers have been cleaned of pollution so you can't blame that. One can only speculate. Perhaps they relished the pollution but I doubt it. They were just as numerous in clean rivers. Modern flood defenses have been cited as a barrier but in my river, access upstream has been improved for the salmon's benefit. I expect the answer to come from their migration patterns. Eels spend their adult life in our rivers and ponds, feeding and growing. When they are mature enough to breed, they slip back to the estuaries and begin a fantastic 5,000 mile journey across the Atlantic to the Sargasso Sea. There they lay their eggs and presumably die. When these eggs hatch, they set off back across the Atlantic as *Leptocephali*. What has happened to disrupt their return? The adult journey is an amazing one but presumably they navigate, maybe using the same currents that sailing ships used to and from the West Indies but maybe also using the same sense as the salmon. The *Leptocephali* seem not advanced enough to navigate, although that may be incorrect. There are many surprises in nature. They would be at the mercy of the prevailing current, in the UK's case the Gulf Stream. Perhaps that's why they are the shape they are to catch the current. And it so happens that we have heard plenty of warnings about the result of even small changes in that current and how it would affect weather etc, global warming being the driving force. I am not qualified to say but I am qualified to observe. Scientific study may tell us just how many adult eels are in the rivers of the UK. I am looking as well, in the same places as my youthful observations, and I come up with NONE. If that's the result of man's activities then that's surely a scandal.

Whilst changes in the Gulf Stream may be to blame there could be other reasons. The Sargasso Sea is made up of the golden algae called *Sargassum* and is locked in position by four ocean currents, The Gulf Stream to the west, the North Atlantic Current to the north, the Canary Current to the east and a Pacific one to the south. It's called an ocean gyre, and seaweed is not the only thing that is locked in. Garbage, especially plastic garbage: millions of tons of it, forever circling and growing. The *Sargassum* is rich in micro life and sustains a great deal of marine creatures, providing food and cover from predators.

There is no food source in plastic garbage. Perhaps this can contribute to disruption of life cycles. Whatever the cause you can bet your bottom dollar it is man-made. This disruption to nature is a warning to mankind along with many others. The consequences of ignoring these signs could be dire so we had better take heed.

You may think that all these feats of navigation are remarkable. They pale into insignificance compared to the feats of this next creature: the Monarch butterfly. I have seen them in North America and marvelled at their life cycle. It's a bit different from my local species, some of which hibernate in the garage. These beautiful insects migrate annually from Canada and the northern United States to escape the cold continental winters. The farthest north ones travel up to **3,000** miles: the ones east of the Rocky Mountains, to Mexico and the ones west of the Rocky Mountains, to Southern California. Research findings, only recently, show that populations spend this time in the same trees every year. For an insect that's a great feat, surely. That's just the beginning of the story. On their spring return during April/May they promptly lay their eggs on milkweed plants, on which the subsequently emerging caterpillars feed exclusively and then the adults die. These caterpillars then pupate and by the process of metamorphosis emerge into adult butterflies, a fascinating process but for nature nothing unusual. These then lay eggs around June/July and also die. The third generation, upon hatching, repeats the same process around early October: lays eggs and dies. The fourth generation does the same but this time the emerged adults do not die. They navigate the 3,000 mile journey to Mexico to overwinter ON THE SAME TREE AS THEIR GREAT GRANDFATHER OVERWINTERED THE YEAR BEFORE. When I was a boy kids used to find chrysalises (pupae) of various butterflies and if you squeezed the sides gently they would wiggle their rear end back and fore, proving it was alive, which fascinated us. Occasionally you would squeeze too hard and it burst. Inside there was a milky fluid. No insect parts, no caterpillar parts, just liquid: a liquid that could waggle its tail. The caterpillar was completely broken down and reassembled through this soup medium into the adult butterfly. The Monarch does this three times and still manages the marathon feat of its migration through all that. That's so weird that it beats anything that any theoretical supernatural can throw at the human race. Nature does it all. This is another pointer to life's crux being sub cellular and even sub atomic as proposed.

The mystery of migration is not without scientific scrutiny. This is a recent statement on bird migration from a professor at the University of East Anglia after much research.

Dr Gill explained, 'They can tell the time. We thought that individual birds might migrate earlier or later in response to the weather. But it seems that, whatever the weather, they migrate at almost exactly the same time every year. If you think about it from the bird's point of view, it makes sense. You know that the place you've been to before will be available, and you know that it will be available at that time. Young birds can learn all this from older birds in a flock.'

I've covered that already. Remember the argument re swallow migration times. That correspondent's statement on variation of leaving times is surely false as I suggested. The sun's position relative to landmarks may indeed be the trigger. It's nice to see scientific research backing up my observations. It's a positive answer to what was theory for a long time.

Even if their eyes can 'see' that magnetic field as previously suggested, how do they know where to go? Following other individuals who have done the journey before is a good strategy as in Dr Gill's findings.

So how about the next case? Maybe Dr Gill can come up with an answer.

Technology gives some clues to migration routes but not how it is achieved. You can track tagged cuckoos by satellite, watching their daily progress on a blog, and it is fascinating (*www.bto.org/cuckoos*). Scotland to Equatorial Congo and even into Angola is some journey. The first thing that strikes you is that migration routes vary greatly. Why go east from Scotland to eastern Germany if you want to go to south to Africa? One particular cuckoo's route does, then turns south over the Alps, down Italy and across the Mediterranean, then over the Sahara to Lake Chad before the final leg to the dense Congo rainforest. In spring, it flies many miles west to West Africa before heading north by a completely different route. Different Cuckoos take different routes: a mere 5,000 mile round trip. The males don't linger in the UK after mating. They are here for only one purpose. They take off for the Congo again as early as the **first week in June**. No migrant is recorded leaving sooner. The female stays longer to lay as many eggs as possible, up to twenty-five, in surrogate nests: apparently able to store sperm internally. She then follows suit, normally in early July, leaving the youngsters to grow in the surrogate nests and then make the migration **entirely on their own**. How does the East Anglian university statement cover that? There are no other birds to learn from.

The deeper you look into the subject, the more anomalies you can find. Remembering my childhood racing pigeon days again, a friend started keeping some birds in his coal shed. These were donated as youngsters from his uncle who was an expert. The access was via a gap above the door and they nested on a shelf. This didn't last long as his mum didn't like the mess and he got rid of them. There were two squeakers still in the nest and I was interested, knowing their pedigree, so I was given one. They are called squeakers, for that is what they do before they mature into 'ruckitacoo'. This one had never left the nest and was not quite ready to feed itself so I had to force feed it by hand until it got the hang of it. It turned out to be a beautiful powder blue colour, my pride and joy. Pigeon fanciers call the colour type '*blue bar*' as it had two dark bars on its wings but my mum just called it the 'bloo doo'. This colour is common, pointing to its and all other domesticated pigeons' ancestry. They are all descended from the wild rock dove, which is also a '*blue bar*', although somewhat duskier than mine. This squeaker turned out to be my champion, winning many races including the longest race at the time from Dol in Northern France. When it was three years old, disaster struck my loft. A domestic cat got in and created carnage: blood everywhere and several birds killed. The remaining birds were on the rooftops, terrified to come in. Over the next couple of days, hunger drove them to nervously come back down, encouraged by my soft whistling and shaking the food tin. The 'bloo doo' though was nowhere to be seen. My, now not so young, friend appeared with a cardboard box inside which was my champion. He had found it cowering in his coal shed. Out of all the hundreds of identical coal sheds in the estate it had chosen his, even though it had never seen the outside. Coincidence?

I suspect the answer lies not on the surface but deep in the genome (that's me sounding scientific but I don't know how else to describe it). Maybe that's why it is vitally important to consider provenance when dealing with migratory species. If a European swallow's egg was taken and placed in a nest in North America, to where would that offspring migrate? If salmon eggs were fertilized and put in different river systems, to which river would they return? If an east of The Rockies Monarch was taken to west of The Rockies, where would it end up? If a farmed turtle was released other than on its native beach, to where would it return as an adult? Repeat for any migratory species you like and I hope I have conveyed the message. All the theories of how migration is achieved, to which I was indoctrinated as a youngster, may be part of it but the truth is far from that simple. None of them hold true proof by experiment and that's what fascinates me about the subject. Maybe these creatures do have a built in satnav. Though for a satnav to work you have to key in your destination and that's an unknown to a solitary young cuckoo or a fourth generation butterfly.

Experiments on how all these species achieve it do seem to point to involvement of the earth's magnetic field as in the last chapter. If that is so, then it may be possible for other life forms to tap into this. Maybe some humans can as well, as in my 'supernature' observations. (Divining? Feeling electricity?) Animals and birds have to calculate both latitude and longitude. Remember the Manx shearwater's Atlantic crossing west to east. This is possibly done by considering the sun's position and a clear day is far better for racing pigeons than a heavily overcast one. There may of course be many other factors. It's still all speculation.

So my ambition, if I was a biologist, would be to crack the secret of animal navigational skills. I watch the research in anticipation of a revelation that puts all the old wives' tales I have grown up with, out of the window but will the old wives accept it? I doubt it.

Of all the wonders of nature, migration must surely be the most fascinating: not least for the reason that we still don't truly know how it's done. Will I live to be enlightened by speculation being turned into proof? I would love to. All these wonderful wildlife observations lead me to care about the future of the planet. I cannot contemplate any species being destroyed by us. Extinctions are always going to happen in the evolutionary process but I wouldn't like to think that I was linked to the direct cause. Now, why should I care?

9

EMPATHY AND ALTRUISM

*Animals have genes for altruism, and those genes have been
selected in the evolution of many creatures because of the
advantage they confer for the continuing survival of the species.*

Lewis Thomas, 'Late Night Thoughts on listening to Mahler's
Ninth Symphony'

I am incredibly lucky. I was born at a time to be able to reap the
benefits of modern western society and took it for granted. The
generation before had a terrible time: poverty and starvation
during long recessions and ending with the Second World War. I
have wallowed in the luxury of a National Health Service which
delivered penicillin and other modern drugs to keep me healthy.
The oil age was upon us making life increasingly easier and
more mobile. There wasn't the acute congestion on roads when I
got to the driving stage. I progressed through effort to a good
standard of living with all the modern luxuries affordable. Citizens
in other parts of the world were not so lucky. Why should I care?
It doesn't affect me or my family, I'm all right Jack. It doesn't work
that way. Apart from mental disorders and indoctrination, most
human beings are concerned with others' suffering.
Organisations like the Red Cross, Save the Children and many
others are born from that caring trait. Society is a fragile, man-
made state in which co-operation is necessary to punish those
who break the rules so that a peaceful status quo is maintained.
Not only that, but humans concern themselves with other
creatures' problems hence all the animal rights and conservation
movements. We care because we are human and caring and co-
operation has got us to this level of humanity. All of this concerns
the here and now, in our own lifetimes. The next observation
takes it to a second level. Why should we worry about the future
after we inevitably pass away, some sooner than others as it
turns out? Rachel Carson, author of 'Silent Spring' in the early

89

1960s, was horrified by the atrocities against nature caused by the pollution of the countryside with pesticides and other chemicals in the blind pursuit of profit. She wrote and published it knowing she had terminal cancer. She died the next year. Why should she have cared about the future of a world of which she knew she wasn't going to be a part? So how far are we prepared to go to in a fight to save a future world? If you happened to be a soldier in world wars then you were prepared to lay down your life to protect the freedom of your countrymen. Are the soldiers in Afghanistan today not doing the same thing, justifying killing or be killed for a more liberated planet? The casualties are heroes, but they are dead heroes. It's not new. Since antiquity, the theme's the same. My country's own William Wallace's cry of freedom ended in his execution.

Once again, why should he have cared? Why should anyone care about a future which doesn't affect them?

I had an uncle who was a gamekeeper on a local estate. He had a tied cottage with a large garden which he kept immaculate. My childhood recollection is of drooling over the soft fruits: huge strawberries and my favourite, gooseberries the size of ping pong balls. Another recollection was his shotgun. He had a problem in that he had lost his right eye in the Great War. But he was right handed, so you have to visualise the problem. Fire off the right shoulder with the right hand on the trigger but sight the gun with the left eye. He had a specially constructed gun. The butt curved over from the right side to the barrel on the left side. This oddity sat beside the back door loaded, ready for use, as was the norm then. As a child with a mental picture of guns in western movies it was a question that had to be asked, whence the reply came, 'it's a gun for shooting round corners.' In my naivety I believed him, thinking it was a great idea. Returning to the theme, I visited him lastly in his late eighties and he was still enthusiastically gardening: the garden even then being immaculate. There had been a bit of disease trouble with the old boundary beech hedge. He had dug up the dying section and was planting new seedlings. The bottom line of this story is that he was not going to see the results of his efforts. It's not even his property to pass on to his kids. When he dies, who knows who will be the new occupant? I remember thinking at the time 'why is he bothering?'

His employer, the laird of the estate, 'The Major' was a true gentleman. I bought my own house from him. The old walled garden, which had served the big house previously, was overgrown. Death duties and other taxes had forced him to get rid of the remaining three gardeners. There used to be fifteen. Three acres with an eighteen foot wall surround. Could I have the use of it for horticulture? No problem and in return an avenue of dead yew hedge was to be replanted by me. The man was again in his eighties. I suggested something quicker growing so he may get the good of it, but no it had to be the traditional yew, the effect of which he was never going to enjoy. Once again, I am thinking, 'Why is he bothering?'

Twenty years ago, I planted a beech hedge round my garden: 200 metres of it. As I get older it becomes an increasing chore to trim but the wildlife it sustains makes it still worthwhile. Due to a chemical spraying incident on adjacent farmland (addressed elsewhere) sections of it died out. I am not a youngster but I ordered new replacement seedlings to replant. 'Déjà vu,' echoes in my head. Why am I bothering? And that's just plants.

When it comes to animals it moves up several levels.

Alsatian
Free to good home
Very friendly
Eats anything
Very fond of children.

Dogs, descended by human intervention in evolution from wolves, have to have an endless supply of food and indoor warmth or it is regarded as cruelty. Man's best friend has the most sympathy as they are the closest to our experience of domestic animals. Far too close in some instances. They are dogs and not humans but sometimes you wouldn't think so.

The sheep farm on the north side of the hill where I live has a flock of several hundred animals. They are well cared for and the farming system is not intense, unlike the south side. The hilltop is 630 feet above sea level and is a minefield of tree stumps among the long grass, the remains of the First World War felling of native mixed forest to supply timber for the war effort. This is the summer grazing for the flock. In winter they feed on the turnip fields lower down, sown and maintained every year for the purpose. They have to be rounded up for shearing and moved to different seasonal pastures. This task in the treacherous terrain would be impossible without the shepherd's collies, a task for which we all must admire them.

In neighbourly conversation with the shepherd, I bent down to pat the pair. 'Don't pet the dogs.' I was taken aback as the animals seemed keen to be petted. 'They're working dogs.'

These dogs sleep outside, summer and winter, in a lean to shed. They are fed once a day only and their life is in the back of a pickup truck or on the hill. They are bred from to produce the next generation which take over their roles in the future: nothing else. I am not particularly a dog lover but I am an animal sympathiser and my reaction is a heartfelt one. What a shame that these dogs are being ill-treated to suit human gain. It flies in the face of human ideas of how animals should be treated but, looking deeper, there is much more to it than that.

The wolf is the ancestor of all pet dogs. Somewhere in history, probably due to hunger, mankind made friends with the wolf. It must have been an uneasy beginning as a starving wolf pack would easily dine on a human. Gradually, human intelligence enticed the animal to co-operate for a symbiotic partnership. Wolf intelligence played an equal part. The ones with a more docile nature could be bred from and the offspring could thus be similarly selected for favourable traits. There must have been a few hands bitten off along the way but the result is the modern 'pet'. Lying latent though is still the instinct to hunt and kill. Wild aggression is a historical trend which can easily be resurrected through selective breeding as in the case of pit bulls, etc. In the case of the collies, they are channelled into the traits of encircling and selecting victims. The wolf is never more typified than in the collie except they stop short of the kill, but they would like to. Just look at their eyes when working the flock. In the interests of an easy life without starvation they are trained to play ball.

Now think about the wild wolf and its lifestyle. Company of its own kind, healthy through the exercise of travelling up to fifty miles a day over rough terrain, doing what it is designed for, stalking and herding its quarry and picking off an individual from the herd. Breeding and looking after its family and snuggling down outdoors in a sheltered spot with no one petting them. Isn't that describing the lifestyle of my neighbouring collies? However, I still can't help feeling sorry for them and that's a failing on my part, born out of an easy modern lifestyle.

Most dog owners in the western world love their pets. They have been responsible for breeding every conceivable shape and size, not to suit a common interest but for their own pleasure. Set a Pekinese in a rabbit inhabited area and the wolf comes out. It may chase with gusto but to no avail. That screwed up mouth has no chance of catching, let alone eating one. These individuals and their ilk cannot exist in the wild. They need their owners to keep them alive. Apologies to Pekinese owners but beauty is in the eye of the beholder. New 'breeds' can be created with selected pairings or by artificial insemination: an Alsatian/Chihuahua cross is possible but a natural birth is not. A caesarean is necessary to give rise to this freak.

In the 1960s a daily magazine television programme called 'Tonight' with presenter Cliff Michelmore took up the subject of puppy farming. It is still an issue today with unscrupulous breeders overbreeding and maltreating their animals. This particular clip featured a case not far from me. A honey trap was set. The presenters had answered an advertisement for puppies in a national paper. At that time, life in the countryside was still harsh for families living off the land and this was a welcome addition to the income. The crew descended at dawn to catch the breeder unawares in case he cleaned up his act. They were there to collect their puppy, previously ordered, a Labrador. There were two railway carriages with stalls and straw bedding. On entering, the camera panned in to reveal an area of flaking plaster on the ceiling. There has to be some drama in the programme. It then revealed that a King Charles spaniel had given birth during the night and one of the litter lay dead in the straw. When quizzed on this 'atrocity' which was played on as the highlight of the programme, the breeder replied that he simply had not had the time to remove it as the crew had just got him out of bed and stopped him from doing his rounds. He usually had the beds changed and the animals fed and seen to by 7.30 am. Outside, the carriages were located in a large fenced field with various accoutrements for the dogs to play with. Some were running around as the crew filmed.

They took possession of the purchased Labrador pup, held up to the camera with straw in the grasp for neglect effect. No doggie beddie here. Then it was revealed that it had not yet been treated for worms, scandal again. It was subsequently checked over by a vet who administered the de-wormer. It eventually lands up in the studio looking homeless puppy dog sad, aww . . .

A loving home had to be found. A competition was held. Who could offer it the best home? The winner was a flat dweller from Carlisle. It looked a nice flat when the programme visited to see doggy nicely settled in his basket. All's well that ends well.

So there you have the story. On the one side you have a life with free run exercise, bedding changed every day, your toilet issue cleaned up, company of your own kind to sniff each other at will as doggies like to do, sex in doggy season and no need to worry about starvation.

On the other side, central heating to keep you warm all day as you languish in your blanketed basket bed waiting for your owner to get back from work to take you on a lead round the block to the toilet then back to your tinned 'goodness knows what' for tea. Your master screws up his face as he dishes it up as it doesn't smell very nice. Spend the evening in the basket bed before a walk on the lead again for a sniff round the block to see if any bitches in heat have been around. Dream on, no chance of a leg over. Being not allowed to breed is probably the worst side. You're quickly chastised for even thinking that way, via an embarrassed visitor's leg. A solution to that particular problem is widespread. Male readers will take a sharp intake of breath here. Cut their 'nasms' off. Castration solves the problem and a life in limbo follows. That's what you do to your best friend?

Now, if I were a dog, a descendent of the wolf, which life would I choose? I could put up with the flaking plaster. A dog though has no choice.

I don't know the fate of that particular dog and it may not have been that way but it is that way for many dogs all around the country. We are making our pets do our bidding for our own ends, not for their ends. Dogs are not human and perhaps they shouldn't be treated as such in their own interests. If you are a dog owner, count the number of hours out of twenty-four that your pet spends in its basket bed.

Hare coursing is now banned. The perpetrators are saying the dogs are doing what dogs are meant to do. No doubt about that. So where is the argument against? Well, apart from the preservation of a dwindling species, the activity is carried out for human enjoyment. No doubt about that either. The dogs are not killing to feed themselves, only to please their masters. In my early youth, using a dog to chase a hare into a net across a field gate was a way of putting meat on the table and there were plenty of them. Hare was a delicacy, used to the full. The blood was drained off for stock for 'hare's blood soup'. The meat was roasted and any grisly tough bits went into the soup and also fed the dog. The animal lasted days. In a poor family this was almost a necessity and dogs throughout history have contributed to human survival. In fact it is another triumph over nature that man has turned a wolf, with no chance of catching a healthy hare, into a speed machine with quite amazing agility. It doesn't seem necessary though, in modern times in the UK, and the hunters are well aware of that. The quarry is not landing up on their table. It's a grisly indulgence on their part.

Fox hunting with hounds has met the same fate. The hounds have an acute sense of smell, far more than a wolf ever had. Again selectively bred for our needs and again now deemed unnecessary in a civilised country.

Humans are following their own primordial instincts in hunting and that seems to be why they do it. It's not justified by putting food on the family table, only the pleasure of the kill and in fox hunting the pleasure of the suffering as well. Oscar Wilde described it beautifully.

The unspeakable in pursuit of the uneatable.

Even in the bad old Victorian times there were conservationists shocked at the suffering inflicted for pleasure alone.

Domestic cats, manipulated that way by the same process of human convenience, are rescued if they do not have a warm fireside in front of which to cuddle up to their human slaves. The difference between cats and dogs is that cats manipulate their owners and not the other way round. They have the freedom but choose to stay. They can still carry out their hunting pleasures and have the best of both worlds.

It is surely an inherent trait in us to abhor cruelty to animals. There are many societies dedicated to the cause of animal rights. Deceased sympathisers leave huge sums in inheritance to their kitties. Animal cruelty is wrong. Most of the population seems to accept that. Apparently, it depends on the species of animal whether we accept cruelty or not. Have you noticed?

Let me provide the evidence. Cows and horses are not treated equally. Cattle are frequently kept in horrendous conditions (below), especially during the winter, often up to their knees in their own filth. Veal calves never see an open field lest they put on grisly muscle.

This is unfortunately typical. And of course they are eaten. Just you try that with horses in the UK as in recent horsemeat scandals. The 'eaten' bit is the only unobjectionable part, as no cruelty is involved in the slaughter, but surely their short lives can be made comfortable? Many farmers do but this picture is not an isolated case as I pass such conditions every day. Pie in the sky legislation is paying lip service to action against cruelty. The reality is very different. As Ghandi said:

'The greatness of a nation and its progress can be judged by the way its animals are treated.'

Seeing this common scenario I don't particularly feel part of a great nation.

Any animal lover's abhorrence must be poison. Illegal *carbofuren* is a favourite. Gamekeepers traditionally used it to kill predators. Used? The past tense is not applicable unfortunately. Its use has drastically diminished due to legislation and prosecution but it would not have but for the vigilance of charitable conservation groups gathering evidence and prosecuting. At least the courts are now taking a more sympathetic view due, in no small measure, to the awareness campaigns of television nature programmes. It is still a big problem in my native land.

Now, if you are a conservationist you surely cannot condone the poisoning of wild mammals and birds. It unfortunately, once again, depends on the species. How would you like to hear of an intelligent mammal dying of an internal haemorrhage in extreme agony? There is no campaign against it and yet it goes on daily day. Warfarin (or other anti-coagulant based) baits are legally set for rats and it isn't an instant death either. You can even buy it in the supermarkets. 'Oh, well, rats, urgh, that's different.' The reason being? I have never liked double standards.

The most extreme cruelty to animals in my personal experience happened in the 1950s and the aftermath still persists today. In my childhood one of the staple diets was rabbit, at least once a week. My family was poor and country minded. They would not let a great source of free protein go to waste. Persecution of natural predators for the enhancement of game bird numbers led to a glut of rabbits and rabbits like crops. So the chemists engineered a normally benign rabbit virus to make it lethal. The rabbit was introduced into Australia initially to serve, as it did in my family, as an easy source of protein for the new country.

97

Having no natural predators there, it ran riot: a perfect place to try out the new virus. The effect could not have been more dramatic. It nearly wiped them out. Note, nearly. It was introduced into the UK with the same effect. It nearly broke our hearts as kids. The suffering was unbelievable. A day on the moor was spent putting those poor animals out of their misery. Their intestines hanging out of their anuses, eyes full of pus and swelled up so they could not see, they lurched around in blind pain. No great protest ensued. You try the same thing with hedgehogs or badgers and watch the sparks fly. How this hierarchy of cruelty came to be, I wouldn't know. I only observe that it is so.

For the rabbit nature fights back and, by way of evolutionary mutation, a very few of the population were immune or at least partly immune. Their offspring inherited the immunity and although waves of the virus still afflict today, rabbits are still on the go albeit a decimated population. No one would say that the rabbits weren't in need of control but that's a 'helluva' way to do it.

The UK government, nowadays, seems to fly the anti-cruelty banner but not quite. They have exceptions. We kill animals for food and this is done in as humane a way as possible. Legislation demands strict controls. As a recognised standard they are quickly stunned before being killed. **Except** if your religious beliefs demand that they be killed by cutting their throats without being stunned. A prayer is said and the animal has to hear that prayer as it dies (I presume multi-linguality in animals). Then you can indeed impart cruelty with impunity.

So, in certain circumstances, conservationists and politicians seem even to condone cruelty. Double standards? I don't pass judgement: I only observe that it is so.

The next level is we ourselves. Well, human beings abhor cruelty to fellow humans, surely. This is true empathy and probably at the heart of our feelings for animal cruelty and leaving a better world for our future generations. There are always exceptions but our basic instinct is to protect our offspring. This is projected to caring for the welfare of our extended family and then wider to others of your own culture. Outside that sphere can be very different. Innocent children of Catholic parents going to school in Northern Ireland can suffer a barrage of stone throwing and being spat upon by adults of a different denomination. You can't do that to cats or dogs. The same hatred is evident all over the world with the former Yugoslavian and Iraqi atrocities still fresh in our minds. Racism is still very evident in the southern states of the USA. It is only suppressed and so lingers on. Abolition of apartheid in South Africa has to live with a big undercurrent behind the scenes. In my own country, the same suppression keeps it in check but it still festers under the bandage. These are all first-hand experiences and a simpleton like me just doesn't get it. Brought up in a society where there was no hatred of others, it seems unthinkable that the colour of one's skin is judged before the personality. It hit me right on the chin when I went to India. I have 'baggage' on my travels and it was a difficult task persuading her, as it is hardly a holiday destination. It may be for some in their all-inclusive hotels but she knows me. I am there to 'see'. Nature is remarkable there. Although I saw some amazing wildlife, there is another side which cannot be missed. The small market town of Mapusa in the south was where I went to see day to day life in rural India and to buy a pair of 'Hi-Tec' trainers which weren't. It was a real eye opener in more ways than one. Approaching the town there was an encampment of crude covers and poles. I imagined a refugee camp. I felt sick at the sight of these poor individuals. In town the market seethed with people. Fly covered mounds of rice, spices and other foods probably accounted for the permanent 'Dehli Belly' throughout the stay. Sewer pipes under the roads had broken covers to reveal flowing sewage and a huge population of rats. They were everywhere, running around the corrugated iron roofs of the shops, copulating on street corners etc. A tug at my shorts: I look down to see this tiny girl aged about four years, festered ulcers on her legs and arms, pointing to her mouth and holding out her hand. I shook my head, an action that I have to live with forever. A small boy followed us the whole day, dodging the insane traffic to keep up. He never asked for anything but it made me uneasy and guilty. You see I was warned not to give them anything. I now worked out that they were from that encampment, they were 'The Untouchables'. It means what it says: an underclass to be completely ignored. My 'baggage' shed a few tears that day and will never go back. She wanted to scoop the little lassie up and take her home. You can empathise with the pop stars altruistically adopting a waif. That's a lucky waif, as millions are not so lucky. In general, despite the poverty in India, most people seem happy. Not so the untouchables, never a smiling face. They live like animals because they have no choice. What has happened to that inbred empathy that makes us feel sorry for animal suffering, yet inflicts cruelty on innocent fellow men? The poet Robert Burns described it as 'Man's inhumanity to man.' I will never understand the double standards in the world in that respect. I think everyone should be made to go to India. That would stop them moaning about their lot. My visit has ruled out any chance of going to equatorial Africa. She says that's not a holiday. It's just frustration at not being able to change the world. I have more observations on India later.

Wars through the ages, and still today, throw up a problem. We, apparently, are prepared to die for our principles and a better life. But if you die, then you don't have a better life. The First World War was surely a lesson for mankind. No chance. Today many lives are sacrificed for ideals that cannot be realised if you are dead, but the country is free. Death seems worthwhile for your country's freedom. William Wallace again springs to mind. So humans are indeed prepared to lay down their lives for others. Why? Ghandi again:

'What difference does it make to the dead, the orphans and the homeless whether the mad destruction is wrought in the name of totalitarianism or in the holy name of liberty or democracy?'

No difference than the personal sacrifices ants, wasps, bees, etc make for the greater good of the many. Who can doubt then, that man is just another animal.

If all that comes across as worrying behaviour, then humans should be mightily concerned with another huge problem which has the potential to drastically influence both our and wildlife's wellbeing in future.

10

GLOBAL WARMING

*The conversation on global warming has been stalled because a
shrinking group of denialists fly into a rage when it's mentioned.*

Al Gore

Twenty five years ago I made the acquaintance of an interesting
individual: an inventor. To say that he was eccentric is an
understatement. It seems he had no success in the invention
line, despite numerous patents taken out, but apparently that
was due to the short sightedness of business gurus. Yea, yea . . .
The latest bee in his bonnet was climate change. A doomsday
scenario was that of extreme weather patterns, due to our
continued disregard of the environment by burning fossil fuels.
That was the first ever time I had heard of the greenhouse effect.
What a load of rot was my first reaction. There was no world
wide web then so he must have been up to speed on the latest
science literature. Well, he was an inventor. Nowadays, although
he has passed away, I am not ridiculing his words any more:
shades of the Bran Seer. Now the whole world is aware of the
dire consequences of continuing to ignore that early warning.
This man went further than just talking about it. He designed and
patented a way of extracting energy from wind: wind turbines.
Well you know what they are today, massive erections,
controversial to say the least. Some citizens are affected more
than others and some, including politicians, may think it's a good
idea. The photograph on the following page shows the
panoramic view from the lounge window of Woodlands
bungalow. The owner could change the name to 'Turbine View'
but it doesn't have the same idyllic countryside ring to it. How
would you feel if you were opening your blinds to that sight every
morning?

Sunsets are never to be beautiful again. I don't know the owner
but I would stake my life on his not being a politician. There are a

lot worse cases but I include the picture below for a very good reason.

These erections were considered too far away from the property to warrant even a notice of intention and the owner was not consulted. With this in mind this site is not far away from my home. Having been fortunate, for nearly half a century, to have enjoyed the magnificent unobstructed views of both city and distant mountains (more than seventy miles away) this would devastate my quality of life. It seems to happen almost overnight. Mine is a windy hill, perfect for construction, so I am living in dread. The planet has to be saved so what price my miserable, insignificant existence?

On a hill above Crathie, Aberdeenshire there is a stone pillar: a monument erected by Queen Victoria in memory of her beloved Albert. It's also a windy hill overlooking Balmoral Castle, a perfect place for a turbine. It could cater for all the castle's power needs and the surrounding rural community's. If the turbine was big enough the queen could make money from the excess fed into the national grid. It would be seen as royalty setting an example to the nation. After all, what good is a lump of rock on a hill?

Another perfect place would be the Eden estuary at St. Andrews. Golfers from all over the world come here to play the 'Old Course' at the historic home of golf and they could have the extra enjoyment of seeing these massive blades whizzing round. Neither, I earnestly hope, will ever happen and the suggestion is tongue in cheek. Neither the Woodlands bungalow owner nor I have a choice and the difference is? In a country of supposed equals, it seems some are more equal than others.

It's possibly a sacrifice worth making, as we have to save the planet. Be that as it may, it is a bandwagon. Landowners are cashing in on the back of the green ticket but many of them couldn't give a hoot about saving the planet as they will readily state, 'Best crop I ever sowed.' It's purely for profit. The government on the other hand must surely have diminishing emissions in mind. Here is a recent statement from the energy minister's office.

Scotland has an incredible wealth of energy resources, including our wind sector, capable of both meeting our energy needs and significant exports to parts of the UK and Europe. We have a responsibility to make sure our nation seizes the opportunity to create tens of thousands of new jobs and secure billions of pounds of investment.

In case you missed it, no word that the prime reason for all this was to save the planet. This all seems to have been forgotten in the Klondyke promised. Will the man in the street's energy bills be reduced as a result? I would be surprised but the energy companies will be ratcheting up their profits. To be energy efficient in this country with wind power, many thousands of turbines have to be installed in windy locations, the prime places being the highlands and islands of Scotland. If it saves the planet then we have to accept just that. So it follows that we have to give up our beautiful wild places, sacrificed for the greater good.

My inventor does not have the patent on these monsters. His wind turbines were a lot less intrusive. As a child (as you may also have done) I came home from the fairground with a 'whirlie', a little hand held windmill on a stick with tubular blades. The beauty of them is that they work just as well when held horizontally and that was his construction idea. They can be stacked on top of one another, so one column could handle multiple turbines. He doesn't stop there, being conscious as he was of environmental impact. He envisaged them being incorporated into architecture. Imagine the top storey of a skyscraper given over to providing the power for the forty floors below. The new bridge over the River Forth in Scotland could power the city of Edinburgh. Both situations, by the way, are picked for their windy locations. Even in the windy countryside, selected for today's turbines, columns incorporating many blades would be a lot less intrusive. He envisaged a problem with the gearing and blade balance which he realised would take high tech engineering from people like Rolls Royce. The stakes then were not as high as they are now and his patent fell on deaf ears once again. I can only say I was impressed, not for the planet saving point but just for a cheaper and more unobtrusive way of producing energy. He had sent in impressive blueprint drawings to be granted the patent but would it work? In order to prove it you would have to build a prototype, that costs money and he was personally *'pink lint'*. Industry was approached and I even postured the idea to a well-connected industrialist. Invariably, the answer came back, 'But will it work?' That returns us on a loop to the original question. So the conclusion is 'It doesn't work because we've never tried it.' And there it rests.

Perhaps the desecration of beautiful countryside is the price we have to pay if we are to retain our easy lifestyle with energy consumption taken for granted. The anomaly is that the biggest energy consumers don't have to suffer massive changes to their environment.

There was another acquaintance of mine, not quite so eccentric but certainly not your average Joe. After graduating from my local university, he answered the call of adventure and joined the Hudson Bay Trading Company in Northern Canada. After the demise of the fur trade and the closure of the company, he decided to stay and settle. On his trips home to visit his family he told tales of the Eskimo culture and the fantastic community spirit reminiscent of my own childhood. He married a local indigenous girl, settled in Baffin Island, and had two children. When they were of school age they returned to North East Scotland, thinking of their education. After a few years they decided to return to Baffin Island: the reason? His wife couldn't stand the cold. Forty below in the Arctic is more comfortable than one degree above here in North East Scotland. She just shivered all winter (and summer). It's a different cold.

He always was a go ahead man. If you don't like it, change it. He went into teaching to improve the educational standards which he originally thought were lacking for his own kids: an inspirational move in its own right. Through that inspiration he eventually became vice principal at Attagoyuk School and is, at the time of writing, still living on Baffin Island but with additional duties. He scientifically measures and monitors the extent of the sea ice and reports it to the world. He now holds the post of 'Director of Evaluation and Assessment at the Government of Nunavuk.' He paints a grim picture: massive loss of sea ice over the years leading in 2012 to the lowest ice area ever. It's not only the polar bear that is threatened but the Eskimo way of life as well. It will never be the same again. Oil companies are poised to move in to harvest the fossilised bounty under the growing ocean area leading to even more harmful emissions and exacerbating the problem. Although I have never been to the Arctic, I feel personally connected through this local man to the tragedy unfolding there.

2011 was the driest year ever recorded in the south of England. Hosepipe bans and other water conservation measures heralded, by now well publicised, global warming. As usual, the press had a field day. There were interviews with the 'high heidies' of water authorities predicting that the reservoirs were at such a record low they could never replenish. Desert conditions were the future of the south east so we had better get used to it. It's a feature of nature to buck the trend, to poke in the eye all these experts, and it didn't half. Winter 2013 and their reservoirs are not only replenished but they are running down the streets. You didn't have to turn on the tap to get your water. It came in the front door. It's as if some supreme controlling being from above reacted to the gripes about drought and decided . . . oh, you're not happy, are you? Well, try this. . . One Thames Valley councillor apparently agreed with this scenario and wrote to the

Prime Minister to tell him it was God's retribution for siding with homosexual rights. Such sinning. Apparently, homosexuality is a choice and not a quirk of genetics. Thank goodness we saintly puritans in this part of the UK were spared that ordeal. 'Him' up there seems to be selective.

If we look back at the statements made by my inventor and other scientists, you will find that these scenarios are exactly as climate scientists predicted all that time ago. Extremes are at both ends of the spectrum and they are also predicted to get worse, so we had better get used to it or do something about it. That's easier said than done.

These warnings are of the danger to our very existence. I can add to that the many wildlife changes since the world of my youth. Science can add thousands of others, once scoffed but now proven as fact. Lemmings don't have a look in.

A comment on that lemming statement: it has become a byword for self-destruction. This is an example of the one time out of ten my father got it right to disprove teachings. I learnt at school that Arctic lemmings committed mass suicide to control numbers. That's where the metaphor comes from, but it is a fallacy disproved by investigation. Lemming populations fluctuate on a four year cycle. When it reaches a peak they migrate widely to find new territories. Many may indeed come a cropper as such numbers in motion have a large mortality rate. Swimming across a Norwegian fjord is an unknown distance and it is not surprising some may perish. Predators such as stoats, owls and birds of prey play their part in reducing numbers but serious observation has shown that none are bent on suicide. On the contrary it is a survival tactic. The winners are the fittest, perpetuating the species.

Mentioning Norway, reminds me of another misconception taught at school. Vikings wore helmets with horns and conquered new lands to rape and plunder. The first is untrue to the extent that no evidence exists to support the horn theory. Many helmets have been unearthed but none with horns. Rape and plunder may have happened somewhere, as with invading armies even today, but there is no evidence of mass executions or other atrocities. They may have come in peace but had to fight. That may be wishful thinking on my part as I would like to think that my Nordic ancestors spawned my forebears by love affair and not rape. As there is no proven evidence to the contrary, I shall remain romantic. Global warming is a proven and measured fact affecting wildlife in many ways. In my experience there are many other human caused threats to our own and wildlife's environment, all just as worrying. The countryside has changed.

11

THE FARMER'S IN THE DELL

This whole effort to rebuild and stabilize a countryside is not without its disappointments and mistakes . . . what matter though these temporary growing pains when one can cast his eye upon the hills and see hard-boiled farmers who have spent their lives destroying land now carrying water by hand to their new plantations.

Aldo Leopold

What's he doing there in the dell? The answer depends on the farmer. There are good farmers and bad farmers, as far as nature conservation is concerned. Once again, naturally, his actions are driven by finance. It has to be a commercially viable operation. They may own the land but they cannot do what they want with it. They can only farm it unless they can be granted permission to do something else, as in development around a built up area. Then they can make a fortune but, for the vast majority, they are only custodians of it for future generations.

The 'Countryfile' programme currently on television shows idyllic rural life on the farm, but the reality can be very different. On one farm a tycoon went into pig farming in a big way. Such were the conditions of rearing that the cruelty was repeatedly exposed by concerned animal welfare groups. More than one large fine was imposed and paid with ease. Eventually, to their credit, the campaigners through covert filming succeeded in getting a ban imposed on his keeping of pigs. The improper keeping of pigs has other consequences though.

It sounds like a schoolboy maths problem. *A farmer has enough land to dispose of the effluent from two hundred pigs to fertilise the soil. He then increases his herd to two thousand pigs. What does he do with the excess?* He has a choice. *Pay for the collection and transportation to a safe, lined landfill site or spread the excess onto his existing land and let it be washed away by the rain.*

The former is horrendously expensive, so which does he choose? It's a no brainer. With a slurry tank overflowing weekly the problem increases so, in the name of efficiency, he short circuits the tractor and spreader and runs 100 mm pipes from the tank directly to the fields. All he has to do now is to wait for heavy rain and turn on the pump. Problem solved. Indeed this is exactly what happened and the countryside turned jet black. The problem though was not solved. People who cared noticed dead fish in their hundreds in the local spawning stream fed by the catchment. The main river stank of effluent as it flowed by. The source was easily traced and the farmer brought to task. In defence he pleaded that it was the result of a leaking slurry tank. This was accepted and a heavy fine imposed but it was small fry to the overall budget.

Now, it was obvious to an observer that this was not the case. There was no leak in the tank, confirmed by personal inspection, except for via the pipes leading to the fields. This was only one operation. Other farms were doing the same on other tributaries of the same river and one that also fed to another river system. That particular tributary, used for generations of kids to catch trout and sticklebacks, is now devoid of aquatic life.

The main river concerned though, has another attribute. It flows into the North Sea through an internationally important estuary for wildlife. Extensive mud flats are the domain of numerous species of invertebrates which in turn are an important food source for many wading birds, especially in winter. Mussel beds are the food source for the largest colony of Eider duck in the UK. Sand eels and other small fish feed on the washed out remains of the invertebrates at every tide and, in turn, support a breeding colony of all species of British terns. It is so valuable an area, ecology wise, that it is quite rightly a closely monitored nature reserve. But, for all the rules and regulations, the supervisory powers have no control over what enters the system up country. When the slurry descends to the mudflats, the effect of the pollution might not be immediate but it lasts for decades. Eventually it was obvious that something was up, upriver, so a grant of £100,000 was given to trace the source of the pollution.

Had they given me a fiver for fuel, I could have saved them a fortune and a lot of time and effort. Would you believe it? All the locals could have done the same but they are not qualified. Observation seems not to be important.

Now that the, totally unrelated, ban on keeping pigs is being enforced the situation is slowly improving but the river has a long way to go.

A ban on keeping pigs does not exclude cattle and that was the shift. There seems a hierarchy of cruelty on farms. Reading from the top: horses, sheep, pigs, cattle, although castration to males in all farmed species is still carried out without anaesthetic. In my youth, I knew a farmer who carried out 'libbing' of male lambs with his teeth. As he worked his way through the flock, the blood ran down his apron as he spat out the testicles. That was a long time ago. More recently, I came across a cow giving a breach birth to a calf in a field. The mother was bellowing in agony with the calf dangling half out and writhing. I alerted the farmer as any caring person would have done. Passing at the end of the day both mum and calf, in the same position, are lying dead, totally ignored: small fry to the budget. These are busy people. This is not good farming and as far as the natural environment is concerned, the same disregard applies.

Once upon a time it must have been heaven for wildlife in the UK. The whole of my country, apart from the coastal plains behind the dunes and sizeable marshland, was covered in the old Caledonian forest. When humans started cutting the forest for fuel and construction, this gave way to agriculture. Before the days of field drainage the marshland was left wild. To separate the livestock from the crops, hedges of *Crataegus* (hawthorn/quickthorn) were planted. In rougher terrain drystone dykes had the same function. This created such good habitat and food for all kinds of creatures: individual fields had uncultivated borders where seedling trees, brambles (blackberries) and all sorts of wild flowers thrived, growing through and alongside the hedges. The coastal plains were ideal grazing for both wild and domesticated animals. At harvest time, a feast was available for grain eaters and they timed their breeding to coincide with it. In winter, stubble fields were sustenance for them through the winter. Fruit from the haws, wild woodbine (honeysuckle), dog rose, elder and many more plant species sustained both native and migrant birds throughout the winter. Except for the absence of most of the ancient forest, this countryside is my youthful memory of a bygone age. At my school the rotation of crops system was taught. A cereal was grown one year, then grass and clover the next. Clover, being a legume, 'fixed' atmospheric nitrogen via bacteria in its roots, returning it to the soil in future ploughing. The clover was such an attraction for bees and all sorts of pollinating insects. This crop firstly, though, fed cattle for a year, the throughput of which further fertilised the soil. The bottom line is a highly natural cycle of sustenance for the native population and wildlife. We can all feed ourselves well. The one failing in modern society of that system is that it doesn't generate big profits. The pursuit of that has had a devastating effect on wildlife. The advent of barbed wire meant that the land taken up by the hedges and dykes could be reclaimed giving bigger yields: grossly bad news for wildlife in every way. Food sources disappeared, as well as nesting and shelter, and animals suffered appalling injuries.

Anyone who has tried to untangle a badger or roe deer from being hung up on a barbed wire fence, as I have done, must be influenced by these experiences.

Fencing doesn't address the problem of wastage through disease and insect damage. If you could control these, you could make a lot more money. You could make even more if you could give the crop the nutrients it required for maximum yield: enter the industrial chemist.

Nitrates can be manufactured and instantly applied. Ammonia doesn't have to involve animal urine. Science can assay and provide the requirements for maximum yield. Modern machines can spread these on a big scale. There is an appreciable problem with this. For all the nitrates applied approximately 50% is not taken up by the targeted plants but is leaked, as runoff, into ditches and then streams, rivers and lakes or oceans. If you have seen the result of this, it must leave an impression. The water becomes eutrophic ie overloaded with nutrient. The illustration on the previous page shows the result in Lake Eyrie, USA.

Worldwide 100 million tons are spread. Close to home, just when the shellfish here are recovering from industrial waste pollution, they are affected by a poisonous bloom of *cyanobacteria* making them again inedible, purely as a result of nitrate runoff. My own water supply, used for hundreds of years from the sunken well, became so loaded with nitrates that a mains water connection was the only option. Worldwide there are reports of vital aquifers becoming polluted especially in places like China and India. Many of these people don't have my option.

These artificial fertilisers are not harmful in themselves as they are exactly the same substances as in the real thing but without the risks to health such as *E coli 0157*.

Once again, how much to apply is critical. The problem is that they are applied all in one go, as opposed to over the course of a year via legume and livestock throughput.

Even barbed wire fencing is now becoming a thing of the past, a godsend for animals in one way, but with a sting in the tail as it leads to even more habitat loss. The modern way, to achieve maximum production, is to have huge fields without any borders and cultivated right up to roadside boundaries. From my window, eight fields have become one field in twenty short years. This caters for the massive combines to do their job efficiently: every grain saved and no spillage to sustain grain eaters.

There are so many other big changes in farming practice to go along with all that. These huge fields can be harvested one day, then ploughed and re-sown the next with no stubble overwintering to provide food for wildlife. Winter crops are all the rage for an early harvest next year. Then there are the real chemicals, these are the perfect aid for crop health and maximum yield: herbicides, fungicides, growth retardants, pesticides, bird repellents and goodness only knows what else are spread with gay abandon. Runoff of these chemicals is again evident in watercourses but the effect on the surrounding countryside is even clearer.

Every two or three weeks the sprayers are in action during all stages of growth. There are hundreds of chemicals on the market competing for sales. Surely 'spread with gay abandon' is inaccurate. There are strict controls for the use of these chemicals, aren't there? It says so on the label. That is a disclaimer on the part of the manufacturers but the reality, for all to see, is disregard. Only spray in calm conditions. How calm? Judge for yourself: while walking on my local country road, a sprayer moves up the field and a wet spray hits me on the face. It is far from being a calm day. In fact a calm day is an unusual occurrence in this part of the world. I am aware of a horrible smell engulfing me. I enter the field and flag down the driver. I ask him what he is spraying as I may be in danger. HE DOESN'T KNOW.

I look up the legislation and find there is no legal obligation for him to tell me. At other times, the spray drifts on to roadside wild vegetation, which wilts as a result. Any remaining hedgerows show signs of damage. This practice is not a one off, it is widespread. The result to the fields is the creation of a sterile environment. Unseasonal ploughing and harvesting has upended thousands of years of co-habiting with nature. The demise of the skylark, corn bunting, lapwing, grey partridge, honey bee and a host of others, according to the results of research, seem to be attributed to these modern methods and I have watched it unfold in a few short years. There are three insecticides called *neonicotinoides* that have just been banned for two years pending investigation, although the manufacturers passed them as harmless to bees. It turns out that they indeed do not KILL bees but they interfere with their ability to navigate back to the hive which, in effect, is one and the same thing.

That leaves the 'safe' insecticide *pyrethrum*. It is derived from natural sources so that's ok? So are *curare* and *strychnine* aa well as many other lethal ones. New research into bumble bees has revealed that the shrinking in size of this insect is directly linked to *pyrethrum*. Trials over two colonies, one with exposure and one not, led to larvae hatching at a reduced size. Big, natural sized bees are able to carry much more pollen than smaller ones and this affects the success of the hive, leading to its demise. The 'big bummlers' of my youth are disappearing and bumble bees play a big part in the pollination of both wild flowers and cultivated crops. According to ecologists, any further decrease in numbers will eventually affect our world as we know it. Another serious side effect of *pyrethrum* is that insects can become immune. Rape seed crops are affected by the rape pollen beetle and overuse has produced resistant individuals who can further breed resistant offspring just like my *myxomatosis* rabbits. Farmers are urged to use sparingly and not kill all individuals. Overuse would lead to total ineffectiveness. However, to some farmers, that's the next generation's problems. Carson's 'Silent Spring' is coming home to roost. Surely after her warnings of DDT and other noxious substances, lessons have been learned? Not so, as every year products previously passed as safe are being banned in number when dangers to both humans and wildlife become evident AFTER their use.

So what about the good farmers? They talk a good game. Many I know certainly keep their animals in much better conditions. They are sympathetic to wildlife, they state. They even put out bird feeders in their gardens. Their sympathy is relative. They are doing what they think is good for wildlife. Here is an example of a farmer who professes to care. 'Set aside' was popular a few years ago as it attracted grants to prevent overproduction of grain: so much for the drive for efficiency which changed the landscape. This set aside was deemed good for wildlife but it only lasted for two or three years. Just when wildlife started to enjoy natural meadows, the land was brought back into production. The wild flowers and grasses have to be destroyed first. A miracle of chemistry is at the farmer's disposal: *glyphosate*, another 'safe' chemical weedkiller. Who am I to argue? Apparently it breaks down into harmless substances in contact with the soil. It is absorbed by the plant through its leaves and translocated to the roots which break down at the cellular level, cutting sustenance to the organism. The application is by way of a fine mist rather than soaking of the foliage, so it is very cost effective. Fine mist is easily borne by even gentle breezes a very long way. Considering Sahara sandstorms are carried across the Atlantic Ocean and fertilise the Brazilian rainforest, how far does a fine mist travel? It is certainly evident that it enters the systems of many roadside and woodland plants. You can see the damage, especially if you have an adjacent garden like mine. There are other problems coming to the fore. This chemical can enter the plant through the stem or, in the case of trees, the bark. Beech (*Fagus sylvatica*) is particularly susceptible and many mature beech trees bordering farmland are showing typical signs of glyphosate poisoning. Death over a number of years occurs. City and town councils have also latched on to the 'safe' label for weed control. Employees, untrained due to cutbacks, are applying this weedkiller around shrubberies and hedges paying no regard to drift. Beech hedges are now looking more like rows of condemned houses than uniform healthy hedges. The iconic London plane (*Platanus*) lining the avenues of the capital are suffering from the 'safe' label as well. Many other species in my locality are the same. Spraying around the bases has resulted in the trees showing typical glyphosate damage, from which there is no recovery. That spraying round bases is unavoidable as these are the areas they wish to weed control.

Apart from destroying the set aside vegetation, farmers have found a new use for this product. Rapid turnover of crops is enhanced if you can kill all weeds in the field before harvest as, immediately after harvest you can then plough a clean field. How can this be done without killing the crop as well? After the plants have set seed it doesn't matter. Kill the lot and the seed will still ripen to be harvested from the dead parent plant 'unaffected'. Not even the good farmers see any harm in this. Two or three weeks or so before harvest, the crop is sprayed (my observation) and it is obviously dead at harvest due to translocation through its tissue, hopefully not to the ripened grain. Can we be assured of that? The crop can be used for either human consumption or animal feed. Either way it enters the human food chain. We don't have to worry though, it has been passed as a 'safe' chemical just the same as all the other 'safe', but now withdrawn, products. Another side to this practice is that the spray booms have to be set high. This exacerbates drift and a new spectre has recently appeared. Arable farmers who grow potatoes didn't think they had to worry about nearby grain fields being sprayed with *glyphosate*. Any drift is considered 'a negligible amount' as far as the potato plants are concerned and this appears not to affect the crop in the slightest. If the tubers are grown for human consumption there is no appreciable problem **BUT** if they are grown for seed there is a problem. When planted out the next year *glyphosate*, apparently concentrated in the eyes of the tubers and despite the 'negligible amount', leads to **complete and utter failure of the daughter crop.** So serious is this problem that 'The British Potato Growers Association' has set up a helpline. So what is a negligible amount? Greg Dawson, an agronomist with Scottish Agronomy, admits 'even amounts so negligible below the limits of laboratory detection can cause complete failure'. He also admits 'even very flat, calm conditions can see spray vapour lifting and travelling **several hundred metres'.** As I have mentioned, I can concur with that. So what about the potatoes sold for food which I have eaten? They also store the chemical. Perhaps I don't have to worry, it's a negligible amount.

Well, I could obviously take evasive action and eat organic crops. They may be more expensive but hey, what price good health? They are chemical free and are proving popular. To get an 'organic' label, a grower's land has to have a buffer zone to separate it from chemical based farmlands. How big? **Six to eight metres:** how far did the agronomist say drift could travel even in flat calm conditions? I rest my case. The World Health Organisation doesn't rest its case though. Glyphosate has now been banned in many countries due to that organisation's concerns that it causes cancer in humans. How long will it take in terms of loss of life for legislation to be changed in the UK? Déjà vu.

My experience with farmers is that, whatever their thoughts on the environment, it is not themselves who do the work. Untrained, or trained but apathetic, operators are often the ones left to administer this ever growing cocktail to the countryside. Farmers don't see any damage to plants, birds or animals connected with their operations but I am sure many would be shocked to learn about the devastation. Unfortunately, there will always be a percentage of them who couldn't care less as my previous example highlighted.

I cannot expect the environmentally friendly system of my youth to prevail today. Customers won't buy scabby potatoes or wormy apples. They even expect them to be washed or waxed to perfection. How disgusting to have to wash a potato before cooking. That all comes at a cost to the environment, as described, so is it a price worth paying? Why should we worry about the loss of a species? Our welfare comes first, but it is our welfare that is the worry. Like the canary down the mine, loss of species is a pointer to the dangers to us as the two are inextricably linked. Nature's balance is being upset.

As an example, we rely on the honeybee and other insects for much of our food. They and other insects are vital for pollination. So our fate is inextricably linked with theirs. That's how things work. It doesn't affect grain farmers as most of that crop species are wind pollinated so they can do without these insects. Legislation for the sake of it is no solution, it has to be enforced. These chemicals are not being applied as per manufacturer's safety regulations and that is breaking the law. Big deal, so what, who is going to stop it? If you doubt this, then you are not looking hard enough. I see it constantly all summer.

Taking a farmer to task when one of his employees is spraying near me on a windy day he explains, 'we have to spray you see.' No you don't but it enhances profit and if you do then you have no right to spray anyone else's land, in this case mine. In a friend's garden next to a field of potatoes being sprayed with something, we found ourselves clutching at our throats and rubbing our stinging eyes. Whatever was being sprayed set our airways on fire. Only minutes later the potato greenery shrivelled up and died, as did many of the plants in the garden. What was the substance? Only sulphuric acid: it kills the potato plant top growth at a certain stage to avoid blight. The tubers continue to swell up until harvest. So to whom do I complain? Not to the farmer obviously. Who wants to know? If you are thinking SEPA or DEFRA then forget it, I have tried. The Health and Safety Executive, 'them must be the boys.' They issue guidelines (that

117

doesn't seem like laying down any laws). This is an excerpt:

*Check whether spray drift is likely, taking into account how they will be applying the pesticide and the weather conditions; the law states that the use of a pesticide **must be confined to what is being treated**.*

Consider telling people living and working nearby (this is good practice, but not always a legal requirement, depending on what and how you are spraying);

Take special care when spraying near vulnerable groups such as hospitals and schools;

Take special care where there are public rights of way.

There has to be concern surely about such a statement. Firstly, it shoots itself in the foot. If the law states that you must confine the spray to what is being treated, then why the special care when in some specific situations. The worst worry is that it is almost an admission of guilt. It's seemingly acceptable to spray me and other healthy people, but not hospitalised people or children. Even if I was a chronic asthmatic, as long as I am not hospitalised, it's ok to spray in my vicinity. Of course, always the bottom line, who is going to police it?

Now, mentioning asthma: in the last thirty years, worryingly, there has been a huge increase in cases of childhood asthma and allergies. Whilst there may be many factors to blame, the timescale concurs exactly with the changes in farming practices and the amount of chemical spraying now carried out. Be it breathed in or consumed, it has to be one of the suspects as it turns out that none of our crops are truly chemical free if a 'negligible amount' is considered.

Here is another perceived farming problem - **Erosion**

In the 1930s homesteaders in states like Oklahoma and Texas paid an enormous price for their disregard of nature. Previously, fertile virgin prairie had been put under the plough and, with increasing mechanisation, continued on a larger and larger scale. Native grasses were replaced by shallow rooted arable crops. For quite a time it was idyllic, producing profitable yields but trouble loomed. Drought, every so often for millennia, has

118

always been a common occurrence in these parts of America. If homesteaders had asked themselves the question as to why grasses and not forest naturally predominated, they may have been more prudent. The grasses can take drought on the chin: deep rooted and mat forming they can conserve moisture. They can also shut down to dormancy until conditions improve. A drought affected natural prairie may look like a dry burned out landscape but life sits in readiness. Without the native flora, a period of drought was disastrous. Native grasses would have bound the light, fertile soil but without them the homesteaders could only watch helplessly as their lands just blew away. In fact the dust travelled as far as the eastern seaboard blotting out the sun from many cities, New York included. It is still known today as the 'dustbowl'. Widespread famine resulted in an exodus to the cities and they weren't exactly abundant in jobs in the 'thirties.

As mentioned, cutting down tropical rainforest for profitable hardwood has long been opposed by the western world due to life on this planet's reliance on the oxygen they release and the carbon they capture. Addressing the problem seems easy. Let's plant replacements. It may take a long time but surely the forest can, in theory, bounce back. That's not as straightforward as it first seems. Once again, shallow fertile soil is exposed and this time it isn't the lack of water that's the problem. It's not called rainforest for nothing. Some of the highest rainfall anywhere on earth washes the soil and its nutrients into the massive rivers leaving a barren land on which very little will grow. Felling these monster hardwoods is a one way street. There are other side effects. Increased sediment in rivers and estuaries is damaging the environment of the animals that live in them.

Erosion happens naturally everywhere. Our mountains are gradually eaten away and washed into the seas. That's **gradually**. The two examples above are immediate in terms of the earth's timescale and are caused by us humans. Are we learning by these past mistakes that scientists have pointed out?

When I was a boy the 'tattie holidays' in October were a necessity to gather in the potato harvest: as much a staple crop to my society as oats and barley. The holiday part of the phrase is a misnomer. It was backbreaking work but the additional

119

income to the family was welcomed. The crop was unearthed and collected in baskets. Nowadays mechanical harvesters do the job. There is only one problem. How does a machine know the difference between a potato and a similar sized stone? 'Tattie howkin' kids didn't make that mistake. As the potatoes roll along the riddler they have to be sorted. That's a cost in labour. Not only that, but the supermarkets require unblemished and unbruised specimens: a requirement driven by us, the customers. Rattling along the assembly along with stones is the cause of the problem. The solution was simple, harvest all the stones from the field before planting the crop and so machinery was developed to do just that. Potatoes are not normally grown in the same field two years running so new fields have to be riddled as the years unfold. This leaves the soil on the farms with no stones. Oh dear. I hope we don't get a drought followed by high winds. You get the drift? You probably will if it happens. Droughts of that severity are uncommon in my part of the world but three years of record rainfall have given us the rainforest scenario rather than the Oklahoma one. Yes, without the stones to retain moisture and give the loam substance, the soil is being washed away into the swollen rivers damaging wildlife and impoverishing the remnant lands. To make up for the nutrient deficit, fertilisers such as slurry are spread with scant regard to the consequences: the rivers and water tables taking even more punishment. That completes a loop back to my original observation on modern farming. It looks like we will never learn.

There are even more consequences in the same vein. On every farm there used to be wet areas, small streams and bog land left uncultivated, but wild bog land was a land resource wasted. Modern drainage has drastically reduced these areas. Ditches and natural streams have been piped to encourage fast runoff, much to the detriment of wild flowers such as marsh marigolds, marsh orchids and many more. I already mentioned the estimation that in these parts we have lost 80% of our wild flower species, many of whom relied on these environments. It has also had a devastating effect on animals like bank voles and of course, amphibians. Further up the food chain, kestrels, owls, herons and other predators have all taken a huge knock, number wise. Many relied on the marshy areas and ditches. In the past I have even seen otters foraging in ditches more than half a mile from the river (contrary to belief, they don't confine themselves to rivers). Stoats, weasels and even polecats used the cover and the food that these ditches provided. Marshland birds like oyster catcher, curlew, lapwing, snipe, etc have similarly suffered greatly. As far as farmers are concerned, draining these havens is good for production and they don't consider wildlife whatever they may state BUT there is a proven cost to human habitat as well. These boggy areas were like sponges, storing water in heavy rainfall and releasing it gradually. The modern fast runoff has huge repercussions downriver, the water arriving in a 'oner'. Floods: it is easy to blame global warming or the council's lack of investment but it seems man made, as efforts in some areas procured by conservation groups has helped the problem immensely. They have been blocking the drains and returning areas to their natural state.

There must be a more environmentally friendly way. Drawing the attention of farmers to these problems helps. Some are running better farms as a result, albeit for slightly less profit, but the big tycoons are never going to listen. Theirs is a bandwagon which, if not halted, will exacerbate habitat and species loss. Who has the power to reverse this trend? Who indeed? It may depend on who donates money to political parties or who takes councillors out for lunch (that's not made up, by the way). It may be the pressure of economics or the buying power of the supermarket chains. It may be the pressure of environmental groups but does their charity money stretch that far? Parliament has the power but not the money, apparently, to enforce any of these laws. Giving financial incentives has to be policed as some will take the money and pay lip service to conservation. If it does happen then a great recent suggestion is to compulsory re-naturalise (with possible tree planting and maintaining) a percentage, say 5%, of their land if they farm over a specified acreage. Some farmers are doing just that by leaving uncropped areas at field edges to replicate what it used to be like. It is encouraging to see recent grants for replanting and protecting hedging at field boundaries but spraying near all these areas must be avoided which often doesn't happen. Strict policing of the application of effluents, chemical fertilisers and pesticides is necessary for success. It can be done but it costs money.

My apologies to all farmers who are trying their damnedest to incorporate wildlife conservation but simple observation, by anyone, will see that there are not many of your ilk. There is a long way to go. Perhaps this is the sacrifice that has to be made to feed the expanding world population. Lose our beloved wildlife, both flora and fauna, and endanger human health. You cannot argue with either of those facts. The wildlife loss is obvious and the breathing in of sulphuric acid droplets is not recommended.

All is not completely lost however. The European Union Common Agricultural Policy is considering the problems. They have suggested that agricultural subsidies be linked to 'greener' practices. That seems a great idea, but it's hit the buffers. Not such a good idea according to farmers and Conservative MEP, Ian Duncan, who sits at this time on the *environment* committee of the EU. His statement in the headlines read, 'GREENING RULES BAD FOR FARMING' predicting a detrimental effect on farmers' competitiveness on the world market. Par for the course: the wallet before the environment. In Scotland, in particular, we have another boost to the environment. Due to the terrain, the country has many un-farmable areas although much is being lost through further drainage work (not previously possible). Many areas have little soil and too much rock. These are the havens to which many threatened species are confined, normally in upland areas, but nationwide there is one unexpected bonus in the way of a legacy.

The Victorian era seems to have been categorised by two classes, filthy rich or desperately poor. The first depended on the second for their lavish lifestyle. Servitude was the order of the day. Stately homes and estates were built and maintained by the working classes for little more than subsistence both then and previously. Hunting and fishing were the pastimes of upper class males and estate grounds were laid out to accommodate both. Shrubberies and woodland were planted as cover for game and the importing of rare plants was fashionable as plant hunters scoured the now accessible world. A good time was being had by the chosen few but, for some, it was not to last. As the Victorian era passed first to the Edwardian era and then to George V's reign so the First World War took its toll. Estate workers were mobilised as were the gentry, albeit as officers, and they were expected to lead their men 'over the top'. Many never returned. Those who did seemed to be stirred with a different attitude. Women were campaigning for the vote (there now being more women than men) and labour movements brought home the real value of a man's (or woman's) labour. Many estates were keeping up with the Jones' and all but the richest found estate and mansion management hard going. Many fell into disrepair and now stand ruinous as a stark warning of living beyond your means. The plants though grew on, creating an unmanaged wilderness of shrubs and stately trees. Today the remaining estates are still going under due to taxes and labour costs, or they are being managed by National Heritage bodies. In both cases the trees and shrubs still exist. Around the estates, farmland is still looking like it used to: except the hedging field breaks are more mature, as are the avenues of stately trees. Being revered for their maturity they are not cleared to extend field size for modern farming. The grounds are in a time warp, a glimpse back to a former age.

There is irony here. These once manicured grounds and their copses, laid out as habitat for hunted species to be shot and now overgrown, are the last refuge of many wild bird and animal species. Locally the only places to find an abundance of red squirrels, badgers, fox, deer and many more, all living happily without a gamekeeper's interference. Pheasants, of course, are also in abundance because no one is shooting them. No one is protecting them from predators either and they are doing equally well. There's more good news. These places are the last refuge of some species once common but now in serious decline: spotted flycatchers, jays, wood warblers and stock doves to name a small sample. All the familiar birds are in abundance as well. Nature doing as nature intended. There is a further added bonus. Many of the plants, collected as specimens from around the world are now extinct or nearing extinction in the wild because of exploitation. That means the only source of seed to save a complete eradication of the species is from these private collections and identification with seed collection is being carried out. My own local rundown estate epitomises just these notes. Some tree specimens are, for the UK, awesome. Whilst not in the same league as the Californian redwoods or the giants of the rainforest, nevertheless they are impressive. Noble firs and Douglas firs with a huge girth and height and my favourite, a Sitka spruce, measured by someone I knew with accurate laser measurement at 186 feet. That was twenty-five years ago and, considering the tallest tree in the UK today is a little over 200 feet, it would be interesting to have it re-measured today. Not so easy though. One of the nouveau riche oil barons has moved in and he has no respect for the new Scottish parliamentary law on the 'right to roam'. A barrage of choice words is not what you expect when enjoying a walk in the woods.

The Victorian legacy is not quite dead, however, and hunting for sport in all its forms still exists. It has been seriously curtailed by conservationists with the 'hunting with dogs' legislation and 'protected species' laws. To carry out this sport, a shooting estate requires a gamekeeper.

12

KEEPERS OF GAME

Snaring is probably one of the worst ways in which an animal can die. They are left in agony, perhaps for a long time, dying from the snare injury, starvation, cold or exposure. It is estimated that of animals caught in snares, 50 per cent are species other than the target one. That is very worrying.

Baroness Byford

The first time you see a gamekeeper's gibbet is a shock to someone who has grown up with a respect for nature. A horizontal pole between two forked sticks in the ground is sagging under the weight of all the birds and animals he has recently killed. Hung with string from the pole are two foxes (minus the tails), half a dozen crows and rooks, two magpies, two stoats, a weasel, two sparrowhawks and a buzzard. That was my memory but there were other birds as well: it was in my youth. The fox tails were handed in to the local police station for the bounty of one shilling each. Posters in the station window advertised this. Gibbets are, thankfully, a lot rarer now but not unheard of. Why this macabre spectacle? It is to show the landowner that the gamekeeper is doing his job and earning his wages. These species are not just shot. There are Larsen traps, gin traps and wire snares set. The gin trap is now banned in the open but I have one in my possession found, after the introduction of the legislation, on a walk. A rook was caught by the leg, severed through the bone and held only by the white tendon. It was still attempting to fly off. How long it was like this I wouldn't know, but I cannot contemplate the unimaginable suffering which was put to an end by my hand. The landowner blamed poachers and I believed him, as he didn't hunt himself. They weren't after rooks either, confirming the non-target species statement.

The snare and the Larsen traps continue to be legal but with strict guidelines on their use. One of these is that they must be checked every day. From close observation the reality is that, in some cases, they lie for many days, even weeks without inspection. By covertly springing a snare or removing the attractor bird from the Larsen trap one can check on the periodicity of visits. The interval varies from one to six weeks: hardly daily, as the law demands. Recently, one rabbit had died in a snare, caught by the leg which had been pared to the bone. The remains were weeks old. There is absolutely no policing of these laws. Mention it to the police and there is token interest. Crime is more important but this is a crime, surely.

Are most of these creatures doing much harm in the countryside? Is grain production being hampered or farm animals harmed by them? It turns out that their only sin is that they might take a pheasant chick during the few weeks when it is vulnerable and pheasant chicks are definitely vulnerable. They were introduced into this country from the Far East purely for the sport of shooting by our Victorian forebears. The predators in this part of the world are completely new to them. Eons of evolution cannot be changed in 150 years. They are sitting targets: a fast food outlet for animals that rely on hunting to live, not for sport. There may be no argument in humans doing the same, as pheasant is tasty and we have to eat. A pheasant shoot of eight guns, their owners paying good money for the sport, is expected to shoot more than just one pheasant per gun. Twenty-five per gun is a reasonable day: that's 200 birds and next Saturday perhaps the same again, and the next and the next, throughout the season. Wild birds in an unfamiliar countryside cannot possibly sustain these numbers so the estate turns to pheasant rearing. Eggs are hatched and the fledglings are kept in large cages until old enough to release. Having been reared by hand, they are as tame as domesticated animals, easy targets for the hunters (overleaf, the elusive quarry).

Many of the 'sportsmen' couldn't hit a barn door with a bargepole. They certainly couldn't pot the wild variety so easily. In the short time since their introduction the survivors have wised up and are more elusive.

It comes down to money. Money has to get what money pays for or no more money. A huge economy has been built around hunting, both here and around the world. Well, what's wrong with that? We have to eat and nature is there to be harvested as our ancestors did.

There are two big differences. Firstly this is purely for 'sport'. None of these people have a need to shoot for survival. If they happen to like pheasant there is nothing wrong in having one for the pot, but 200 in a day? That's a big pot. Well they can be sold for food but the second difference, and the bone of contention, is the persecution of anything alive which has any inclination to take a chick to feed itself and its family, and that's the gamekeeper's job. Like farmers, there are good and bad varieties of these. On one estate, to sustain the slaughter 24,000 birds a year are bought as chicks, mainly from France, and reared to shooting size. I don't have the evidence to back up this next statistic but the story goes that only 60% are shot. That leaves nearly 10,000 birds for native animals and birds of prey. So why do keepers have to decimate these?

You would think that a gamekeeper would have an excellent intimate knowledge of the countryside and its inhabitants. Not many of the ones I have met. They are quick enough to pay lip service to conservation to appease critics but their only motive is predator v game bird chick. Coming across one who was resetting his Larsen trap, a magpie dispatched and lying dead on the ground beside it, I asked if it was really necessary. He made a big thing about magpies taking song bird eggs and they were the real reason for their decline: nonsense, surely, as the species have co-existed for millennia. His proclaimed ambition is to wipe out the species and good riddance. The truth is that he is not interested in the slightest in song bird conservation and he certainly didn't have the evidence of predation I asked for. It was purely a personal opinion. This was on an extremely cold winter's day. The snow lay a foot deep on the fields and was crystallised. At 11.30 am the thermometer at my north facing back door read -20ºC. A buzzard soared on high. This was a rare sight in those days. Persecution and the DDT scandal had put paid to them for many years but this was the start of the comeback. It was now illegal to kill buzzards by an act of Parliament passed a few years earlier. I marvelled at their survivability in these harsh conditions and happened to mention my thoughts to the keeper. 'What do they feed on in this weather?' Back came the reply, 'they hunt cushies (wood pigeon).' I couldn't believe the extent of his ignorance. Buzzards are carrion eaters in the main: one of the reasons for their previous demise is because of eating poisoned bait or DDT accumulation from dead animals. Their diet includes small rodents, beetles, earthworms and young fledglings including, occasionally, very young pheasant chicks. Well, there are 24,000 vulnerable specimens running around. They most certainly do not catch anything as fast as a woodpigeon. In fact woodpigeons treat a soaring buzzard with complete disregard. If a peregrine appears, then that is a different story. Of course buzzards will feed on a dead pigeon but the killing would be done by others. A female sparrowhawk will often pounce at high speed on a pigeon but it cannot carry it off. It severs the head and neck with the dexterity of a surgeon and makes off with that. I have seen it happen more than once. The body is the target for scavengers including crows, magpies and buzzards. I have to add that buzzards will take young pigeons from the nest and also can drop on an unsuspecting grounded one in wooded areas but in general this is not their winter sustenance. No point in explaining that to this keeper. He makes out that he is an expert on wildlife and many people accept that, purely because he is a gamekeeper.

My admiration of the buzzard's survival in such harsh conditions is also misplaced. It is the harsh conditions that provide their food. There is a bonanza of animals and birds which perish in these icy wastes. Little birds like wrens and robins take a huge knock but there are many more animals and birds at the end of their lifespans. The old, infirm and sick succumb to make up the buzzards larder. It's an ill wind in more ways than one.

There was another species which would feast on pigeons but they were wiped out by the Victorians, possibly contributing to the glut of pigeons and rabbits in the early part of the last century. The very mention of the name sends shivers down a gamekeeper's spine. The goshawk. It didn't just take pheasant chicks. It could take the adult bird. Interestingly, the past tense doesn't apply anymore as they are making a comeback. Imported in more modern times from the continent for falconry, they were trained into subservience for the sport. This isn't a domesticated species. It is a true wild animal and if some didn't conform, they just took off. Escapees bred and the comeback is now progressive, much to the horror of the gamekeepers. Being a wild, indigenous, threatened species they are given legal protection. The keepers don't agree and persecution (and thankfully, prosecution) continues. I personally have only seen one and it indeed happened to be the killing of a woodpigeon which caught my eye. Silently and swiftly it carried the kill into and through the tree canopy as if it wasn't there, so agile was the flight. It is said that a tree canopy is ninety percent air, a fact not borne out by the flight of any of my errant golf balls.

On grouse moors the shooting target is a native wild species, but it is legal, and estates work hard to sustain the population by burning moorland to create lush green heather shoots on which red grouse feed. Whatever other insects, reptiles, amphibians, mammals and wild flora are destroyed in the process is deemed irrelevant. Predators are still persecuted but with the new law, some, like the hen harrier are protected. The trouble is that if you have a hen harrier nest on a hillside you don't have any grouse. Grouse that the estate has encouraged by their efforts then move to another hillside on perhaps another estate. In casual conversation with another keeper I asked about the hen harrier situation. The one word reply, 'verrminne' summed it up.

It's a dilemma, and here's another: the capercaillie is a highly endangered species. Their plight is directly the result of man's activities: felling of the native Caledonian pine forest habitat it needs and of course, shooting. You would think all country people would be working to save this ancient species and yet up until five years ago there were still regular capercaillie shoots going on. I have the testimony which I have no reason to doubt. It has stopped for the time being, not for any conservation reason but purely because there are so few left that it is not commercially viable. This is the attitude of the custodians of the countryside. Nature groups and the Forestry Commission are working in the face of this to re-establish the species. New pine forests, their natural habitat, are being planted but are eaten by red deer. Deer fences are erected to keep them out and sod's law, capercaillie are being killed by flying into them. There is a strong case for culling the burgeoning red deer population which has escalated hugely since the eradication by us of its only natural predator, the wolf. They have the same problem with elk in North America. They settle in fertile valleys where felled forests in the past are trying to regenerate themselves in vain. They graze them flat with nothing to move them on. Enter the wolf, reintroduced to its old ranges. The difference is dramatic. Although the elk graze young trees, they only have a small bite of the cherry before they are kept on the move by the pack. The native forest is making an amazing comeback, completely naturally. Of course the policy is not without controversy and the conservation battle rages on.

Another dilemma concerning the capercaillie: the native pine forests are reduced to a very small proportion of their former range as required by not only the wolf, but other predators as well. A patch of pine forest has an encouraging caper' count and a, nowadays, rare predator moves in: a pine marten. High on its dietary list is capercaillie eggs and young. Previously the forest was so vast as to sustain both but not anymore. There's the dilemma. Does a gamekeeper or conservationist let the caper' inevitably die out or do they control the pine martens, both being a protected species. I am keeping out of that argument.

There are definitely gamekeepers who are more knowledgeable than others and some work along with conservationists to find a balance, but as stated there are good and bad on both sides. Recently a keeper, on checking his pheasant cages, found a sparrowhawk inside which he caught and released. For the life of him he could not find an entry point. Next day it was back in the pen. Sensing something fishy, he caught it again and put it in a bag in the back of his Land Rover. After he finished work he drove to the local village police station with the bird, showing it alive before releasing it. 'That's strange,' said the officer, 'someone anonymously handed in a video of you supposedly disposing of the bird this afternoon.' There are two points here. First, this sort of honey trap gives the true conservationists a bad name getting them tarred with the same brush. Second, interfering with a sparrowhawk is against the law and two wrongs don't make a right.

All these laws I have mentioned so far are contained in the Wildlife and Countryside Act 1981 and it makes interesting reading especially with regard to birds:

Schedule 3 Part III	
Birds which may be sold dead: 1 September to 28 February	
Capercaillie	Pochard
Coot	Shoveler
Duck, tufted	Snipe, common
Mallard	Teal
Pintail	Widgeon
Plover, golden	Woodcock

Coot? Golden Plover? Have you ever tasted Golden Plover? Have you seen them on any restaurant menu? I for one am horrified.

On the following page is another table from the act detailing which species can be shot legally in season:

Species	England and Wales	Scotland	Northern Ireland	Isle of Man
Pheasant	Oct 1- Feb 1	Oct 1 - Feb 1	Oct 1 - Jan 31	Oct 1 – Jan 31
Grey Partridge	Sep 1 - Feb 1	Sep 1 - Feb 1	Sep 1- Jan 31	Protected (ban in force)
Red-legged Partridge	Sep 1 - Feb 1	Sep 1 - Feb 1	Sep 1- Jan 31	Sep 13 – Jan 31
Red Grouse	Aug 12 - Dec 10	Aug 12 - Dec 10	Aug 12 - Nov 30	Aug 25 – Oct 31
Black Grouse	Aug 20 - Dec 10 (Somerset, Devon and New Forest: Sep 1 - Dec 10)	Aug 20 - Dec 10	--	--
Ptarmigan	--	Aug 12 - Dec 10	--	--
Duck & Goose inland	Sep 1 - Jan 31	Sep 1 - Jan 31	Sep 1 - Jan 31	Sep 1 - Jan 31 - Ducks July 1 - Mar 31 - Geese
Duck & Goose below HWM (see below)	Sep 1 - Feb 20	Sep 1 - Feb 20	Sep 1 - Jan 31	Sep 1- Jan 31- Ducks Jul 1 - Mar 31 - Geese
Common Snipe	Aug 12 - Jan 31	Aug 12 - Jan 31	Sep 1 - Jan 31	Sep 1 - Jan 31
Jack Snipe	Protected	Protected	Sep 1 - Jan 31	Protected
Woodcock	Oct 1 - Jan 31	Sep 1 - Jan 31	Oct 1 - Jan 31	Oct 1 - Jan 31
Golden Plover	Sep 1 - Jan 31	Sep 1 - Jan 31	Sep 1 - Jan 31	Protected
Coot/Moorhen	Sep 1 - Jan 31	Sep 1 - Jan 31	Protected	Protected

Other lists are just as shocking to me:

Schedule 3 Part I - Birds which may be sold alive at all times if ringed and bred in captivity.

Blackbird	Goldfinch	Redpoll
Brambling	Greenfinch	Siskin
Bullfinch	Jackdaw	Starling
Bunting, reed	Jay	Thrush, song
Chaffinch	Linnet	Twite
Dunnock	Magpie	Yellowhammer
Goldfinch	Owl, barn	

A song thrush in a cage? I cannot imagine. Well at least it is illegal to kill a wild one, isn't it? Not true. You have to apply for a quarry licence from DEFRA and that's nothing to do with extracting gravel and sand. Then you can kill thrushes, blackbirds, skylarks and a host of others within the law with your pet merlin. But the law says you cannot kill wildlife purely for sporting reasons. So what excuse does it come under? In the light of the public being increasingly conservation minded especially the upcoming generation, it may be time for a review of all this contradicting guff.

There is another justification for gamekeepers to kill whatever they want. It comes under the term 'VERMIN'. There are some animals protected by law. Others such as foxes, crows and rabbits seem outside the protected tag. Gamekeepers consider many species as *just* vermin and their prime aim is to eradicate them: hen harriers, goshawks, stoats, weasels, badgers, foxes and many more. This is disputed by conservationists who vigorously defend the animal's right to live. To where can we turn for guidance? What can we eradicate as vermin and what not? Parliamentary law is a good place to start, surely. In 2003 that very question was asked in the house.

[8 Oct 2003: Column WA60

Vermin

Lord Selsdon asked Her Majesty's Government:

Which mammals and other animals are classified as 'vermin'? [HL4559]

Lord Whitty:

There is no definition of the term 'vermin' in UK law. In such a situation the Oxford Dictionary definition should be applied.]

The Oxford Dictionary defines 'vermin' as 'animals of a noxious or objectionable kind, originally applied to reptiles, stealthy, or slinky animals and various wild beasts'.

So that clarifies it, does it? Some of these categories describe a few girlfriends I have been out with in the past, especially the last description. Basically it gives carte blanche to gamekeepers to please themselves and in any sane person's judgement that must be a serious flaw. It probably should be expected because it is the aristocracy who have been making the laws for hundreds of years and it suited their hunting pursuits. Many would say the time has come to be more precise in the definition, but the class system hangs on. The only way change will come is if it becomes a vote winner and the only way to achieve that is to make the general public aware of what goes on. I do wish I had a video of the rook in the gin trap. It would have converted half the nation. Public awareness is the goal to which conservationists strive and they are making inroads. Firstly they have to win over that public and some are difficult to win over.

13

MISCONCEPTIONS

Education should prepare our minds to use its own powers of reason and conception rather than filling it with the accumulated misconceptions of the past.

Bryant H McGill

Human beings have mastered the art of conversation propelling them to the level in nature which, in that respect, makes us superior to other animals. That doesn't mean that we are at the top of an evolutionary tree for it depends on the particular tree. We can never hope to master the air like the swift or the water like a salmon. Language and conversation, however, have given us the power to dominate other species by sharing acquired knowledge. These attributes have their drawbacks as well. If someone makes a bold statement to another, is it a true statement? Let us take this example that I encountered not too long ago. An acquaintance of mine came to me with a bit of wildlife news. 'You will be interested in this as you are a wildlife lover and bird expert.' I am neither, just an observer who doesn't miss much. A humming bird had been spotted feeding from a flower in a west end suburb of our north east Scottish city. I told him that it was an impossibility and he became indignant. 'The whole community knows about it, not just me, and they can't all be wrong.' Oh yes they can, but my explanation didn't get far as he was having none of it. Humming birds are native to the Americas and are found throughout the new world. They have to feed constantly just to stay alive and can go no more than twenty minutes without nectar from the flowers of particular plant species. At night their systems shut down into a torpor state until the warmth of dawn. Crossing 5,000 miles of wild Atlantic and arriving here in a healthy state is just an impossibility. I got a phone call two days later. It's the acquaintance. 'Have you read this morning's paper? You were wrong.' The article headlined:

'Humming bird sighted in city suburb'

I was in the process of composing a reply to the article but wasn't quick enough. Next morning's paper contained a rebuttal from someone more knowledgeable than I (from the university). Not only that but with a suggestion that the obvious sighting of something was probably a humming bird hawk moth, a mainly southern European species but not unheard of in these parts. This subsequently proved to be correct. The reason for the confusion is obvious. Convergent evolution has these two species looking, feeding and acting in the same way. They are also the same size. A clarification was subsequently printed in the paper. My acquaintance was strangely silent.

It is for the recipients of statements to analyse and make up their minds. How do they do that? It seems simple. As I have said, and as I try to do, they need to look to see the facts behind the statement. Again not so simple is to separate fact from, not just fiction, but from what at first glance appears to be facts. There is also the subservience side previously mentioned. A university professor must know more than them (in this case correct). It depends on the subject, surely. Don't sell yourself short. Although the eye can certainly be deceived, it is a better judge than hearsay or opinion, especially if there is no motive to deceive. Many of nature's mysteries are not easy to solve but some are not so mysterious, although you still have to look deeper than first impressions. Certainly, some misconceptions can be explained by presenting facts instead of opinion but you have to be aware that there is no personal leaning towards a selfish outcome, such as the gamekeeper justifying killing magpies to save the songbirds.

A newspaper article by the RSPB on the plight of British birds attracted this reply.

'Your article informs the public that dozens of British birds are in sharp decline. The RSPB blames farmers, foresters and climate change. Has the RSPB considered that it is their own policy that is to blame - and that policy is its protection of birds of prey?

There are more birds of prey now than in living memory, and their numbers increase every year, and now the RSPB plans to introduce even more. Unless the numbers of birds of prey are controlled, then the numbers of all British birds will decline.

The RSPB needs to understand that it should stand for the protection of all birds and not just birds of prey'.

It brings a tear to a nature enthusiast's eye. I take it, for a start, that by *'protection'* the RSPB means protection from us and not from other wildlife. Also the RSPB **DOES** stand for protection of **ALL** birds and not just predators.

The statement by the RSPB on the reasons for the decline is not given lightly. It is based on scientific investigation over a long period throughout the whole country. Although the article does not give the details, they can be obtained. This is not a fanatical opinion biased towards bird welfare.

The correspondent makes bold statements.

'There are more birds of prey now than in living memory and their numbers increase every year.'

No corroborating evidence. Does he/she refer to surveyed evidence nationwide, surveyed evidence in the local area, or even in just his/her garden through the kitchen window? It doesn't say, so how are we to believe this?

'Unless the numbers of birds of prey are controlled then the numbers of all British birds will decline.'

Sounds like an unscientific opinion to me. No substantiating facts. The correspondent has supporters. This next letter writer agrees.

'For many years we have had the pleasure of watching goldfinches, siskins, blue tits, chaffinches, sparrows, blackbirds and even a song thrush at times feeding in our garden. Months ago, the loud chirping of a frightened sparrow alerted my husband who found a sparrowhawk trying to get at it in a thick bush. Since then all the small birds have gone, probably eaten. Now all we seem to see is a blackbird or sparrow occasionally. Surely these beautiful, defenceless small birds should be considered by the RSPB. In this area we never used to see birds of prey, now they are common.'

Disappeared from their garden, I presume it means. *'Probably eaten'* is pure presumption. It also infers a fantastic sparrowhawk appetite. I would also hazard a guess that the observations were made in the autumn (late September/October). Tits especially disappear from gardens at that time of year. It seems that they prefer their natural food then, as all the insects of summer skies are laying eggs and dying or finding crevices to hibernate, but it may be the fact that the birds are going through the annual moult and keep a low profile. The moult is a progressive process starting with body feathers and ending with the primary wing and tail feathers. These latter stages affect agility and make them more vulnerable. Safety in the cover of leaves in the garden has also been removed. Dense woodland gives them extra protection and provides the crop of overwintering insects. They will return to the feeders in colder weather, resplendent in their new costumes. Of course they won't all return. The reason there were so many in the first place, making their disappearance so obvious, is that numbers had swelled throughout late summer with this year's progeny. A tit brood can consist of up to ten chicks and with all the garden nest boxes nowadays this swells the numbers in the vicinity. There are only so many places to nest and feed so members of the new generation have to make their own way in the world and set up their own territories around new nest sites. This they do in winter in preparation for spring. The ones now using the feeders during winter are the adults back to defend their nest sites and territories or, if any have passed on, there may be new occupants.

The RSPB conducts a nationwide survey of garden birds every year in January, a lean time for small birds. They have over a million members covering the whole country. Many schools also take part giving a snapshot of how birds are faring. These results are published and contradict the writer's findings. Most garden birds are doing just fine. The first correspondent missed the point in that he/she didn't consider the particular species that were in decline. Mostly it is farmland and wetland birds, as well as BIRDS OF PREY, which are in decline.

Then to the final sympathising letter under the heading: *'Time for a rethink on predators.'*

'Your correspondent expressed concern regarding the disappearance of small birds due to the predation of sparrowhawks. Here on the Island of Mull, my neighbour and I feed hundreds of small birds during the winter months. It is heartbreaking to see our lovely wee friends killed on a daily basis by ruthless, but protected, birds like the sparrowhawk, in a horrible, cruel fashion. For over a decade, the re-establishment programme of sea-eagles in the Hebrides has been exploited relentlessly on almost a daily basis by a small pressure group, claiming that sea-eagles are a substantial source of visitor revenue. Make no mistake, like foxes, these horrible predators were removed by our wise forefathers for very good reasons, not the least being for taking lambs, goat kids and other farming livestock. I have lived on Mull for fifty years and I have not seen a single hare since the sea-eagle reintroduction programme. Have landowners, gamekeepers, farmers, fish farmers and bird lovers in the Inner Hebrides got it all wrong, or is it time for a major rethink on sea-eagle proliferation. When is it going to be enough? 40 or 400 pairs.'

Well at least this corroborates the survey, and contradicts the previous correspondent in that they feed HUNDREDS of small birds in their gardens. The horrible, cruel fashion referred to is instant death. You know, like we do to cows, sheep, pigs, chickens and a host of others. The gripe obviously is the sea-eagle reintroduction.

'The re-establishment programme of sea-eagles in the Hebrides has been exploited (?) relentlessly on almost a daily basis by a small (?) pressure group, claiming that sea-eagles are a substantial source of visitor revenue.'

A pressure group of more than a million is hardly small. The campaign is also backed by government. The statement on revenue implies that he/she has the figures to hand. I won't comment as I don't. However, on my visit to Mull on that monsoon October day, for that very purpose, I met many others on the ferry with the same reason for their visit. That's successful tourism.

They have a thing about foxes as well, obviously. In fact it looks like they want to reorganise the world to suit the most important species: theirs.

Modern humans are new to his part of the globe. For millennia before they arrived nature took care of itself. In fact even after that, there wasn't a problem. Only in very modern times came a clash and the writers should know from recent history that it didn't exclude their own species from persecution. The Highland Clearances made way for profitable sheep. These sheep were at a premium and anything which threatened them was ruthlessly eradicated, including the human inhabitants who were trying to eke a living. Modern persecution of nature was born. The inference is that these eagles, wiped out to suit us, killed lambs and kids. Well I wouldn't blame them as we have created a fast food outlet. Let's stick to the facts. As part of the reintroduction programme compensation can be claimed for any lamb killed, if it can be proved that it was a sea-eagle that killed it. There have been very little payments but a lot of disproved claims, some laughable. One crofter claimed to have lost 200 lambs. To investigate this, a conservation group attached radio transmitters to fifty of his lambs and not one was taken. His argument was that the eagles were put off by the black boxes on their backs. It was suggested to him that he had just come up with a solution to his supposed problem. Fit black boxes to all his lambs. In nearly every case, it has been stillborn lambs eaten as carrion. If a crofter comes across a half-eaten newborn lamb, the eagle gets the blame. With that amount of sheep, abandoned to lamb in the harshest land and climate in the UK, a percentage of stillborns and casualties are inevitable, just like humans before modern maternal care.

The writer's comment on hares is irrelevant to the eagles. I can concur with the loss of hares and there are no eagles here. Scotland wide there is a massive reduction in hares, well out with the eagle's range. It was noticed first by the hunters who shot them for sport. A hundred or more shot in a day cannot be sustained. What's new?

Good news on the hare front just lately. Some areas have seen a remarkable comeback of white mountain hares. Bad news follows. The grouse shooting lobby is blaming the increase for spreading body parasites to their hallowed grouse targets and are calling for a cull. Here we go again.

The real misconception in these letters is in nature's way of coping with predation. Serious observers of the natural world appreciate this.

If the offending sparrowhawks eat all the small birds as predicted, then what are they to eat? Starvation would surely follow and a decline in their numbers. This would allow any remaining small birds to recover and proliferate. Any remaining sparrowhawks are in for a bonanza and so on. The populations have to stabilise at a sustainable level in both species. It's not a new term, 'balance of nature'. It is the essence of how life on earth works. Messrs Darwin and Huxleys' revelation hasn't convinced the whole world yet. It probably never will.

I have already mentioned the final anomaly. The writers are condemning the hawk for killing to live and feed their family because they don't like to see cute birds being killed for food. Perhaps they are watching this from the comfort of a centrally heated lounge window whilst enjoying a coffee and chicken sandwich. Maybe they have decided on a fish supper for the luxury of not having to cook tea, or if they are more industrious, they may be preparing their family meal of shepherd's pie with not a thought of the hypocrisy.

Finally, it could be that these nature loving writers like beautiful butterflies as well and may also be concerned with their recorded decline nationwide. The biggest part of a blue tit's diet is caterpillars. I see no letters calling for a cull of blue tits to protect butterflies.

On the whole though, the evidence seems overwhelming that the activities and greedy attitudes of the human race are having an adverse effect on the natural world on our planet. Without our interference the sparrowhawk and blue tit will, and always have, managed just fine. Gamekeeping is not a necessity for balance in the countryside. I mustn't be so hypocritical though. A mole in a bowling green is not welcome, neither is a rabbit in a flowerbed. Also, we have to eat. Humans have harvested wildlife in our prehistory and still do today. I like fish, grew up on rabbit and shellfish and am partial to a bit of venison. If the 'sportsmen' on shooting estates want real sport and a real challenge to their skills then here's the gun, there's the hills, go shoot yourself your tea. Rational conservationists would accept this if no cruelty is involved, if no wholesale killing of natural predators happens and there is no overharvesting to threaten any species. It comes under the heading of sustainability.

14

SUSTAINABILITY

Only when the last tree has been cut down,
Only when the last river has been poisoned,
Only when the last fish has been caught,
Only then will you find that money cannot be eaten.

prophesy of the Cree Indians

It may be just me but there is great peace of mind to be had of a summer evening in visiting my local river to try to catch a trout for tea. It may be some primaeval instinct for a male to hunt to provide food for his family that drives this pleasure, and I am not immune to that force. The pursuit is called dry fly fishing and the wonder of nature that makes it possible is as follows.

Aquatic flies hatch from their larval stage, either in the river bed or among aquatic plants, at intervals to mate and reproduce. This has to be co-ordinated, for a single fly is no use for reproduction. There are many types of fly. Olive duns, olive quills, march browns, iron blue duns and many more species spend the vast majority of their lifespan as larvae in the river. All of a sudden there is a 'rise'. Metamorphosed flies of only one species swim up and break the surface. They then spend a brief time drying their wings whilst riding the surface film before taking off and flying UPSTREAM. They mate, re-land on the surface and lay their eggs which quickly sink to the bottom to perpetuate the species. The adults then die: all this for reproduction in a few moments of 'pleasure'. Can a fly feel pleasure? The upstream direction is irrespective of wind direction. This has to be, otherwise the eggs would eventually end up in the sea rather than colonise the length of the river. That's the weird thing. The 'hatch' is co-ordinated throughout the length of the river, and only for one species at any one time: a pretty good achievement for a tiny fly. As usual there are many theories masquerading as facts on how this is achieved. We seem to know through television nature programmes that coral reproduction in the oceans are timed to coincide a few days after a full moon, even if they are 1,500 miles apart as in the Great Barrier Reef. That seems correct as it can be predicted. So what triggers the aquatic fly? Water temperature is one theory but that implies that precise temperature slots favour a particular species. Olive dun hatches can happen in April or in July and the water temperature certainly isn't the same. Air temperature is another. 'It's too cold for a hatch' being a popular phrase. How can larvae on the river bed tell the air temperature above? During an April snowstorm, a huge hatch of flies is common and the same thing can happen on a balmy summer evening and that's where I come in.

Filleted brown trout, butter fried with oatmeal dressing, is the tastiest tea on the planet but maybe that's just me. Traditional fayre is how I was brought up and I was used to many wildlife dishes. Hare's blood soup, roast pheasant, rabbit or boiled parten (red crab) along with buckies, (whelks) and cod or whiting. All provided by the males of the family for necessity rather than luxury. Home grown vegetables and fruit made up the complete diet. That seems how it was in antiquity in human history, the diet that sustained us to where we are now.

On the river the quest isn't easy on a balmy evening, of which there are not that many in these parts. I have to determine which fly is hatching and floating briefly on the surface and try to imitate it with a feather replica. Suitably treated to float and attached to an unnatural nylon leader, I cast out to try to fool the fish. They have been gorging themselves and are not in the least bit hungry so they can afford to be picky. They come up to have a look as I am poised to strike. Most turn away. 'Can't fool me, it's artificial and trailing on a line. It doesn't look right nor smell right. Pass.' 90% of casts end up futile but then one, perhaps a short sighted, trout makes a mistake and it's tea for two.

That's not the only reason I am there. Only fifty yards away a heron is on the same mission, standing statue like with its grey and white plumage merging with the clouds on the trout's visual picture from subsurface. An otter slips into the stream and disappears under the bank to reappear way upstream. A dipper likewise takes the plunge to walk along the river bed in search of caddis fly larvae. Overhead, swifts scream in their mad chases, skimming the surface and hoovering up the hatching flies. Likewise in a quieter manner, swallows and martins do the same. An osprey proves it is a better fisherman than I and plunges into the downstream pool to grasp and carry off a monster. It may seem a well-worn phrase but 'at one with nature' seems to apply. Anyway, suffice to say that I enjoy it. It's a bit more than that. All these species are doing exactly as I am doing. Harvesting nature for the purpose of eating to survive and feed their families, including the trout and myself. As far as these other species go, they are content with doing just that. Myself, I have a choice, born out of superior brain power leading to human ingenuity. I can throw a net across the pool, fill my freezer and sell the surplus at a profit. In the wilds of the countryside, no one is going to know. So why don't I? Well, I am a conservationist at heart and do not agree with exploitation. I have to eat but I respect nature. Until very recent times the vast majority of the population did exactly that, as in my family upbringing. 'Nature provideth' to keep the family nourished and different populations had their own sources to feed the 'LOCAL' population. Many societies in the third world are still doing that. It comes under my heading 'sustainability'.

Mankind nowadays has kicked that into touch. Now it's not about survival, it's about wealth and profit margins. Big business can make big bucks from traditional natural foods. 'West coast' prawns are now imported from Malaysia because it's cheaper than buying local. You have to wonder about the logic of Scottish lamb being exported to continental Europe and New Zealand lamb being imported into Scotland.

Atlantic salmon has been a source of food in this part of the world for centuries. It was a healthy part of the population's diet. Caught on their way back into river systems to spawn, they were harvested easily by netting or rod and line. Runs of fish were legendary as the newspaper cutting (see following page) from the 1950s shows. Halcyon days for the salmon fishers:

Coastal and estuary nets grew in number and produced bigger and bigger harvests. This, alas, was not to feed the local population but to grace the tables of rich guests in hotels in London and the continent, refrigeration technology eventually making this ever more possible. The price of Scottish salmon soared to record levels as demand grew and at the time of that newspaper article, spring run fish were fetching anything up to £3 per POUND. That's more than it fetches today.

In 1952 an early Spring run of salmon brought big catches to all the salmon fishing stations on the east coast of Scotland. Here Robert Fiddes holds two 30lb salmon, part of an astonishing catch of more than 2,000 fish in a 30-week season. Earning less than £10 a week, the fishermen were on an end of season bonus per 100 fish caught. In just two days they made half their usual bonus!

Now, the average weekly wage then was around double that figure so a twenty pound salmon was worth three month's hard graft. Caviar has never fetched that much. Little wonder then that the poor man in the street turned to poaching. When you couple that with the invention of fish finders and factory ships at the oceanic feeding grounds and the golden egg was being harvested at every stage. That is until supply began to run out, seriously, and no wonder. Not only were the adults being slaughtered in huge numbers, but that meant that the eggs from them were not being spawned to provide future adults for the market: creating a one way street to a dead end. The netters, under license by the government, would have caught every last fish driving the species to extinction under the excuse of it being their livelihood and their right. There are no livelihood and rights arguments if there are no fish. On my local river, a favourite salmon pool called 'The Saugh' is below a weir which impedes runs of fish. The owner of the land couldn't believe his luck: an income on his doorstep. This is from another old press cutting:

'The haul that night was 999 salmon. Mr John Paton suggested another cast to try to get the round number of 1,000. But the pool had been cleaned out.'

Not knowing the total weight it is impossible to estimate the value of such a haul but, at prime prices as stated, it's akin to winning the lottery, even at today's values. Unsurprisingly, future scarcity followed which drove the price up even further to record levels until a saviour appeared in two forms, one a double edged sword.

In 1967, in response to the desecration of salmon stocks, the Atlantic Salmon Trust was formed to address the problem. Due to their efforts of buying up coastal and river fishery licences and campaigning successfully for a reduction in ocean factory ships, stocks are recovering slowly but the condition of many salmon shows that undernourishment at sea is a new factor due to the possible effects of global warming on their food supply.

However, although stock number improvement was good news for the trust, it was also good news for the poachers, still enjoying the ready black market for fresh fish at huge prices. Enter the second saviour: fish farms. Fresh fish could now be obtained far cheaper by hotels and restaurants and the bottom fell out of the market. There was less incentive for illegal activities to risk the prison sentences and poaching drastically reduced, further helping the species, but with a sting in the tail. There is now a campaign against the fish farms. Problems arose once again through greed for profits. It became a new Klondike in itself, especially with the rise of supermarket demand.

It's now not the odd fish farm but a multi-million pound industry. Salmon cages were built in more and more sea lochs and river estuaries where they came into contact with native migratory fish. Escapees in their hundreds of thousands competed for resources and even interbred with natives to genetically weaken stock and, more to the point, interfere with the homing ability as covered in my 'Migration' notes. The sea beds became polluted with the effluent. Unused food attracted young seagoing salmon smolts and all sorts of other fish and the spread of sea lice became a huge problem. The delicate young skin of wild smolts cannot endure so much infestation and it is estimated that around 80% of them die because of sea lice alone.

Once again greed spoils it for everyone.

It's no surprise to me because I have seen it all before at a very young age. My granny stayed in a little stone floored one bedroomed cottage in the country (which is now town). The seventeen pregnancies gave four miscarriages: thirteen births with eleven survivors and then nine reaching adulthood was about average for the percentage survival rate then. How they managed, I have no idea but I know how they were fed. Home grown vegetables, chickens for eggs and meat and a trade deal with the local butcher: swapping produce for red meat and all the usual rabbit, hare and fish caught in the countryside. There were two staple diets in the winter. One was oats, grown extensively then. An oatmeal 'girnal' sat in the washhouse to store the meal, rodent free, to make the traditional porridge every morning, never missed. The last thing done at night was to soak the meal overnight in a pan to soften the coarseness. Amounts were judged by handful or part handful, depending on how many breakfasts were required. This was also how I was fed two generations on. The second staple, which fits with this chapter, was herring: common and cheap as chips. Salted in barrels, my grandmother's one sat next to the girnal. It was cooked in many ways, even as soup. There was a seemingly unlimited supply from the east coast drift net fleet. The 'silver darlings' and their processing was a traditional industry for centuries. The numbers were taken for granted until of course the inevitable happened. The well ran dry. Nowadays, even with numbers recovering, it's a dead industry here. People have lost the taste for it, which is good news for the herring. Not so for cod, whiting, haddock, sole and mackerel.

The fishing industry then concentrated on trawling to survive and here was another huge resource ripe for the plucking.

Memories of casting a line off the breakwater in the harbour and catching huge cod for tea are just that, memories. When oil was discovered in the North Sea continental shelf divers were required and big money drew experienced ones from far and near. One from Canada became a friend. He tells of the abundance of fish in the early seventies 'down there' but by 2000, 'there's nothing there anymore'. First hand observation confirms an unsustainable industry going out the door fast. Scientists were saying the same but the trawlermen were saying different. They have fish finders, so can track whatever is left.

Above all that is common sense. You are shooting your industry in the foot. Remember the herring. Maybe they are too young. The battle continues: conservation and sustainability on the one side and jobs and livelihoods on the other. Scientists, however, persuaded governments to take action by encouraging decommissioning and imposing catch limitations, much to the fury of the fishermen, and the situation because of these measures is slowly improving. Success is measured by the tonnage of fish landed. Hmmm.

The very same argument is raging with prawns and scallops. The sea floor is being damaged beyond belief by the dredging and scientific proof is still being denied by the race for profit.

The worst, the very worst, story follows.

As a boy, the fish market was a place to go for free cod heads from the barrels of waste left outside the fish houses: then anything for free was treasured. They were boiled for soup or used as bait for crabs, being tied into a net stretched across a spokeless bicycle wheel (a gird). A triple string and line attached, they were lowered over the side of the breakwater and pulled up at intervals with the crabs on board. That's why we were there early in the morning and that's when I became aware of another party interested in the barrels of heads and guts, The Caledonian Fish Meal Company. Their lorries collected the barrels and their factory processed the remains into animal feed and fertiliser. Waste not, want not. There's money in muck. The factory had a huge appetite, far bigger than the heads and guts could satisfy. Constantly running in and out of there were huge high sided trucks, so full that the loads spilled over onto the roads. Sand eels, hundreds and hundreds of tons of them: if ever there was a staple food, a daily bread or whatever, as far as oceanic life in the North Sea is concerned it is the sand eel. Not quite at the bottom of the food chain but very near it. They feed on krill, which feed on smaller plankton which feed on . . .

As far as higher organisms are concerned, it's what keeps them alive. Many of the fish on which we depend along with dolphins and seals and a huge variety of seabirds rely on them. The iconic pictures of a puffin invariably feature a beak full of them. All these cannot live without the sand eel, and we humans are using them as **fertiliser**.

If you want to sustain a fishing industry and if you want to have a healthy population of animals and birds around our coasts and seas then anyone with half an eye can see that the sand eels should be left alone. It's the only way.

It still continues to this day. Money, money, money and to hell with the future: this is still an observation and not an opinion.

Earth provides for every man's needs but not every mans greed.

Ghandi

There are more observational pointers to changes in the North Sea and the sand eels. The easiest statement is to blame global warming, which admittedly plays a part, but there is no doubt the biggest changes are the direct result of man's activities. The UK is home to some fantastic seabirds, especially around our rugged coasts and islands. Well of course the land is not their home. The ocean is their home but you cannot lay eggs in the ocean, the same as the swifts cannot lay eggs in the air. Seabirds have to come ashore for that reason only. The decline of our seabirds in recent years is dramatic across all of the species, but the most marked is the Kittiwake. 65% of Europe's black legged kittiwakes nest here. A survey in their stronghold of Orkney reveals that since 2000, numbers have plummeted by **87%.** There are three reasons why a species would decline: disease, shortage of nesting sites and starvation. There was no evidence of disease, abundance of nesting sites has never changed, so it is shortage of food that is the culprit and that is obviously fish: including, in a big way, the sand eel.

Kittiwakes are the most oceanic of our gulls and cannot scavenge inland to supplement their natural food, unlike other species.

Herring gulls have become a declared pest in coastal cities nowadays. They nest on rooftops and scavenge everything. It is said that the emerging generations of city dwelling gulls have lost connection with the ocean. They have earned themselves the nickname of flying rats. On 'You Tube', you can watch them walking into shops and stealing food. The influx can certainly be in part attributed to rubbish tips and fast food throwaways but could it be that this recent phenomenon can be attributed to the decline of their staple diet at sea?

A recent episode of the 'Springwatch' programme on television delighted nature lovers: dolphins in the harbour. People flocked to see the spectacle which has now become a regular occurrence. It is now being marketed as a tourist attraction with organised seal and dolphin sightseeing sailings. It was not unknown in my younger days to spot one or two dolphins on seasonal occasion around the outer breakwaters chasing sile (young herring) but this was new behaviour. This is a highly industrialised harbour serving the offshore oil industry from 'The Oil Capital of Europe'. How nice to see the BBC pick this particular harbour out of hundreds. The dolphins can only be there for one reason, food. Now why would they come so far inshore to a busy port to feed? Could it be lack of oceanic food? There is irony here. They are herding and rounding up young salmon and sea trout who, collecting in large numbers in this harbour mouth and other estuaries, are feeding to gain strength before setting out on their ocean wanderings. That's the same species that the Atlantic Salmon Trust and anglers have had success in protecting. Their improvement of upstream access and spawning beds, including stripping adult fish of eggs and milt, has had fantastic success in producing young fish so they should be happy that their efforts are succeeding but they are not amused. The dolphins are taking THEIR fish.

Another species has caused concern: the grey seal. According to anglers their numbers have rocketed, so much so that they are found well upriver from their marine habitat. The reality is that their numbers have declined: it is only they are now conspicuous in areas previously unoccupied.

In my younger days Sammy the seal was a resident at the harbour mouth. It was friends with the harbour pilot who threw it titbits on occasion: there was no abundance of river seals. More recent observations: sawbills (so called because of the tooth like insides of their beaks allowing them to grip slippery fish), the red breasted merganser and the goosander are more common upriver in recent years. Cormorants are equally more prevalent upriver. It's not unusual to see groups of around twenty as opposed to the odd one seen previously. All these species are not in the rivers taking returning adult fish. They are after the shoals of youngsters which have proliferated in the face of other species' decline at sea. If you watch them, that's what is evident.

Anglers should be delighted that their efforts have brought wildlife in to share in the spoils but many are calling for a cull of all these species. How selfish can you get? For some reason they hedge on the cull of dolphins. Another anomaly is that the whale and dolphin trust, set up to protect these sea mammals, doesn't include that other sea mammal, the seal.

Another discovery of scientific endeavour is that the average size of haddock in the North Sea has diminished over the last forty years, the time span that the research covered. An article in a local newspaper reported this story. There was no interview with the scientists. They interviewed an award winning fish and chip shop owner and his reply was published. 'Nonsense, they want to stop peddling this scaremongering trash. It is doing untold harm to our fishing industry.' I am in a quandary. Whom do I believe, forty years of scientific research or the off the cuff remarks of a chippie? This type of sensationalist journalism doesn't help the search for a prosperous and sustainable future.

All these changes in animal behaviour mentioned must surely be attributable to one cause. Lack of oceanic food of all types but in particular, they all like sand eels.

That's what the divers say and that's what the scientists say. My observation of wildlife patterns concurs with theirs.

There are many other factors contributing. The North Sea oil industry is regulated. No pollution allowed. There are mixed opinions over a substance used in drilling: mud. It serves many purposes not least as a lubricant for the drill. As you will know, when using a drill, the particles from the cavity come up to the entry point, in this case the sea bed. A mixture of mud and waste issues from the hole and it is the mud engineer's job to dispose of this. If synthetic or oil based mud is used, then by law this has to be taken ashore for disposal at great expense. Natural substances can be left on the sea bed after testing for toxicity by using the amphipod, *Leptocheirus plumulosus*, as a guinea pig. There is controversy here. The species is a North American one and does not occur in the North Sea. Also, apparently, it can survive one test sample but die when exposed to another. Which one would the oil company prefer? Let's say that the sample is cleared of toxicity. Then the mixture flows out of the borehole to cover the seabed like a slow moving massive teardrop. Any life is smothered. It may not be toxic but it is just as lethal, according to eye witnesses. Records show that there are more than 10,000 drill holes in the North Sea.

All is not lost. There is some real hope for the North Sea on the horizon: government backed MPAs, ie designated 'marine protected areas'. No fishing, no dredging, no oil drilling, no anything. Note government backed, not government initiative. That came from a worried Marine Conservation Society. The evidence for their concern came from varying sources but in particular the scientists at the International Council for the Exploration of the Seas (ICES) who were extremely worried about the state of cod stocks. MPAs fit the bill for all species' recovery. It has even been suggested by the Scandinavians to have sand eel hatcheries incorporated. They recognise their huge importance. Let's hope this all comes to fruition before it's too late but already the greedy, wealthy, dissenting voices are being heard. 'How dare you exclude us from plundering a sea area?' Livelihoods could suffer. It is livelihoods that are surely being protected, future livelihoods. There is no agenda to cut anyone's throat.

This is another unsustainable activity indulged in by myself in my youthful naivety.

'The oyster lives down in the sea,
You can't tell the he one from the she,
But he can tell and so can she,
As they revel in the joys of procreation.'

They don't only live in the sea. One species lives in the clean rivers of the UK. In antiquity the freshwater pearl mussel must have been endemic in every river. They suffer from the same affliction as their saltwater cousins. A grain of sand lodges within the shell and their reaction is to coat it in mother of pearl thus forming a pearl. A freshwater pearl was much sought after through the ages as a precious rarity. In 1507, King James V of Scotland remodelled the Scottish crown: made of Scottish gold and along with the jewels from the old crown, included pearls from many Scottish rivers. One of these was a rare black pearl from one of my local rivers, the Ythan pronounced (eyethan). Today you can see the Scottish crown in Edinburgh Castle, the oldest crown in the UK. You would be hard pushed to find a specimen pearl today. They didn't spread slurry on the countryside in the sixteenth century. In the cleaner rivers that drain mountainous countryside they still exist but they are under threat. I am a guilty party. In my ignorant youth my friendship with the travelling community, through my best friend, introduced me to pearl fishing which was an exciting day out on the river. Actually, they were travellers who didn't travel, but wished they still did. They were reduced to a day out on common ground. It was a tradition of their forebears, living as they did on opportunism, to seasonally hunt for the pearls. Wading into the river, waste deep with your 'joog', you searched the riverbed. The joog was a quart milk jug with the bottom cut out and replaced with a crude, puttied in glass bottom. When a trained eye spotted a mollusc, you used your 'clook' to capture the target. Another genial device, this was a rowan stick with a split end. A stout rubber band round it gave it a spring. This was the grommet from a lemonade bottle screw cork, common at the time. Locate the stick over the shell, twist and extract. The waist storage bag full, you returned to the community seated round the campfire and prized them open. Out of a hundred shells opened you may get one pearl. Out of a dozen such pearls you may get one perfectly round marketable one. My claim to fame was a matched pair of pear shaped ones which 'apparently' raised the princely sum of six pounds. I suspect I was 'done'. The thrill of the chase was the driving force but it soon became clear that such wastage cannot be sustained and the freshwater pearl mussel is now an endangered species, courtesy of the likes of me. It's now illegal to disturb them. Just like all the other endangered species in the world it is we who stand alone as the reason for that status in every case.

It all seems a bleak picture for the future of wildlife and indeed for ourselves. In the UK, what are we and other organisms doing about it?

15

WHERE EAGLES DARE

If future generations are to remember us with gratitude rather than contempt, we must leave them something more than the miracles of technology. We must leave them a glimpse of the world as it was in the beginning, not just after we got through with it.

Lyndon B Johnson

Desecration of wildlife and habitat is not happening completely unnoticed. Tycoons, hell bent on making a fortune rather than a comfortable living, are not in the majority and caring people do care. Governments are swayed by the voting public who are made aware of conservation issues by excellent television programmes. Action is being taken on various fronts. There is a new awareness of our place in, and our responsibility for, the future of the natural world. One of the biggest aids to that end is in the formation of national parks and protected areas, both on land and in the seas. It's ironic that we seem to have taken that lead from one of the biggest polluters, the United States. The John Muir Trust is working wonders (he happened to be a Scots ex-pat). My own Cairngorms National Park does not just include the Cairngorm plateau, such a special place, but a wide area around it. Visit it and see the spectacles to be seen nowhere else in the UK. It's a place *'Where Eagles Dare'*.

The golden eagle is symbolic of wilderness in the UK. Many people would love to see one in the wild. In fact although they may not have seen one, the chances are that an eagle has seen them, especially those who have been in their home territory which is vast, meaning anywhere in the highlands and islands of Scotland. If you have been there as a tourist then you could have seen one as, although not numerous, they are common. So why didn't you? You may have scoured the mountain tops and heather clad hills and glens from the car whilst driving through the magnificent scenery. You may just be lucky but if you want the best chance, then that is not the way. Golden eagles spend the vast majority of their day soaring for that's how they are designed. 'But I was watching the sky as well' is the usual reply, but that's still not enough. Even if you are walking the hills and watching the sky you may miss them because they are UP with a capital U. Lie on your back in the heather, refocus your eyes to the lowest clouds and then you may see them: mere specks in the sky. After the young have fledged is the best time, as the maximum number of birds will be in the sky. I could suggest the best places to you. The upper Deeside hills in Aberdeenshire are where I have seen the most soaring, around the village of Braemar on the tourist route. A flick of a wing and they are in Kincardine, Angus or Perthshire. A flick the other way gets them into Inverness-shire, Moray or Banffshire. It is remarkable that from all that height they can detect a movement among the heather in any of these places. Luck plays a big part in seeing them catch and kill, for it is quick. On that weeklong trip with Feeky as a teenager, high on the Perthshire hills, we spotted a magnificent female floating over the hillside below us, precipitating a mad dash downhill by hares and grouse. Further behind and lower down, the male takes his pick and pounces on a hare. (My deduction of sex is that the female is normally larger than the male especially on wingspan). This co-operation by a pair is beautiful to see and I feel privileged to have witnessed the spectacle.

There is another memorable place to see them in my experience. Glen Lee in Angus is beautiful in every way, not least because of the variation in scenery in a single glen. You can drive to the car park at the east end of Loch Lee and enjoy a lovely walk up the loch side. If you continue walking up the glen you are now past dog walking distance and people become a rarity. At the head of the glen are the Falls of Unich. The flat valley floor below has a large population of rabbits, as do many remote glens, the inhabitants shielded from the ravages of myxomatosis by virtue of their geographical isolation. There are many warrens, easily excavated in the sandy, gravelly soil created by the scouring of the glaciers. These are bread and butter for golden eagles, a bounty right on their doorstep. Wary adult rabbits may not venture far from their bolthole burrow but the impetuosity and adventurous nature of youth leads the offspring into danger. An eagle from its lofty vantage point is just a speck in the sky but the expression 'eagle eyed' is not for nothing. It can monitor many warrens in many glens at the same time and if one individual looks vulnerable, being slightly further away from its burrow in the eagle's judgement, this big bird can lose altitude in a flash. It can also work out the attack strategy and this is where I come in. I was taking in the scenery of the falls and the rabbits in a warren. They were aware of my presence but as long as I didn't take any more steps towards them, they were happy. I didn't see the eagle in the sky but watched, as if in slow motion, as it came in at ground level from behind the mound and pounced on its target. A kill, suddenly there is a screaming and two more birds appear from nowhere to share the spoils. I assume these were the year's progeny. All this spectacle from a mere hundred yards away, no need for binoculars, one of my most memorable moments.

There are more interesting nature points about this particular glen. It has its own unique features as indeed they all have. As you climb slowly from Loch Lee, the scenery changes as does the wildlife. A steep sided valley with rocky crags and a beautiful green fertile floor, bisected by a winding stream, provides ideal habitat for the eagles and also for peregrines, hen harriers and more, and of course their prey. Looking down at you with a watchful eye are the herds of red deer, the UK's largest mammal.

The craggy sides are also green in season with *Alnus glutinosa* (common alder). This is known as the waterside tree due to its habit of colonising stream banks. These trees are stunted specimens, not just because of the weather but also due to the poor, rocky nature of the soil on these steep sides. The roots have nothing to travel in and are curtailed, giving the effect of natural bonsai. Wait a minute, did I mention the beautiful fertile valley floor with the winding stream. No trees: all these seeds raining down on pristine soil and no trees. Why? The answer is really obvious, the red deer as previously mentioned. Grazing of the emerged seedlings does not allow any growth and confines the species to their rocky prison to which, no doubt, they have adapted through natural selection. It's not just the deer. Sheep have grazed here since the people were displaced in favour of them in the highland clearances. The argument still rages that the deer have to be culled because of overgrazing but it seems that it is not quite true. Red deer are a forest animal, so have evolved in that environment. The highlands used to be completely wooded with forests of Scots pine, alder, birch and aspen. Man felled the forests and forced the deer into the hills. They also did a little more to protect their introduced cash crop, sheep. They killed off the timber wolf which left the deer without a predator. Note 'timber' wolf denoting their preferred and natural home, as illustrated by the animal below (centre left).

Their predation would have had some effect in keeping numbers down but much more importantly, as previously mentioned, the wolf kept the deer herds on the move meaning they didn't overgraze a specific place. This let the indigenous forest regenerate without any help from us. In the long term, remember, all these species of plants, the deer and the wolf benefit from forestation: beautiful.

So why don't we just reintroduce the wolf into the UK as some would advocate for the reasons given. Well, it may not be just as simple as that. There is one big advantage that the US has over the UK, millions of acres of wilderness. United States Congress is presently in the throes of declaring more millions of acres as wilderness. It would be difficult to find even a few acres of that in the UK. In this small island man has colonised, or at least farmed by grazing, most of it and livestock would immediately be at risk. Even national parks have their farms and even then wolves don't recognise boundaries. I would, however, love to see it but sadly it looks like it's not to be.

All is not completely lost, however. What we can do is to keep large areas free of deer and let the forest regenerate. Small area experiments are really encouraging. The Lairig Ghru is an old drove road through the Cairngorm Massif. It winds up to over 3,000 feet through surely some of the most spectacular scenery in the world (if you are lucky enough to get a fine day). At its highest point there are remnants of the old Caledonian forest. Not anything living, unfortunately, just petrified stumps. These do not show signs of being raggedly blown over by severe storms. They have been felled by man. You can still see the chop marks (no chain saws in those ancient times). Also the climate may have been a little warmer with natural cycles in the planet's weather. A small area was fenced off to see what would happen if the deer were excluded. That was thirty years ago and the area today is a remarkable mixed woodland, an island in a sea of heather. No trees grew outwith that fence. The solution then is simple, use fences. Commercial forestry uses them but that is a short term measure for financial gain, the trees being felled after thirty years or so. Small areas cause problems for capercaillie, owls, etc with their flying into them. What may be the answer is huge, even monstrous areas being fenced so that a fence for a capercaillie would be a rarity. The opportunity has arrived on a plate with the creation of national parks with the authority of central government behind them. It may anger a few crofters but most would say, hey, move over and co-exist. These fences, of course, would be very short term as the forest will quickly grow to the extent that it will not need protection and they could be removed. The deer, bless them, can then return to their natural habitat. It seems simple but it needs money and commitment. The fences need maintaining and, eventually, properly removing instead of the usual degeneracy that becomes a danger to wildlife.

159

There are fifteen national parks in the UK, born out of that fellow Scotsman's dream in America. John Muir campaigned and succeeded in setting up the first national parks in the United States to protect the wildlife and their environment. At last our government are investing money in nature and the public are responding. John Muir's philosophy is winning through, albeit a battle against money.

'Saving the American soul from the total surrender to materialism"

My adventures in life can concur with that. National parks on land and offshore in the form of marine protected areas are not only wildlife's salvation but ours as well. All are equally important but the one which is close to my heart and history is 'The Cairngorms', now ten years old. It encompasses a huge area of wilderness at 1,748 square miles. So I am keeping an eye on progress.

I return to the aspen being a long term indigenous species. Attempts are being made to encourage its recovery and with the aspen not setting seed the task is more difficult. Firstly, why do they not set seed? They produce flowers in the way of catkins, so what's the problem? Aspens are *diaocaeous*, meaning that there are male and female trees requiring cross pollination. Obviously, in a stand of aspen, there must have been a seedling in the first place and that seedling if allowed to grow can send out root suckers as much as forty metres from the main growth. Whole woodlands can be created from one seedling. With the felling of ancient forests, aspen became compartmentalised. With the aforementioned grazing deer running riot they became confined to rocky places, as with the Glen Lee alders. A female clone in an isolated gully may have no male partner for fifty miles making fertilisation impossible, so it spreads by the sucker method, hopefully reducing the distance between partners. It is impeded in this task by the grazing. If the national parks are to correct the imbalance caused by lack of predator, as previously mentioned, they have to either control herbivores or fence them out. The photograph overleaf shows my observation of the aspen dilemma and the ongoing conservation attempt at reestablishment. Here we have a stand confined to a rocky gully and hopefully you can see the numerous lighter coloured sucker growths, sent out each summer in the grass in the foreground. These are not seedlings. In winter when food is scarce, the vigorous new growth protruding from the snow hasn't a snowball's chance in hell. The suckers only have to be protected from the deer to survive and below you can see the new fence being erected to protect the gully and surrounds. It doesn't take long for the new trees to be large enough to fend for themselves and I hope to live long enough to see the aspen forest which will inevitably result from the national park authority's efforts.

Another gift to nature is not what others may agree with, but the proof of the pudding is in the eating (and the observing). It seems every bit a national park to me with wildlife protection and conservation.

In ancient times, when forest covered this land, there were still areas devoid of trees. These were the coastal strips where shifting sand dunes and salt spray made it unfriendly for most tree species. Certain grasses and wild flowers, though, adapted to thrive which would have been good news for herbivores. Wild cattle, sheep, rabbits and hares would graze here and their droppings would fertilise the poor sandy soil. The grasses have probably evolved with the grazing to cope with it. Their strategy is to send out lateral roots in response to being clipped and propagate new shoots from them. The sand is thus stabilised and eventually a turf mat is formed. The seaward side and dry tops of dunes are the most inhospitable and here only marram grass can survive, but on the landward side, in the lea of the worst conditions, bent grass and other species thrive. This gives such places the name 'bents'. When our ancestors progressed from hunter-gathering to farming, and the domestication of animals, these areas were common grazing land. This still happens in many parts of the world today, as herders move their flocks and herds to find the best pasture.

Some wild species of animals and birds have evolved with the grazers to exploit this short cropped greenery. Choughs are known to require herbivores and pastures to thrive which has confined them to small coastal areas where this still takes place. Swallows and wagtails mop up the plentiful insects that hatch from the turf. Many other birds find sustenance in the seeds of the flowers and grasses of the areas not so closely cropped.

Someone in Scotland in the fifteenth century, possibly a bored herder, had the idea to pass the time by knocking a ball along with a stick and into a target hole, challenging his mates perhaps to do so in as little hits as possible. From there, more holes would have been added to make a course. There were obstacles to overcome. Exposed areas of sand, where rabbit activity had let erosion get a grip, formed hazards (bunkers). Uncropped marram grass areas became 'the rough'.

Tidal coastal streams and ponds formed water hazards. Some rules would have been made up and the game of golf was born. For quite a time the herbivores were necessary to keep the grass short and some courses today still use this method. Now it matters not to the bent grass whether it is cropped by teeth or by machine and with the advent of the latter, better management was possible and similar conditions could be created away from the coast by seeding land with bent seed. All aspects of the natural original design, though, have never changed to this day. It seems all very harmless activity but what about the plants, birds and animals?

In a recent controversial application to build a golf course, the RSPB had their say. Headlines in the local paper reported on an official statement from a spokesman. 'Golf clubs are bad for wildlife.' Once again there are extremists on both sides of any argument regarding wildlife and here was another one. I can only hope that it was a journalistic mis-quote and not an extremist view as, once again, the statement is not borne out with facts. It is true that they CAN be bad for wildlife if not properly designed and managed, or if they are built in the wrong place, but that is not what the official statement says. It is also one 'helluva' kick in the teeth for the golf clubs who are striving to make their land suitable and friendly towards wildlife: encouraged by the environmental policy of golf's governing body, The Scottish Golf Union. The RSPB and other environmental groups should surely be working hand in glove to help implement this policy using their expertise to advise as, in most cases, advice would be welcomed. After all, we all know the push to get people outdoors, off office seats and away from computers to enjoy fresh air and exercise, and golf seems to be a perfect option.

It so happens that locally I have experienced the reality and feel qualified to comment.

In the 1980s a group was formed to create a golf club in this part of Aberdeenshire as growing leisure time was making it increasingly difficult to play the limited courses available. An area of farmland was made available and an application made for planning permission. It was refused on the grounds that it was grade 'A' agricultural land and against council policy. After several bites at the cherry, a public hearing was held and the reporter decided in the council's favour to refuse. End of story? Not quite.

Pressure continued for the council to provide leisure facilities and they came up with a possible alternative site, an area of ancient indigenous woodland and marshland. Totally unproductive, farming wise, this was given planning consent and the course built. Marshland was drained and many trees felled and bulldozed. In any conservationist's mind, including mine, a hugely bad choice and this obviously fits in with the RSPB statement. I emphasise, this wasn't the golfer's choice. It was the council's.

It so happened that in central government at Westminster policies were changing. They too were concerned about increased leisure time and growing obesity problems. There was also a massive grain surplus being produced. The new policy, loud and clear, was to encourage farmers to take land out of production in favour of leisure facilities. Westminster is a long way from Aberdeenshire and pony express takes a while. This policy was announced two years **previous** to the initial application. That's just not enough time, to have enough council meetings, to change local government policy which is why the original application failed. Eventually, however, policy was changed in line with Westminster which is why, ten years later the golf club took up an offer to purchase adjacent **grade 'A'** farmland for a second course. Not only did the council approve the application but they BOUGHT the land and leased it to the club for development with a grant thrown in. It just takes time in politics, a lot of time. Eventually the club purchased the land outright from the council.

So where are we in the initial argument?

In the first case, today there is no way that pristine virgin wild land of that nature would be granted permission. The farmland option would be favoured. The second case would have been thrown out if applied for ten years earlier.

However, in the first case, although the bulldozers did enormous damage to the forest, much of it was preserved including some of the peat bog as a conservation area. Water features of streams and ponds were created and many indigenous young trees were replanted. Today it is still a haven for wildlife and I can report thirteen species of birds alone that are new to the area with not a loss of a single original species. It is mainly the ponds that have introduced these new residents and visitors, such as tufted duck and little grebe. Badgers and hares abound. Rabbits and golf courses don't get on well so there is an element of control but the surrounding net fence keeps most at bay and the many foxes help keep numbers low. Red squirrels love the pine forest and bats are everywhere. The drumming of great spotted woodpeckers heralds the spring each year. This course, for one, is in your face GOOD for wildlife and good for humans too. They even have a resident oystercatcher nest each year in the middle of the car park and staff put a chair over the nest to protect the brooding bird.

The second course took sterile farmland out of production and planted 25,000 indigenous trees. That's a lot of trees. That turned a council planting plan of ornamental rhododendrons and azaleas on its head. The club wanted it as a natural part of Scotland, the same as the first course, and they succeeded. It opened with mixed golf reviews in 1996 and seventeen years later it is a most enjoyable walk in the woods. Not only that but the song of the skylark is common, a rarity nowadays. Many other birds and mammals now inhabit and breed in an area that was practically devoid of wildlife.

In recognition of their contribution to conserving and creating natural habitat the club was presented with the 'Green Butterfly' award. Not quite the prestigious 'John Muir Award' but a step in that direction.

Golf courses are bad for wildlife? Not around here, RSPB.

While respecting their ideals, no good comes out of hard stances. Those conservation groups should have been a part of those projects. Golf and other leisure pursuits are not going to go away, so best to help rather than to down cry.

One more thing about golf courses: if the green keeping staff stopped cutting the grass then it would be unrecognisable as a golf course in a year. A few years later it would just be a wild part of the countryside once again. It is completely reversible.

Wildlife is amazingly adaptable. As long as there is adequate food and lodging, that's all it asks for.

Another letter in the local newspaper: this time a protest against a housing scheme on the outskirts. 'If they don't stop all this building on the natural countryside, soon there will be no green fields left.'

There are many kinds of countryside - farmland, natural or commercial woodland, scrubland, heathland, etc, etc – contributing to a big variety of habitats. Observation of wildlife, as previously covered extensively, reveals modern farmland to be the least favourable to wildlife. The letter writer mentions natural countryside but green fields are the only unnatural areas albeit what she has grown up to think of as natural. So, out of all the various habitats, better to build on 'green fields' than anywhere else and there is a huge advantage for wildlife in doing so. It's true. Suburbia is one of the richest wildlife areas nowadays. Conifer hedges and shrubberies are quickly planted for privacy giving ideal nesting habitat for many bird species and cover for many animals. Hedgehogs, badgers and foxes are after the slugs, worms, voles, shrews, mice and many more which benefit. Lawns, established and kept mown, are a new feeding ground for birds such as blackbirds, thrushes, robins, dunnocks, wagtails and a host of others. The population is protective of its wildlife and are providing feeders and nest boxes and are encouraged to leave winter habitat for hedgehogs etc. Couple that with garden ponds for amphibians and a host of other invertebrates and it is Nirvana for most. It's a huge improvement on habitat over sterile farmland. It doesn't help the farmland species, though. Corn buntings and skylarks have no new homes to go to.

So, even suburbia fits the criteria of a national park. It doesn't have to be as grand as the Cairngorms one and it is cost free.

It doesn't stop with suburbia. Industrial estates, built on previously intensively farmed land, have become home to many species. Rabbits are not shot in these environments and find a refuge in the storage yards of pipes and other equipment. Having no burrows to facilitate the spread of biting insects, and thus *myxomatosis*, they proliferate. Yards have security fencing, easily breached by tunnelling but they still keep foxes out. There is no feeding in these yards, so the bunnies have to go in and out to the wide roadside verges, sown with grass as the planning consent decrees. The fox is there and takes his share but the boltholes are impregnable.

The hardcored yards are a boost for another species that was struggling in numbers in the modern countryside, the (not so common) common gull. Along with the black headed gull, they are inland gulls that have taken a population knock with increased drainage in the countryside. There are many colonies that have set up locally in the storage yards. Oyster catchers, of course, share these gravelly nesting sites: again all benefitting from fenced protection against predation from badgers and foxes. These are doing the same job as national parks with protection and habitat and I had better include my own wildlife oasis garden. I can say that I live in a national park. It's a pity there are no golden eagles.

*Note: Would you believe, there is a downside on this suburban paradise for wildlife? Garden feeders attract many birds and animals and close proximity means easier spread of disease. In recent years, house and tree sparrow populations dropped to alarmingly low levels. The populations are showing recovery from a beak and mouth disease which proved fatal. Recently a huge crash in greenfinch numbers point to the same type of cause: a parasite called **trichomonas**. I personally became aware of this through a campaign of awareness advertised on television which stated the cause of spread was dirty bird feeders. Well, clean feeders are a good idea but a peanut feeder is unlikely to get that dirty. Contamination of bird tables is much more likely. The campaign, though, misses a point and that rang bells in my brain. Déjà vu: when I kept racing pigeons all those years ago, **trichomonas gallinae** was on every fancier's lips under the heading 'canker' and it probably still is today. Keeping a large amount of livestock in close proximity, just the same as my nursery plants, means that any infection spreads like wildfire. Race birds are transported in panniers to the release point and are fed and watered en route via clip on troughs. Every fancier knows that it is the water and not the feed that is the medium, the same as the famous London cholera well. Closing it down stopped the spread and pigeon fanciers know this. In my day Condy's crystals (potassium permanganate) were used to sterilise drinking water. Any bird returning infected was treated with a miracle cure from the vet. Left untreated they died. SO there is no doubt in my mind, through hard experience, that the cause is water borne. Bird baths are the media. Many enthusiasts cannot install a garden pond which doesn't concentrate the disease, so they should either sterilise the water and change it daily, an unlikely chore, or forget about the bath/drinking water source. Shut down the 'cholera well'. There are plenty of natural water sources they can find.*

Despite these obvious problems, all in all, it could be worse in this country and campaigns continue for better awareness and improvement but we are a part of a wider world. Attitudes in other countries may not be the same but their actions may matter for both our good and for wildlife's.

In part two, I recount my limited experiences with that wider world's attitudes.

Part 2

INTRODUCTION

It's all very well observing and documenting nature locally but when you see these vivid images on television showing wonderful wildlife in the wider world, it whets the appetite to see their lives first hand. Early in life it was an ambition of mine to see these lands and their flora and fauna but I didn't think it would ever be possible as there was no money or opportunity to do so. Now, even if you only have a modest income, if you search for the cheapest deals you can go to most places. When I get there it is in my nature to avoid the tourist trails and do my own thing: break away from the pack and a different world is there to be discovered. It's modestly satisfying my childhood thirst for adventure. It is not in the Sir Edmund Hilary, Captain Scott or Ranulph Fiennes league but it is out of the norm. This has to be holiday combined with adventure for one big reason: I have my baggage with me on my travels. Whereas I would love to go to the Arctic and see polar bears hunting seals, I am confined to warmer climes because, you see, my baggage likes to be warm. It's not her fault. She can't help the genes she inherited.

It's intriguing how old Adolf would have categorised her. Fair hair and blue eyes definitely puts her in the Aryan race league. In 1936, that very nice gentleman, Heinrich Himmler introduced the *Lebensborn* in an attempt to breed true Aryans. Homes were set up to raise and breed true. Child candidates were rounded up from across Europe by looking at family documentation back two generations. They had to fit the bill, being physically examined from head to toe for any irregularities in Aryan ideological attributes. It's not just dogs and pigeons which can be manipulatively bred for certain characteristics. The whole thing falls flat if love affairs cross type so the 'opposition' had to be eradicated, spawning the holocaust. My baggage, however, would have been spared the gas chamber if the invasion of Britain had succeeded but if Herr Himmler could have researched back one more generation of her family history, as we can do today, he would have been less praising of her. Her great grandfathers on both her mum and dad's sides were Negro immigrants from Barbados, both marrying British white girls. Physically, three generations later, there doesn't seem much trace but embedded deep is an inclination to be warm and a severe reaction to the cold. She loses heat at an alarming rate and her chances of survival in a cold crisis are slim. One wonders how far back Mr Hitler could trace his own *'pure'* Aryan forebears before discovering a fly in the ointment.

'We're a' Jock Thamson's bairns' is a saying in Scotland, meaning we are all related: all brothers and sisters under the sun. There is no such thing as a 'pure' race.

Her inherited traits, however, are not that bad a constriction for me: being confined to warmer climes for my adventures. I have a reciprocal problem with temperature which is never considered. I don't like being too warm. My ancestral genes are Norse, and probably many others, and my fair skin is sensitive. I have to acclimatise slowly and drink a lot of liquid (beer or rum) with my feet up: such martyrdom.

So how is nature doing in the wider world? Closest at hand is continental Europe.

16

THE EUROPEAN ECONOMIC COMMUNITY

We are bound by European law. Member state governments have to comply with the same wildlife laws as we do in the UK. Walk down the Ramblas in Barcelona and you will find the people interesting. It's a nice experience until you come to the cages of captive wild birds for sale. Finches, warblers, sparrows, etc are crowded together and panting with beaks gaping in full sun in the sweltering August heat. In the UK the RSPCA would surely intervene but they are a charity, not the government. Their mission would be to stop the suffering but what about the wild bird angle? Selling wild songbirds for profit to any prospective buyer is surely illegal?

The Island of Fuerteventura in the Canaries comes under Spanish jurisdiction and thus part of the EEC. A travelling act does a tour of the resorts as part of the evening entertainment for tourists. An eagle owl and a steppe eagle are trained to do tricks for the audience. It seemed to me that they weren't exactly enjoying it and, if they weren't tethered, they would wing it. How well would it go down in a UK nightclub?

Let's see what the legislation says:

Directive 2009/147/EC of the European Parliament and of the Council of 30 November 2009 on the conservation of wild birds (this is the codified version of **Directive 79/409/EEC** as amended) is the EU's oldest piece of nature legislation and one of the most important, creating a comprehensive scheme of protection for all wild bird species naturally occurring in the Union. It was adopted unanimously by the Members States in 1979 as a response to increasing concern about the decline in Europe's wild bird populations resulting from pollution, loss of habitats as well as unsustainable use. It was also in recognition that wild birds, many of which are migratory, are a shared heritage of the Member States and that their effective conservation required international co-operation.

So where do these two examples fit in? No pollution, no loss of habitat and, perhaps, not even unsustainable use. It looks like this activity is legal as long as they are not migratory species. It is quite unequivocal about that. Any new state joining the EU must comply by signing up to agree and uphold that law.

Most UK migrants have to cross either the Pyrenees or the Alps on their journey. As in my migration notes, their movements are tuned to exact times of year. The birds expect, from generations of experience, to find food in stop over places. In northern Italy 'sportsmen' are waiting. They are fully conversant with the influx during autumn and spring when these tired birds descend to rest. It doesn't matter size or species. All are fair game. From tiny warblers, through swallows to rare honey buzzards, all are shot down merely to test shooting skills.

The island of Malta GC (George Cross) lies in the middle of the Mediterranean Sea. Many migratory birds use it as an important stopping off point on their long voyage. Unfortunately the guns are waiting there as well. You can watch covert filming of the shooting of swallows on *You Tube*. With increasing pressure on the government from charity run conservation groups it is, apparently, decreasing. The benchmark is the number of cartridge cases left at shooting sites. They have decreased but it may be that the shooters, under increasing pressure, are now covering their tracks. This atrocity has been known about and fought against for a long time by conservation groups but, eventually, it was highlighted by BBC television's Chris Packham. Recently the Maltese Constitutional Court has allowed a referendum on a ban (very nice of them considering it is illegal under European law). It seems that the majority of Maltese oppose this slaughter. I can only hope it goes close to unanimously agreeing with the conservationists. The Mediterranean, though, is a big expanse and, believe it or not, there are worse Mediterranean places in our EU community. Cyprus: a favourite holiday destination for vacationers from all over northern Europe and a favourite resting place for huge amounts of migrants. Blackcaps and whitethroats in particular use the olive groves as roosts and a source of insect food. So called 'hunters' use mist nets, erected on poles, to catch these tiny warblers. They are totally indiscriminate, catching and killing a wide range of species including owls and bats. Again, watch it on *You Tube*. This is not just for sport, warblers are a delicacy.

'Four and twenty blackbirds baked in a pie.'

You may have thought it was just nursery rhyme fantasy. Not so in Cyprus: it's called *Ambelopoulis* and is in great demand. More than a million birds each season are sacrificed (see the following pictures). It could be argued that this is a natural resource being utilised for food but it is ILLEGAL and has been for forty years, not least because of the migrant directive but also because these are endangered species. European law is quite specific about that. If the slaughter is not stopped then these species, already in huge decline, are just as endangered as the tiger or white rhino.

The government of Cyprus, at the moment, has more important things like economic survival to think about but occasionally, due again to covert operations by conservationists, a case gets to court. The penalty is so paltry that it is quite unbelievable. It is obvious that the magistrate has sympathy for what is regarded as a national pastime. He possibly goes home for *Ambelopoulis*

for tea: so who polices this legislation? Well there is an EU committee subgroup which does just that. No doubt the members spend a lot of time in meetings deliberating the best course of action and much more writing reports about it. In the real world the slaughter goes on under the gaze of a paper tiger.

If you don't like cruelty to animals, you may like to think that EU legislation agrees with you. Spain has more than cruelty to caged wild birds to answer for. Bull fighting: it's ancient but barbaric. Abject pain and extreme suffering, played out in front of a cheering crowd: every bit as bad as throwing Christians to the lions. They mitigate that it's tradition and part of their culture. Rome could argue about the lion/Christian thing being traditional.

Then don't join the EEC as they stand against this sort of thing: Yes?

More legislation - Animal welfare law in Europe

The Treaty of Amsterdam which came into force on 1st May 1999 includes a protocol on animal welfare designed to 'ensure improved protection and respect for the welfare of animals as sentient beings.' Impressive, but read on:

In formulating and implementing the Community's agricultural, transport, internal market and research policies, the Community and the Member States shall pay full regard to the welfare requirements of animals, while respecting the legislative or administrative provisions and customs of the Member States relating in particular to religious rites, cultural traditions and regional heritage.

There's the cop out: cultural traditions will suffice. It seems you can have it both ways. Just to confirm that, when taken to task by caring people, a spokesman comes up with:

The commission has no competence to take initiatives in relation to the matter as bullfighting is out of the scope of legislation on the protection of animals at the time of slaughter or killing.

There seems to be a brick wall erected by our public servants.

Many will be aware of the spectacle but just to remind you: an animal is impaled, repeatedly, in front of a cheering crowd and suffers, in extreme pain, to the point of sheer exhaustion whilst being taunted by the matador and his fellow torturers. The end comes with the matador's sword thrust deep into its body. It's not an immediate end either.

Taunting continues until the miserable wretch finally falls to its knees and keels over, when internal haemorrhaging finally takes its toll, to the sound of the screaming crowd who are on their feet at the point of death. To people who care it seems all the worse that nowadays you can watch every gruesome moment on television, and it has top ratings. It is still advertised openly with cruel graphic pictures on street posters (previous page).

175

It may all be synonymous with Spanish culture and many outsiders are aware of its existence. See it live though and if you say that you enjoyed it, many would class you more of an animal than the bull. And there's worse.

Toro Jabillo or *Toro Embolado* is carried out in Valencia and Southern Catalonia under the same 'cultural tradition' banner. The bull is tethered in the street and fireballs are attached to its horns, often fireworks as well. Cut the rope and watch the antics. It is then further tormented by the cheering crowd as it frantically crashes around. This is not just cruelty to, or neglect of, an animal: this is wilful torture.

Cruel sports are condemned today by civilised society. Badger baiting, cock fighting, hunting with dogs, etc are all banned. So the question has to be asked by caring people: why, oh why are we living with these atrocities in our midst?

Just to rub salt in the wound, Spain's parliament is currently debating a new law which would declare bullfighting as a protected national pursuit, a move that would overturn existing bans on bullfighting in the Canary Islands and Catalonia and would guarantee public subsidies for the industry. Further, the EEC common agricultural policy provides a subsidy to bull breeders in Spain, a subsidy paid out of your tax and mine to sustain this cruelty.

Killing endangered species, even for food, and abject cruelty should surely not be part of a supposedly civilised first world. There are more insights in my experience of attitudes to wildlife and cruelty from other 'civilised' countries'.

17

HOUSTON, WE HAVE A PROBLEM

In the most recent census for the metropolitan area of Houston, Texas, USA it had a population of over six million. That's more than the population of my home country, Scotland. Its jurisdiction covers an area of 10,062 square miles (26,060 square kilometres). That's not surprising as Texas is big state, more than three times the size of the whole of the UK. Everything there is big. Cars, roads, stores, buildings, steaks and meal portions and, dare I say it, some of the population (no doubt as a result of the latter). Because of the expanse of area, nothing is local. When my cab driver says, 'I live not far from your address', he means twenty miles away and when I have time to come to terms with the place, I find out he is right. The roads, of course, make the journey seem shorter. Sixteen lanes is a daunting prospect for a country 'teuchter' from rural Scotland as are the dozens of interchanges that make spaghetti junction look like a country track. The sat-nav must have been born here. It is nigh impossible to do without it. 'Make a legal U ahead' dictates like a long playing record from the dratted thing and a woman's nagging voice adds to the frustration. It means, of course, that you have missed your turnoff. What a legal U in the US is, I never figured out. There's another thing you cannot do without: the car itself. Without it you are going nowhere. A fifty mile round trip to the DIY store is normal, as may be the trip to the grocery store. There is no heart where you can do the school run and shop in the same trip. Everything is separate. The morning school run is worth seeing in action. Synchronised swimmers couldn't do better. The line of cars stretches a quarter of a mile. No-one even gets out of the car. Dedicated pupils with identifying sashes stand at the drop off area and open the doors of the cars as they progress in a one way system. With 1,000 pupils to be delivered the rules have to be strictly obeyed, otherwise chaos would reign. If you are lucky enough to be handy for the school, that's not going to be handy for anywhere else.

Now, it's not new information that you need a car in Houston. That's the culture. It is totally alien to my early upbringing but if you are born into that culture, it's the way of life and it's accepted. Suburbia is endless. The policy being *if you have the land use it* and they certainly have plenty of that - endless housing schemes with manicured lawns and street grass areas all connected with broad concrete sidewalks between the road and the houses. Community association inspectors patrol regularly (by car) to see that everything is just so. Occupiers pay for the upkeep. If a bag of garbage is left on the driveway this inspires a letter of complaint, as does parking on the street. The whole setup is clinical. It seems, I am afraid, all for show. My walking to nowhere is a spectacle. Crossing a road is a big risk. Traffic is congested, lightning fast and endless at any hour. But the housing schemes are like ghost towns. No-one is using the sidewalks except the fire ants. They are the only interest to me. There is no community. It is exceptional to know who lives three doors away. Cars are king and they are not small. They make the UK 4x4s look like dinky toys. You may not see many people on the sidewalks but this doesn't mean to say that Houstonians are locked away in their houses. There are plenty of amenities. The gymnastic, football, swimming and athletic facilities are world class, far outshining the UK's but to get there, there is only one choice of transport: the automobile.

So what does this mean for the industrialised nations' commitment to lower carbon emissions as laid down by the Kyoto summit on climate change. The US toils to meet targets. I don't mean to pick on Houston in particular as all over the US, and indeed the world, there are problems meeting targets. Houston's population is tiny compared to Shanghai's twenty three million. But in emission levels per head of population, they beat them hands down. Not that the US aren't trying. There is a huge effort to supply sustainable energy. California seems to be leading the way in hybrid cars, etc. In New York there has been a big increase in cycle ways and the population have responded, although there is still a car/cycle clash of culture. Inroads have been made into having a greener culture but what of Houston. Forget walking or cycling. Apart from the safety issues, the distances are just too great. Couple that with the price of fuel: at present $2.85 per gallon (£1.82). That's 40p per litre and they

178

are complaining, demanding a reduction in tax which seems to be imminent. They don't believe me when I tell them the UK price is over $10 a gallon. If you were a Texas politician standing on a platform of reduction of emissions, that would be like turkeys voting for Christmas. Not a snowball's chance in hell.

So Houston really does have a problem. Fossil fuels are finite but this generation of Texans don't have to worry. They have the money to see themselves out. Oil has made them rich.

Out from the ground came a bubbling crude
Oil, that is
Black gold
Texas tea

That's from the theme tune of the comedy television series 'The Clampetts' (if you are old enough to remember). I still laugh when I think about that 'fancy eating table' when they used the cue rest to pass the salt along the green felt tablecloth. Texans' wealth can sustain them far beyond Texas oil. Exploration around the globe continues, even into nature sensitive areas. There is a huge outcry against the Alaskan pipeline. Oil spills in the Gulf, and many other places, are unbelievably destructive. The very cause of the Arctic ice melting has opened up new drilling opportunities which will further exacerbate the situation at an increased rate. Then there are the even more sensitive areas. There is a big outcry by conservation minded groups and governments over an area in the upper Amazonian rainforest. The government of Ecuador is under pressure from big companies to allow extraction of crude. Conservationists are up in arms. The number of species which abound there is colossal. One hectare of land contains more species of tree than there are in the whole of North America. Many species of primate, including indigenous *Homo sapiens* live there. You cannot blame the Ecuadorian government for wishing to exploit reserves. It's OK for the western world to plunder their natural resources to create wealth, to decimate the forests and bleed dry their fossil fuel reserves as if there were no tomorrow, then turn to a poor nation and say you cannot exploit your forests and oil reserves?

'Why can't we better our lives as you have done?' Ecuador has asked for a deal: there is an estimated eight billion dollars of oil reserves there, so give us 3.2 billion and we will not extract the oil and preserve the forest. To whom are they offering the deal?

The outcome at the moment is unclear. Desecration can be averted but there are other sources of oil around the globe: *at the moment*. What happens when, inevitably, they cannot sustain the present consumption? Ecuador would be again under pressure. Big bucks will be the winner.

The world's major oil companies have been extracting oil from the North Sea for a long time. Rumours are that some of the biggest ones wish to pull out soon. They estimate that there are not enough reserves left to make enough profit, despite politicians' predictions. Well, who would know best? There are also considerable decommissioning costs to consider. There are other areas in the world to be exploited. One is the continental shelf of West African countries such as Equatorial Guinea. There are huge reserves there. These countries are hardly the most stable. More rumours are that companies will have to resort to bribery unofficially, of course, as it is highly illegal throughout the western world's industry. This is not paying government as a whole, as in Ecuador. It's not building roads and play parks which are deemed legal bribery. This is for plain brown paper parcels to individual politicians. It's what people, in general, in these countries are used to. If you bring up the subject in social conversation, it's met with a wry grin. The reality is that if Western companies don't pay, then the Chinese will as they have no such righteous scruples. They may be doing it throughout the Third World and it seems to be common knowledge. I also had it explained how the bribes could be done with no tracking back to the companies: very clever. It's a rat race of big money. So as long as all this money and corruption exists, the Houston car culture is safe. But it is hardly saving the planet. Don't ask me for a solution, I am merely an observer.

I apologise again to Houston for seemingly singling them out but this is the culture Houstonians are born into, with no alternatives. They get on with life as it is. The rest of the Western World is going the same way, although Houston strikes me as the epitome of the problem. I include myself in this same problem, as I include the Greenpeace diesel powered ships sent to prevent drilling in Arctic fields. It would take a long time to get there under sail. It's not only fuel that comes from oil: familiar items from tooth brushes and toothpaste to hair combs and rollers, cosmetics and clothing, packaging and every conceivable everyday accoutrement. The world would be a vastly different place were it not for oil. These goods would not be available, as we know them, without crude oil extraction. They cannot be manufactured from wind and waves. Oil consumption is not the only problem Houston has, and it's not confined to Texas.

The second amendment: the right to bear arms. They are proud of their free country and their democracy, just a little bit different from my idea of a democracy. They will readily tell you that there are four boxes that keep them free:

1 The soap box
2 The ballot box
3 The jury box
4 The cartridge box

Recent massacres of schoolchildren have prompted some suggestions from central government to control guns. This doesn't go down well in Texas: so much so that they are proposing their own measures. An armed deputy sheriff stationed in primary schools is one suggestion and worse, arming schoolteachers. Who, one wonders, would be a gunman's first target? At the moment there is nothing to stop someone walking into a primary school with a gun. Visitors are told not to (see previous page). You don't believe me? This is a deterrent? No one is checked. I have been in many times (without a gun in case you wondered).

The sign behind says, 'Through these doors walks our future.' I can only hope they continue to exist, let alone walk. The local health centre has added a polite 'please' to their request. One of the biggest sellers of guns is Walmart. You can pick up your weapon and ammunition with your groceries. You can even get a scaled down weapon for your child. There's nothing like starting them early. Salesmen don't seem to worry about, when selling an assault rifle, who the purchaser is planning an assault on.

I mention this because this culture is pertinent to my notes on nature. Hunting is what many of these weapons are supposed to be for. It seems inbred into American culture despite rendering the passenger pigeon extinct from a base of a billion plus in fifty short years. Martha, the last individual bird died in a Cincinnati zoo on 1st September 1914. We have just 'celebrated' the centenary of her death. Americans were on the brink of doing the same with the North American bison, saved at the eleventh hour by conservationists. Texas is proud of its hunting tradition. One of my childhood heroes, star of Western movies, was Davie Crockett, King of the Wild Frontier. There was a song every kid knew and one of the verses included the line *killed him a bear when he was only three.* Why a three year old would want to shoot a bear never entered our young minds. Although the hunting mind-set is changing in the western world, even in the USA and in particular California (observation only based on literature), Texas seems intransigent. An example is the threatened species *Puma concolour*, the North American cougar or mountain lion. 'Mountain' is actually a misnomer as their range used to include the entire American continent but it was driven by the settlers into that habitat, much like the red deer in my part of the world. It became an endangered species but conservation measures have had a real effect in increasing numbers. In many states it is illegal to kill one, excepting danger to humans, where an element of control is allowed. Not so in Texas. Blast away. They are still referred to as 'varmints' and the Texans I spoke to were of one voice. Conservation is a dirty word. I may add that there may be inhabitants of the lone star state who think differently but I didn't meet any.

They are not alone in their mentality. In another Southern state, Mississippi, this culture is even more intense and hunting is big business there.

An outdoor equipment store is the biggest I have ever seen. Not according to the staff, 'Hell no, this is a small one, we have some twice the size of this.' Even with American exaggeration of size, I believed him. On the wall, on the way in, there is a huge picture of a hunter with rifle holding up the head of a dead grizzly bear. It's an advert for their products: guns, ammo, crossbows, modern bows and arrows. The range stretches for about fifty metres along the store wall and they are flying off the shelves. There is even a dedicated programme on just that theme on television, 'Mississippi Outdoors- It's a way of life.' Let me try to describe it.

It is obviously a commercial programme as there are many sales pitches for products. One is for a coyote attracting scent in a bottle, followed by a pitch for gin traps. This hunter takes you through the process. He digs a hole in the forest floor, sprinkles in the attractor, which obviously smells like carrion, and sets the gin trap. He then fills in the hole. At this point, my baggage has seen enough and exits the room to be sick before the inevitable which is worse than expected. He returns 2 DAYS later and a coyote is caught by the front paw, whimpering in agony, trying to get away. It looks like the foot is hanging off. He poses in front of the coyote to pitch the trap's efficiency for a few minutes. Then he pulls a handgun and shoots it through the head. With it lying dead, he re excavates the hole and then explains in more detail about the setup. His closing remarks are, 'there you are, I have just saved myself a whole lorra white tailed deer and a whole lorra wild turkey.' Note, 'saved myself' meaning: they are saved for him to hunt. That follows in the next part of the video.

He is on a deer hunt. Shooting is too easy, and we have had a previous sales pitch on guns, so he is using a bow and arrow to challenge his skills. This is one of these bows used in the

Olympic archery events. He is dressed in the most effective camouflage gear I have ever seen and climbs a tree to blend in perfectly. I assume the cameraman is dressed likewise up another tree. He then has to sit and wait. Even on the film it is a long time, so I should imagine in real time it is hours. Eventually, a buck comes along, browsing. Every step nearer is made to sound exciting by his whispered commentary. When it is at point blank range he fires and sticks the buck in the side. If you are maybe thinking that was it over, not a chance. The buck leaps in the air and takes off at a rate of knots. Now to show off the hunter's real skill: tracking. A little bit of blood on a leaf, a hoof print with more blood, etc all very well recorded until he eventually comes across the finally dead body. Triumphantly, he holds up the antlered head, reiterating his catchphrase, *'Mississippi Outdoors- It's a way of life.'* No it's not, it's a way of suffering and death.

I won't even try to describe the abominable suffering in the hunting with dogs bit.

Maybe you want to buy hunting products, so I will point you in the right direction.

Want to set jaw traps for bears, wolves, mountain lion, coyotes, racoons, etc?

Visit *www.fntpost.com* - catch 'em by the leg and watch them suffer, great fun. Setting gin traps this way has been banned in the UK for many years, thank goodness, but unfortunately I have evidence that it still goes on. America is a great country but it can be scary, so I'll try north of the 49th parallel.

18

ROCKY MOUNTAIN HIGH

'Whatever you do, promise me, you won't mention religion?' 'I promise.' We are going across the Atlantic again and I have been warned. The trouble is, I never do mention it and I certainly am not going into the pros and cons in these notes. It's always THEY who bring it up and I very politely (and embarrassingly) try to side step it. They, being anyone I meet. Having previously been overwhelmed by it in the Southern states, I am forewarned yet again. This time it's Canada and I can thoroughly recommend to anyone interested in the natural and physical history of the world to take this particular trip. Nowadays it is very popular. The 'Rocky Mountaineer' train. I must say I wasn't entirely looking forward to two days on a train. It turned out that I could have taken much more. It was fantastic for someone like me who cannot get enough experience in such subjects. For a modest sum (by today's standards) you get an unforgettable experience. Two nights in a five star hotel in Vancouver with dinner, an overnight stay with dinner and breakfast halfway at Kamloops, another two nights at five star Banff Springs and a further two nights in Calgary with breakfast and dinner. Lunch is provided on the train. Your every question is answered one to one. Throw in a couple of nature trips with very knowledgeable guides on the way, a bus trip to Lake Louise with lunch, a helicopter flight into the Rockies and a cable car up Sulphur Mountain with a swim in the hot spring spa: all this for the price of the same week's holiday sunning yourself on the Costa del Sol. Both are enjoyable but as far as interest goes: no contest. This left a free day in Calgary to which I will return.

Although the scenery is second to none, my interest primarily was the flora and fauna. The geology, as well, turned out to be just as amazing. The train leaves Vancouver at the respectable hour of 8 am. It takes the Canadian Pacific transcontinental line to which Scots have a natural affinity, as our forebears were hands on builders of it along with Chinese labourers. My first reaction was, 'why Chinese?' The geography of the world comes flooding back: China is nearer to Vancouver than Scotland and in those pre air travel days, accessible by a single boat trip. I don't forget to mention the work capacity of these seemingly diminutive people: try Hong Kong and be amazed at their capacity. Every view on that journey reeks of Scotland but grander: many of the place names are Scottish in origin. The last spike of the railroad was driven in at a grand occasion at Craigellachie, named after the highland village in Speyside of the same name. The train stops there and as you look around, you can see why that name. If you didn't know you were 6,000 miles away you could be easily fooled. Couple that with the conversations with every local you meet, beaming and exclaiming, 'Oh, you speak just like my granddad.' It makes a Scotsman feel special. To any train enthusiast this trip is a must as well. The engineering feats are remarkable including how they conquered steep inclines with spiral tunnels a mile long inside the mountain. You can watch a freight train longer than that enter, and then re-emerge at the top, with the last carriages still outside the entrance.

It winds its way up the mighty Fraser River valley, past 'Hell's Gate', a canyon with waterfalls and rapids so fierce you could not even contemplate any fish ever migrating up there. But Pacific salmon do just that, and that's near the start of their journey. They travel 400 miles up that mighty river to spawn. Compare that to the seventy mile journey of the Atlantic salmon of my home rivers: it seems like a trickle in comparison. You pass where the Adams River joins the main stream. That's where the television coverage of the bears wading in and catching the fish takes place. We continue through forests of magnificent broadleaves, primarily aspen (*Populus tremulosa*) and birch (*Betula pendula*), with these eventually giving way to steppe country. These dry grasslands are reminiscent of 'western' television programmes like 'The High Chaparral' and 'The Ponderosa'. Features like the 'lonesome pine' (*Pinus ponderosa*) turn thoughts to how such iconic trees can survive such harsh extremes but then nature is full of such species.

Of particular interest to me, pointed out way up a valley at an elevation of 8000 feet, was the site of the Burgess shale. Until the discovery of this fossil site science was of the opinion, in the absence of any fossil evidence, that in the history of life on earth complex life didn't start until around 400-450 million years ago but this discovery was a shock. It was in rocks over 500 million years old and the creatures certainly were complex and well developed. Creatures so weird that they could well have been from some other planet. I asked if there was any way I could be taken there on a trip. The answer was no but as it turned out, I didn't have to. I was informed I could see the fossils and reproductions of these creatures at the Tyrell museum in the badlands of Alberta. I would have to look into that.

The scenery and the climate change again: more moisture from a higher cloud base and colder of course. This is what I have been waiting for, the iconic natural conifer forests of British Columbia, and what a shock was in store - vast mountains all around, clothed in a covering of . . . brown? What is this? Pine bark beetle or, at least, the work of the fungus it spreads. There are still lesser green patches of Sitka spruce but the magnificent lodge pole forests are dead: all of them. The scene continues for mile after sickening mile, until elevation gives way to high peak vegetation and then to the continental divide. Here drops of water on your left run to the Pacific and on your right to the Atlantic, depending on which way you are facing of course. This divide runs the length of the Americas from northern Alaska to Tierra del Fuego at the extreme south. The grandness of scale is overpowering. We leave British Columbia and enter Alberta. As we lose altitude the slopes are green, as I was always expecting, but apparently not for long. The beetle has already struck and attempts are being made to contain it. Experts speculate that the only thing that is going to stop its relentless march is the Atlantic Ocean, 3,000 miles away and I sure hope it does, for in the age of round the world trade, if a few of these little demons ever get to Scotland, it's bye, bye Caledonian forest and all that iconic scenery.

What is happening here? Surely this is not a new species. In fact the beetle and the fungus have always been around, so what has changed? Rise in global temperatures have allowed the beetle to move further north and into higher latitudes. Combine that with mankind's attempts in the past to conserve this natural forest as a resource, not allowing any forest fires which are so much part of the forest ecosystem. Fires clear and fertilize new ground for seedlings to regenerate. This process must have been going on for millions of years: enough time for evolution to provide for a certain percentage of the seed to lie dormant for a long time, only germinating when subjected to temperatures of 1,000° or so which can only come from forest fires. Trees are not the only things destroyed. Beetles and fungi also perish. Fires also create a barrier between forest areas which contain the beetle. In short, it's our fault. Interfere with nature's balance at your peril. Of course, once again, this is not my opinion. Scientists throughout the Americas now acknowledge the vital part played by forest fires in managing natural forests. It brings home to me, as an observer, that the human race tends to think of conservation as here and now in its lifetime, but the reality is that nature's story is played out on a much larger timescale.

So we arrive in Banff named, of course, after the town in the north east of Scotland. We book into the Banff Springs hotel. OK, so I paid a little extra for that privilege but not a lot. At dinner we are offered the full a la carte menu. 'Are you sure this is OK?' 'Yes sir, and would you like to look at the wine list?' 'Well, err, what are we allowed?' 'Anything you like sir.' And, of course, I took up the offer two nights on the trot. There must be a mistake. A quick calculation of prices from the menu takes the total way above what I paid for the upgrade: and the tour company has my credit card details. They never used it. All included. What a bargain. From the room the view to the west was breathtaking and through the binoculars you could pick out wild mountain goats on the rocks far above and raptors soaring overhead. The view to the east was even better, a panoramic view of the magnificent Bow River valley. There surely wasn't a better room in the whole hotel. I can only hope that the tour company got its money back from my advertising the pleasure and value for money of the whole experience.

After experiencing all the other goodies previously mentioned, including encountering the three different species of bear, I find myself with the free day in Calgary. Now there may be a charm in a huge ultra-modern city once you get to know it, but I wasn't there long enough to find out. I was originally intending to explore the Bow River as it flowed past in a milky, glacial melt, torrent on its way to the Hudson Bay far to the north east. But I now have a new goal in mind: the Tyrell Museum and the Burgess shale. What was that all about? A good place to start was with the hotel literature. Every tourist attraction is always found there, but nothing. Ask at reception, but never heard of it. She asks her fellow workers, but blank expressions. Surely this can't be a popular attraction then? Probably some ill-conceived hair brained scheme to fleece tourists that has fallen flat. The world is full of them. The quest for information, however, is overheard by a hotel porter who steps in and saves the day just as I was about to abandon it. He has heard of a man who runs a taxi tour service for Chinese visitors as he speaks Mandarin. Chinese visitors are thick on the ground in Western Canada as many have relatives there, left from the aforementioned construction of the mighty Canadian Pacific Railway. This entrepreneur had taught himself Mandarin for that specific purpose and had cornered the market with his particular skill. He had also been known to take them to the Tyrell Museum. I got his firm's name and tracked down his taxi service business card from the many adorning the notice board. I rang him up. Would he take me to the museum? He hummed and hawed a bit, 'How many people?' 'Two.' 'Nah, there has to be a minimum of three, preferably four, to fill the cab.' He took my room telephone number and said he would ring me back if anyone else inquired. This was teatime and I only had the next day. Chances were slim. At ten o'clock, the phone rings. He has another lady interested and he would take us. We would have to leave early as it got really busy around eleven o'clock. Really busy and no one locally even knew of its existence? Next morning we were picked up as planned with the third person already in the car. Conversation with her was a bit like drawing teeth. I got to wondering her agenda but that wasn't fair, I must stop categorizing people. The driver's mouth soon got into gear though and broke the uneasy silence. It sounded like he was an educated and knowledgeable man. Not to downplay taxi drivers, but it seemed unusual. Well he had taught himself Mandarin and that's an unusual skill for taxi drivers as far as I know.

We pass through the never ending outskirts of the massive city, grown to that size due to the oil beneath that part of the country.

As we enter the seemingly endless prairies there are nodding donkeys everywhere, pumping up an also seemingly endless stream of oil. A rich state is Alberta. The farms are huge, acreages totally alien to my conception of a farm at home. They socialize with friends by aeroplane which is a must have. We drive past the curious Amish farms with their horse and cart culture and biblical lifestyle. I wonder if they have ever heard of my destination. Oh yes, the destination. Where were we being taken and why way out here? After all, there are remarkable paleontology museums I have visited before, in London and New York, conveniently brought to the people. You just take the tube or bus, so why bother having one out here? What and where are these badlands anyway? The name conjured up all the western movies of my childhood. The badlands were where the bandits have their hideouts and the good guys track them down. That's where the name comes from, surely? Wrong. I have been living with this misconception for sixty years. The badlands are bad because they are un-farmable. No use for anything: poor soil and bad terrain. 'I'll show you,' says the well informed driver and, as the terrain changes from fertile prairie, we stop briefly at a dry river valley. It certainly lived up to the name but what were these curious layers in the strata? That's not unique in North America, the Grand Canyon being an excellent example. They were exposed previous soil surfaces, a long time previous. 'That's why we are here as you will soon see,' the taxi man explained. In the distance I spot a model of T-Rex looming, tacky and far too large for the real thing. Here we go: another tourist trap. But this is nothing to do with the museum. These are the profiteers that surround any popular site. It turns out this is advertising a fast food outlet selling Brontosaurus burgers with 'The Flintstones' as a theme. I felt like screaming. There were no Brontosauruses in the human stone age of the Flintstones. I contained myself. That fact was to be beautifully demonstrated later.

We have arrived. The car park is big and is filling up. Best get going. I make straight for the Burgess Shale exhibit. The experience is better than expected. There are interactive shows to take you through the history, more fantastic than any story, fact or fiction, I have ever read. Animals were living on the sea floor 505 million years ago. They normally do not fossilize, having no really hard parts to last the slow buildup of sediment required for this process. But there was a huge mudslide, engulfing the creatures in the area quickly, short-circuiting the normally slow process. That's how it happened. Then the whole slow buildup of sediment, eventually turning to stone, sealed it all in. But wait a minute. How the hell did that seafloor end up 8,000 feet up in the Rockies? The interactive screen portrays the whole process: tectonic plates. That's a reasonably new term. A geologist friend recounted his university days in the early 1970s when the theory of 'Continental drift' was first mooted. His professor's words were, 'I have to tell you about this theory as it has been included in the curriculum but disregard it. It's a load of rot.' Nowadays, new technology has uncovered the undeniable facts. Given the new name, tectonic plates, they can be traced out precisely with a pencil line on a world map. In this particular case, the Pacific plate pushes against the North American plate, pushing up the Rockies. Pushing them up to a height which was once three times what they are today. That's two and a half times the height of Mount Everest. Also pushed up and tilted at an angle went my Burgess shale. That would take a long time, surely? Well yes, around 500 million years. The higher the mountains were pushed, the more glaciated they became and therefore the more erosion took place. Rivers like the Fraser carried the sediment out to sea to continuously form new rock to be pushed up again in a never ending cycle: a cycle, of course, which continues to this day. The same erosion cycle exposed the Burgess shale from its time capsule to be discovered by excited paleontologists. If that lot failed to amaze, the next room housed the animals which were unearthed: exact replicas of these creatures, seemingly of myth and legend but very real. Creatures like *Hallucinogena*. I presume the man who named it thought he was dreaming. Many more life forms right before your very eyes in a reconstructed seafloor vista. I could only stand and marvel, probably with mouth open.

The Burgess shale is only a small part of the museum's exhibits and it has been transported there from the site on the Pacific side of the continental divide. That's 'West Side Story'. Not so the rest of the museum. It deals with the other 'side' of the story, literally. Sediments flow both ways from the high peaks and right where we stood the landscape is the result of further erosion of these sedimentary rocks: The Badlands.

To the east of the Rockies, which were being pushed up, was a huge shallow inland sea dividing North America in two. Over eons, sediments from the rivers would fill that sea. Plants and animals that lived and died during all that time were fossilized as these were the perfect conditions for that process. For a large part of that time, only plants would fossilize, as soft bodied animals would rot before the process began. No mudslide here. Eventually, with the evolution of more complex animals, they did leave fossils. This continued right up to the era when sea levels dropped and the climate changed from tropical to cold and ice became locked up at the poles. The sea dried up and the soft sedimentary rocks were left at the mercy of erosion from glaciers, then river systems and weather, giving rise to the landscape seen today. That erosion, though, exposed the layers and they can now be read like a calendar showing all the ages. But it also exposed the fossils, an abundance of them. That's why the museum is here. These fossil finds, of course, run the full length of that ancient sea throughout North America so this tiny area is a drop in the ocean. Fossils abound everywhere.

The huge car park is filling up. Busloads are emptying. The place is getting busy as predicted. It now becomes clear why this is happening. It's over ninety miles from Calgary, not a long way in this vast land. It's mainly school kids travelling from goodness knows where but, obviously, that was the time taken to get here from their school day starting time. That was encouraging, children of all ages being shown the history of life on earth. But this museum does more than that. Doors open onto the fossil beds and these kids can become paleontologists. You can organize to stay overnight in a tepee then, armed with picks, etc they go to find their own fossils. Kids are fascinated with dinosaurs and playing around with models doesn't convey to them their antiquity. Fossils of dinosaur bones are found aplenty here but where to look? The seams go down many metres. The staff and the TV screens give them a clue. You see this line in the strata? It runs all around everywhere you look, like someone has drawn it with a crayon. Below that line: plenty of dinosaur bones. Above that line: none. That's the K-T (Cretaceous-Tertiary) boundary and if you do find a dinosaur bone above, or a modern mammal bone below, it will turn modern science on its head. That's the children's quest. They find plenty of dinosaur bones but no science threatening phenomena. When they find a bone, they bring it in and have it identified. Can you imagine the thrill of a kid going home and telling his mum he has found a Tyrannosaurus Rex tooth or an Iguanodon leg? Wouldn't it be wonderful if every kid in the world could experience this at an early age? They would have to reconcile this with any other information subsequently fed to them. In addition to this, there are technicians going about their daily business of identifying, preparing and plaster casting the finds made every day. You can ask questions about their work and they take the time to explain in great detail. Exciting finds of previously unknown species are also a possibility. It has been done before by kids. There were very many dinosaur species walking the earth. Asking how many would be like asking how many mammal species live today. We might determine the latter but never the former, but it is estimated to be around the same amount. Only a tiny amount of fossils exist. Fossils are a very rare occurrence in nature.

The rest of the halls are filled with specimens of many dinosaurs. There is a T-Rex mother and baby, nest and eggs all found complete on site and re-assembled. Many more fill the place. Kids are told that dinosaur descendants live today. These are the birds. This was of particular interest to me because I have heard of, and seen pictures of, the 'missing link' which corroborates this. *Archaeopteryx*: a bird with teeth. Would you believe, before my very eyes, there it was in a glass case: the actual complete fossil of *Archaeopteryx*. It was so beautiful, loaned from Washington State University across the border. It was such a privilege.

The taxi driver tracks me down. The single lady wants to go. I have to drag myself away, missing out many more interactive shows. I could have spent a lot of time there. It was a shock to the system that, but probably the biggest shock of the whole experience to me wasn't all the fossils. That precise line in the strata, as you probably will know, was the event which finished the dinosaurs sixty five million years ago. Of all the metres of exposed strata, that line was very near the surface. In short a very recent event in the history of life. The black seams of coal, formed by the fossilization of a primaeval forest, appeared way, way down in the strata. On the way back to Calgary the lady didn't say anything. Maybe she couldn't get a word in edgeways with all my questions to the driver who seemed to know it all and took it for granted.

Next day we flew off to visit long lost friends and their subsequent families back across the Rockies in the Fraser valley near Vancouver. Very nice hospitable people: the barbecue is lit and a feast is laid out on our behalf. Before we eat, though, there is a little matter of a prayer. It wasn't a little matter as it dragged on: enough to expose my unease. Now to the inevitable grilling. 'You don't say prayers in Scotland?' 'Well err, not me personally.' There then ensued a conversation about how I should read this book that changed some hero's life. Would I like to read it? No problem. It may be of interest, who knows. The subject was about to drag on when I happened to say, 'Well, of course, the Bible [story] is not factual as the Amish believe.' Oh yes it was, was the response. Aiming for the middle ground I reasoned that, perhaps, six days in Genesis was just a period of time. Noah's ark could be representative of one of life on earth's great extinctions. Six thousand years ago, the time it was worked out from scripture that the universe was created, may only be symbolic. This is my keeping the peace. By this time my leg under the table was getting black and blue. I still have notches in my shinbone. So I throw in, 'Have you heard of the Tyrell Museum?' It was as if I hadn't spoken, so I try again. 'Err, um, have you been to the Tyrell Museum?' Same response: zero, I get the message. Yes they have heard of it, the same as all the receptionists at the Calgary hotel. It's a dirty word not to be mentioned. They have blotted it out. They have no answer to this age thing, so it doesn't exist. I am living in a scary world with the only light on the horizon being the work done with these school kids at just the right age. It was a great barbecue though and I thank them for their kind hospitality. That seems guaranteed in North America.

Vancouver Island is the last trip. I took the one train per day upcountry and back from the capital Victoria, which was another great experience I can recommend. Flying back by seaplane to the mainland, the sediments of the Fraser River spread out for miles into the ocean below me, was a reminder that Earth's processes still and always will continue whatever we humans do to the planet.

Canada is a huge but beautiful country. A small population shares a massive land area, a luxury not afforded to the people of my next destination.

19

INDIA

If you are a wildlife enthusiast, you may have been on safari in Africa. It's very popular nowadays. If you haven't, then you must surely have enjoyed the numerous nature programmes featuring iconic places like the Great Rift Valley or the Okavango Delta. I, myself, was more fascinated by India. Having been brought up with the stories of Rudyard Kipling it was a lifelong ambition to visit the home country of 'Shere Khan' and 'Rikki-Tikki-Tavi,' such ingenious and colourful names. On the whole I wasn't disappointed with the experience, and it was an experience. Kipling's India has changed. It wasn't the picture I had in my mind for all that time.

With a population of over a billion, you cannot escape the people. Even in rural areas they are everywhere. Their lifestyle is of necessity basic and that's the first impression you get of the wildlife. It has adapted to the hordes of people and even thrives because of it. Birds like kites scavenge the waste, which is mostly organic. The paddy fields are alive with herons, egrets, snakes and a multitude of other wildlife. Hunting eagles, hawks and falcons soared overhead, balancing the populations. No intensive farming. No chemical fertilisers or pesticides, at least in the areas I visited. The pests are kept at a tolerable level by predators. The food chain beautifully plays out in front of your eyes. I was even a part of it. On one outing to the jungle we stopped for lunch at what was just a cookhouse, apparently recommended. Leaving the car at the roadside, we walked a hundred yards along a track. There was a ditch at the roadside where pigs and chickens foraged about and we had to 'shoo' them away to get to the path. On the menu were pea and ham soup and a choice of chicken or pork sandwiches. I had just seen the chickens, scabby looking things with very little feathers, so I plumped for the pork as the pigs seemed healthy. I mentioned the permanent 'Delhi belly' when referring to India in a previous note and the stomach cramps started again, as usual, the moment food went down. 'Was there a convenience?' 'Yes there was' said the proud owner. It wasn't unusual not to have one. He pointed me out the back and up to a hut on the hillside with a large rain fed water tank on the roof. No hole in the ground squatting affair as normal, but a western toilet bowl. No cistern though, or a wash hand basin. A tap on the wall fed tanked rainwater to a bucket on the ground. You washed your hands under the tap and then used the contents of the bucket to flush the toilet. I was impressed. Returning to the car the pigs are agitated, furiously rutting around the ditch competing for whatever had arrived in there to eat. I then noticed an open sluice running down the hillside from among the trees, feeding into the ditch. Peering through the trees I could just make out a familiar little wooden hut with a water tank on top.

A natural cycle it may be, but the thought of it doesn't make your stomach feel any better. These hordes of people feed themselves from the land. Simple diets based on a staple of rice and a multitude of fruits (with of course, pork and chicken). India is the biggest banana producer in the world but not the biggest exporter. That's Ecuador and we eat theirs. India needs most of its own as home consumption is huge. You can have real fancy meals using banana as a base and the leaves can be used as plates. Fishing in the huge opaque estuaries draining a sub-continent is primitive but effective. It is also sustainable. No fish finders here.

In big cities, capitalism breeds wealth and along with that obesity. These are the 'lucky' few.

Throughout the land the first impression is of people looking like supple bits of wire, just like my recollections of people in my childhood. They mostly seem content with their lot. The many acquaintances I made were not after charity from a westerner, as in many other countries. They were eager to strike up a conversation about the historic British rule, of which they were curiously proud. One Hindu temple attracted me because of the thousands of people waiting to get in: apparently, a place of pilgrimage. My sandals are added to the huge pile outside the doors. 'I probably won't see them again' I thought. I did. Stealing from outside a temple was abhorrent to them, I learned. Indeed stealing anywhere is a rare occurrence. One old gent in a long white robe approached me, a relic almost of Victorian times. He looked, and probably was, over a hundred. I put the beggar guard up. 'What country you from?' he asked. I have to be polite but am expecting the sell or beg pitch. I mutter, 'Scotland' accompanied by a go away look. He then relates to me his life in the BRITISH army in colonial days and is truly proud of it. I didn't go into the fact that we had been sucking his country dry with nothing in return. The commonwealth was a misnomer back then. It wasn't common at all. The wealth all went one way. He said, 'I am from Calcutta, have you ever been to Calcutta?' 'No.' 'Oh, you should, lot of people, lot of people.' Well yes, that's why I am not going. I humoured him with 'one day perhaps' waiting for the obvious beg and trying to show little interest. He finishes by shaking my hand and saying, 'Really nice to meet you, I hope you manage to visit Calcutta someday.' I felt like shrivelling up and dying. It was a lesson in humility. I should have shouted him back and bought him lunch. How many stories could that old guy have told me? Better than any history book. I went there to learn about India and I had missed my biggest opportunity, but too late, he had disappeared into the billion plus.

The whole of my experience of that country reminded me of my simple childhood, both the human inhabitants and the wildlife. It really felt as if you were a part of nature. Wealth is not necessary for survival or happiness. In fact, as the world changes, as it inevitably will, perhaps even suddenly as has been the norm in the past, the western world has no plan B. The people of India have a much better chance of survival in such circumstances. In nature terms, humans are just another rung up the food chain which stops with us as there are no predators to keep us in check, at least not since the invention of the gun, hence the billion population. Some of the predators of our ancient ancestors still exist but they cling on to that existence. Habitat loss and poaching could soon finish them off. Any child nowadays in the western world is aware of the threat to the tiger. Some species have already become extinct. It was the Victorians who started the ball rolling in the name of sport. Big game hunting was in fact just a big game. All over the commonwealth this 'sport' was practiced and royalty set the example long afterwards. The illustrations overleaf, taken at the 'Delhi Durbar' in the early 1930s, show King George V on a tiger shoot:

198

One is entitled 'The king is an excellent shot.' No he isn't. Although firing at point blank range, the poor terrified animals having previously been driven in by beaters, a servant is reloading a second gun for him meaning he has missed by at least one shot previously and is obviously expected to miss again. A total of six tigers were shot that day.

Well, it was a must have then. A tiger skin rug in front of the hearth or a head mounted on a plaque on the wall. It seems barbaric now but it was barbaric to nature lovers then, only they would not dare speak up against the aristocracy and royalty. Tigers today are in big danger of becoming extinct completely and campaigners work tirelessly to stop it. Let's hope they succeed. There is not much hope of my ever seeing a tiger in the wild.

King cobra I did hope to see in the jungle but alas, although I was assured of

a sighting and was pointed to the likely areas, not a single one. I did see plenty being piped out of wicker baskets at the markets. No wonder I didn't see any wild ones. It looks as if they have all been captured.

The wild forests of Kipling's 'Jungle Book' are what I had hoped to see but the forests I visited were so full of people. Even fuel for cooking fires, out of human necessity, put the old forests at risk. In other tropical forest countries, it's not necessity but Western greed that puts them and their wildlife at risk through needless exploitation. One such place is in Indonesia.

20

RAINFOREST

I'm off to Indonesian Borneo to explore the rain forest. No intrepid explorer me, I'm too old. I don't intend to go to the interior. Suffice to do the periphery and, of course, see how my close cousin the orang-utan is faring. As I fly from Singapore at 30,000 feet the landscape below intrigues me. Pristine rain forest and winding, sediment filled, mighty rivers as far as the eye can see: and from that height, that's far. Individual tree canopies sticking out higher than the surrounding forest makes you realize the size of these organisms. If you can see an individual tree looking big from up there, then that's big. It doesn't change for three whole hours until it finally changes into palm oil plantations for the last twenty minutes of the descent into East Kalimantan. Now that's a lot of rainforest. I had previously read that if deforestation continues at its present rate in Borneo, there will be no rainforest left in ten years. How can that be possible? That's what THEY say and I won't argue, but if it is true then that's a disaster on a massive scale. Help is on the way though. The Indonesian government, to whom this part of the Island of Borneo belongs, has banned any new rainforest clearing. So that's OK then? As I am about to find out, it's far from OK. Corruption is evident from the minute you set foot in Indonesia. You have to literally smooth talk your way out of the airport. It also relieves you of a few thousand rupiah (not as bad as it sounds as inflation is runaway). At least in India the army only threatens you on the way out for money or goods. The customs officers and the police force are one thing but their shady dealings pale in comparison with that of the Indonesian army. Whatever the good intentions of the distant government in Java, the army reigns supreme in Borneo. All bow to them, or else. The mafia doesn't have a look in.

The people tell many terrible tales: here are a couple of examples. The terrible disaster of the tsunami, which decimated Banda Aceh in Sumatra a couple of months earlier than my visit, resulted in aid from the western world finally getting through. A picture in the local paper is of a badly beaten man's face. It was horrendous. Also printed is a whole list of injuries which he suffered. The following is a newspaper report of the inquest into the event:

The army had caught this man trying to steal a whole lorry load of aid. The soldiers were so incensed at this act that they lost control and beat him up. In his defense, the culprit pleaded that he was only delivering the aid, as he was the official driver and had never even deviated from the route.

The assault had taken place, in fact, on the very route to Banda Aceh. The magistrate's ruling was that . . .

Although the victim should not have stolen the goods, the army was wrong to take the law into their own hands, so, as the man had suffered enough, he would be let off with a warning.

End of case. Defense council asked what had happened to the lorry's contents as they didn't arrive at Banda Aceh, but this was ruled as irrelevant.

This is one of many personal experiences. I met with an ex-patriot French woman who played golf. When she knew I played, I was invited for a game at Seppingan Golf Club. Sitting on the equator as it does is not good for my game. It's cooking but I cannot forgo the challenge. It was an experience. The course is carved out of jungle, wall to wall. I am warned that if my ball goes in there, forget it: cobras and all sorts. If my ball goes into the water hazard, even at the edge, forget it again: crocodiles. Of course I am intrigued. Wildlife: that's what I am here to see. I have lived long enough not to be afraid of these things but to respect them. After all back home, as I mentioned earlier, people are totally unnecessarily afraid of bees. I have to remember this is a western WOMAN warning of these things. That's not meant to be sexist but it is a fact that their fear is normally more intense, so I take it not quite with a pinch of salt, just with a little less regard. We start off. There is a water hazard at the first hole. The whole surface is covered with floating weed and algae. Her ball goes in. There is a swirl: crocodile, surely. A human head appears. This is a local making a living off selling found balls. He spends all day, every day, in that pond. Every pond had its own resident but sadly, no crocodiles. We play on. My ball goes in the jungle. I had a cursory glance in the general place, minding the warning. A rustle in the undergrowth: cobra? No, two eight year old boys scraping around looking for my ball IN BARE FEET. Every fairway jungle had its resident boys. In fact the horror story told by my female opponent about a king cobra appearing in the school playground the day before summed it up. When I asked the outcome, apparently the kids threw stones at it and it went away. What an anticlimax.

I return to my story about corruption. I was asked if I wanted a return match. I had just beaten a woman and could hardly refuse: bad losers the French. A time was booked and we met to prepare. Caddies were obligatory and part of the green fee. I had enjoyed the information from my last one and hired him again. We walked to the first tee. Six soldiers turn up and commandeer six sets of clubs lying outside the clubhouse belonging to golfers waiting to play. They then appropriate six caddies, one of which is mine. They then cut in front of us taking our tee time. 'Hey, wait a minute, what do you think you are . . .' A fair French hand is placed on my shoulder and a fair French mouth whispers, 'shhh.' The caddy, whom I had befriended, never looked my way and the twelve of them walked down the fairway showing, also, that they had never even played the game before.

So it is hardly reassuring to learn that the task of policing the ban on the felling of the rainforest fell to the army and it was not surprising to subsequently find out that felling goes on apace, the only difference is that you now have to pay them for the privilege.

I manage to get a driver to take me to the orang-utan sanctuary. I wouldn't drive there myself. Dual carriageways are just that. Use both lanes in ANY direction and after dark it is plain madness. The orang-utan, a close relative of we humans hasn't been treated as such. Apart from habitat loss, young ones are regularly sold in the market as pets, being like cuddly human babies. They wear nappies (diapers) just the same but the cuddliness fades and adolescents are abandoned. Not having had the opportunity to learn any knowledge from their mothers as to how to look after themselves in the wild, and the wilderness becoming further and further away, they perish: either being shot for scavenging, run over by traffic, or dying of starvation. Here's where the sanctuary comes in. They rescue these unfortunates, many of them being handed in. They are bonded with a surrogate human mother. They have no other contact with the outside world until deemed naturalized enough to be released back into the wild: except that is, for being gawked at by the likes of me. But this is not a tourist attraction. I had to 'persuade' the driver to get us in and we had to wear masks to prevent the possible spread of diseases, they being so closely related to us and susceptible to the same colds and flus, etc. It is a labour of love for these young girls, acting as surrogate mothers, who spend all their days cuddling baby orang-utans. It was a humbling experience and worth the driver's bung and the donation (and the price of the T shirt of course). Surely it is time to make this trade illegal? Apparently it is, overseen by the army. Enough said.

'Take me to the rainforest.' The driver knows the ropes. A nature reserve, part of the original forest saved by some means, to show the world that the government is serious. Apart from the fact that it is surrounded by palm oil plantations it is breathtaking. Massive buttressed hardwoods alive with the sound of cicadas and draped with flowering epiphytes. These are the trees seen from the plane. How high are these trees? My guide takes me to another part of the forest with a series of steps up to a platform in the canopy. There is a monkey bridge from this tree to another about fifty metres away. You are dared to cross it. How high is the bridge? At least 100 feet: I never measured it but that's what I was told. These trees, at that height, haven't even started branching. The canopy is a dizzyingly long way above. Of course I crossed it. Some things just have to be done in life. Indonesian authorities have just got to stop paying lip service to conservation and put money where their mouth is to see it really taking place. That is, of course, if they are serious in the first place. That's a difficult concept in Borneo.

There are many other places that are awesome in their natural beauty and wildlife. I am spoiled by having the Scottish Highlands on my doorstep which must be high on the list: attitudes to conservation here is hugely better now than it was, many times better than in Borneo. This next destination must rank among my highest on both counts and it was a surprise.

21

VIVA EL REVOLUTION

Fidel Castro and Che Guevara are Cuban heroes who fought for the same principles as my own country's hero William Wallace. How dare oppression be forced upon a population? There should be no class distinctions. All men are equal. They had an argument. The fight for freedom from colonial rule was hard fought in Cuba but ideology does not pay the bills. At last they were liberated but unfortunately, no better off. In fact worse off as the western world cuts you off. Supply chains are destroyed and life becomes a bitter struggle. After fifty years of 'freedom' and looking at eternal posters of 'the famous pair' plastered around Havana, that ideology is wearing thin. Ninety miles from the US and it's a different world. They are not a happy people, but they cannot say it. The words on everyone's lips are, 'we love Fidel but we hate the policies of the government.' It is, of course, one and the same thing. The principle is there, the same as my William Wallace hero worship, but the reality is very different. Communism is an ideal but it seems everyone is a capitalist. That's an observation again and not an opinion. The world was nearly destroyed in the early sixties by a nuclear war caused by Cuba's idealism but they were an oppressed nation. They had a legitimate cause to be angry. How do an oppressed people fight back if it's not through idealism? Everyone has a dream: Martin Luther King Junior, Nelson Mandela and many, many others all fought for it. Too many people disagreed with their dreams and, unfortunately, some still disagree today. Indoctrination has a powerful and long lasting influence.

Cuba is on the brink of change. It is not an easy road but it's almost there and it will happen soon, for sure. Unfortunately capitalism comes at a price: inequality, big money and corruption. To these people, I wish the best of luck. They deserve the best after what they have been through. Me, I agree with some of Fidel's policies. Not with his politics but on his love of his country and all the preservation measures that have been put in place to protect its environment. They have nature reserves second to none. The world could learn from him.

There are many wild places on earth that I have seen, and many I haven't. It's not my fault: it's just too cold for the baggage. Arctic and Antarctic wildernesses must be special places. I can only savour what I have experienced and Cuba is high on the list. Tourists flock to Havana and Varadero, the two centres that make up the package holiday. I wanted to see the real Cuba. I enlisted the help of a Cuban travel agency. Tell them what you want and they will arrange it. They made a good job of it. I wished to see Havana of course and then fly to a string of cays off the north coast 500 miles away. The attraction was the nature reserves. I picked the hotel, unfortunately: it was on one of the cays nearest to the reserves. Five star: it was lucky if it made western two star grade. It was opened as a first on the cays by Fidel, way back, to boost tourism and has a plaque to prove it. It may have merited the five star rating then but, sadly, not now. The hygiene was an issue. When you see a tanker emptying a cesspit and carelessly spilling contents on to the path to the swimming pool and kids splashing through it, you know there is going to be trouble. Sure enough, nurses with red crosses on their hats were soon taking samples from the buffet for analysis, holding up the queue. Yes, eventually everyone suffered, inevitably.

I got in touch with a fisherman who could take me bonefishing on Cayo Romano, one big reserve. I wasn't geared up for a fishing trip but it sounded good and arrangements were made. Sure enough, bacteria got me. I had to postpone the trip. The bug lasted and lasted causing many postponements until I either had to go despite the tummy or not at all. The last day of the 'holiday' was arranged. I was picked up by an old American limousine, for which Cuba is famous, and driven many miles. A causeway led to the cay: Cayo Romano at last. There was a steel wire across the road which was a patched up dirt track. A honk on the horn brought a little old man (oh, probably the same age as me) sleepily from a block hut. No words were spoken. He just dropped the wire and we were in. Twenty minutes later the car stopped and we got out. The gear was unloaded and it did a U-turn and drove away. There was a mangrove marsh of black mud on both sides of the road, such a hellish place as I have ever been. This felt like the real 'middle of nowhere'. I thought if someone was to hit me on the head now, I would never be found. It didn't look like a nature reserve to me. I scanned the horizon. I didn't see any water. We had to walk and I stood in my holiday sandals and T-shirt. The fisherman had all the gear. I was kitted out with a pair of tight fitting ankle boots and away we went into the marsh. It was hard going, a mile or so of slogging and squelching and still no water. Not far now, he said. Through a mangrove thicket and then a vista opened up to take my breath away: a massive lagoon of clear blue water. 'We will fish over to there and then have lunch.' 'Where?' 'There.' He pointed again. 'There' is the far shore, just discernible in the distance. 'How far is that?' 'Less than two miles but there is no boat, we walk.' And we did. A quick spasm reminded me of the ongoing health problem. How would I cope with that in the middle of the lagoon?

The whole lagoon is no more than eighteen inches (450 mm) deep. It was just awesome that place. Flamingos just moved over as we approached. Eagles and fish hawks fished all around. Herons and egrets of all descriptions showed no fear of us. A huge barracuda, thirty pound or so, checked out my bare legs and cruised around shark like. This was indeed nature worth saving, so well done Fidel. The day was magical, despite the stomach cramps. The photograph on the previous page is deceptive. The nearest shore is in the background. I am standing in the centre of the lagoon. Can you imagine a 1·2 metre long barracuda checking your legs out in that depth of water? I spent seven hours wading before trekking back through the black mud to the road. I was glad to see the car turn up and it duly delivered me back to the 'hotel'. Transport and all equipment provided: the cost of that wonderful day's experience? US $60. I have been to many wild places but that place topped them all for sheer beauty and loneliness (and price).

We left for the airport next day to fly back for another stay in Havana. The bug still lingered but we would surely manage as it was only an hour and a half flight. An announcement: the plane has broken down and we are to be bussed back to Havana. Only TEN hours of bumpy roads and stomachs bouncing up and down. Well, that's communism for you.

There is another island in the Caribbean that I can say is equally wildlife conscious and is a destination inspired by a television programme.

22

THE 007 CONNECTION

Ian Fleming and I have something in common and I don't mean literary talent.

Another David Attenborough gem on television was his series on the life of birds. In one episode he is on the tiny island of Little Tobago off the north east coast of Tobago. Red-billed tropicbirds (*Phaethon aethereus*) nest there, one of the few nesting sites in the world. They are a race apart: white plumage with bright red bills and streamer tails. David is crouching down very close to the nesting bird incubating its eggs whispering the story, as is his trademark.

He is here to see the actions of, not the tropicbird but, the magnificent frigatebird. If any bird epitomizes the tropics to me, it is this one. It could well be a pterodactyl were it not for the wrong era. It looks primitive and ghostly. It is fantastically agile and if I were a kite designer, it would be my blueprint (previous photograph).

This ocean wanderer nests on only a few islands in the world, none of which are anywhere near Little Tobago. An enigma is that, although it is an oceanic species, it cannot swim or even land on water. If it did, it couldn't take off again. But it doesn't have to. It is an opportunist and a pirate and that is what Mr Attenborough was there to see.

The marvelously filmed action shows the red billed tropicbird, an excellent fisher, returning to its nest with a crop full of fish. It has to run the gauntlet of frigatebirds. Noting the ones with full crops the frigatebirds chase and harass, even catching and shaking, the tropicbird until it regurgitates its catch, whereupon the fish are caught before they hit the water. Any that do, are deftly picked up without the bird contacting the ocean. The aerobatics were superb. I thought I could have a slice of that as I hadn't been to Tobago. So I talked the baggage into another holiday trip. It wasn't difficult. It's warm there.

As you drive up to Speyside, Tobago (yes, Scots get everywhere) you pass deep ravines with winding roads and spectacular views across the ocean. There are remnants of large trees but it's mostly quite young rainforest. Getting friendly with the locals always comes up with interesting stories and one of them recounted the history of the forest. When he was a young lad there used to be a pristine mature rainforest on the island. Then a hurricane struck. He was huddled under the mahogany kitchen table. The roof blew off and a wall caved in on top of him but the stout table saved him. When the hurricane blew over he dug himself out to emerge into what he says could have been another planet. There were no buildings left standing in the village but most noticeably, there were no trees left. All gone: the whole mature rainforest. What I was looking at now was the natural regeneration of the forest. The first instinct is shock at such devastation but look closer and you can see that this is just another natural event, probably doing the dense rainforest a favour by making space for the next generation of trees. The same process as the forest fires of North America. The older generations die off, in all species in nature, to make way for their youngsters and that includes us.

210

This is a strange fact about how most humans perceive life. In all walks of life, humans will acknowledge that the younger generation is the most important. They are revered as the future and we give preference to them, even our own species. Surgeons have to continually make difficult decisions as to who will live or die, and the recipient of a transplanted organ will almost always be the younger patient. A parent of a child dying of leukemia would gladly take their place in sacrifice. The young are more important for the future. That's not how humans treat trees. The older a tree is the greater respect it commands while saplings will be trampled underfoot. If a mature tree has to be felled for a new road, there is a huge outcry but no-one considers the hundreds of seedlings bulldozed away. They are the future forests requiring protection. Our lifetimes are nothing in the grand picture. Of course I wouldn't like to see magnificent trees destroyed but if it has to be, my wish would be for laws to see that for every mature tree felled, a hundred are planted and PROTECTED until properly established. However, in Tobago, the forest does this itself and I am happy to report that in Tobago, government protection is given to this young forest.

Eventually, in the north east corner of the island we have lunch in 'Jemma's Kitchen', unusual in that the whole restaurant is built up a tree. From there you can look out across the bay to Little Tobago and Goat Island.

Goat Island is tiny with a two storey house and beach (left). You pass it on the way to Little Tobago which has been made a bird sanctuary by the government.

There are three locals, with small power boats, hoping for trade. They are willing to take anyone snorkeling as the bay has an untouched coral reef, again protected by the government. I ask them to take me to all three: Goat Island, the coral reef and Little Tobago. An argument ensues between them for the trade and the price is dropping by the minute. I tell them to sort it out and let me know and I feign a walk back to the car. It's arranged. That's how it works outside the UK. We are off. Snorkeling was great with a pristine reef and an abundance of fishes and turtles, as it should be. Brain corals are huge, apparently the biggest in the world but I think I can challenge that. Goat Island is private but the beach is not (I hope not because I didn't ask permission to be on it). Ian Fleming is reputed to have owned it but the truth is not clear. He certainly stayed there and it is a perfect hideaway. The Beatles and Princess Margaret have also stayed there. What was the attraction for Mr Fleming apart from the privacy? After all, he had plenty of privacy in his home in Jamaica. Well, you see, he was there for the same reason as me and Mr Attenborough. He was an amateur naturalist with a special interest in birds. Although Jamaica is really fantastic for bird life, he too was overawed by the raw nature of this place. He may have got some inspiration here too, as you can just imagine a blonde in a wetsuit and flippers walking up the beach. He had a copy of a book on birds of the area. It was a concise encyclopedia called 'Birds of the Caribbean'. I also have a copy. He must have enjoyed reading and using that book, both here in Tobago and in Jamaica, because the author's name was none other than one JAMES BOND.

It is only a few hundred yards from Goat Island to Little Tobago and you are faced with a long steep climb to the top of the cliffs, past thimble sized humming bird nests in the bushes and the nesting burrows of Audubon's shearwater, another rare bird. The vista opens out onto the sheer cliffs and ocean. Right beside the end of the path, tucked under a bush, is a red-billed tropicbird on its eggs. There is nowhere else to walk to, so this is the place and this is the nest featured in the television programme. I crouch down, feet from the bird, as was portrayed. It is completely unperturbed by my presence. My photos (following page) are taken: been there, done that. Then I relax and enjoy the spectacle, exactly as Messrs Fleming and Attenborough did. I am pretty sure my elbows were in the same indentations made by both.

Tobago has other treasures. At Arnos Vale, on the other side of the Island, there is an inshore coral garden just yards from the beach. It doesn't look very special until you look underwater:

spectacular, undamaged and protected.

The main government here is in Port of Spain, Trinidad and they seem to be doing the right things, conservation wise. But they have it a bit easier than some. Tobago is not heavily populated and development is not overdone due to the lack of Caribbean type beaches. One larger hotel has bulldozed the shore to create an artificial beach of imported sand. Boulders at each end contain the sand and it looks hellish compared to natural features. Nevertheless, tourists feel safe in the all-inclusiveness and confinement (it's not for me). Fishing methods are traditional and non-commercialized. The Island can maintain itself simply and naturally, a joy to see. There seems no rush to make millions and the 'laidbackness' is the best in the Caribbean. You feel on holiday and long may that continue. Mind you, it has been a few years since I was there and other islands used to be like that, so no guarantees. Mr Moneybag's big business has more than just a tendency to sway governments.

No more so than on this other infamous island.

23

A TAX HAVEN

On the face of it, the Cayman Islands in the Caribbean are an eco-friendly island group. That is what is professed to visitors with an array of dos and don'ts to protect coral reefs and wildlife. Grand Cayman is the main island. Here, the saving of the indigenous blue iguana from the brink of extinction is a significant achievement. From as little as fifteen individuals in 2003 there are now several hundred. Predation by cats, dogs, humans and competition from the invasive non-native green iguana caused their demise and the new botanic park provides the protection needed. However, this work was mainly carried out by conservationist volunteers who cared. Tourism is big business for the locals, especially cruise ships, and the premier attraction is Stingray City: two sandbars behind the northern reef. Hundreds are taken out in boats to swim with, and feed, the rays. It would appear that no damage is done and it is a great way for people to come close to wild sea creatures. The rays are there by their own choice for the food provided by the tour company. There is a similar facility on the island of Antigua too which I would prefer, as there are only three or four people in a boat as opposed to crowds. Another attraction is the Atlantis submarine to view the deeper reef corals. Environmental wise, these seem to be harmless attractions. Unfortunately there is another side.

The second most popular attraction is the turtle farm. This was acquired and has been run by the government since 1983. Losses in the last financial year were $7·9 million. This cannot be due directly to the recent world financial crisis as the loss has been less each year. It is reported that a light on the horizon is the 13% increase in the sale of turtle meat. Did I say turtle meat? Oh yes. Most restaurants on the island have turtle steak on the menu, costing as much as £40 a course (this is an expensive island). Considering that green turtles are on the **endangered species list** how can this be justified? Cayman used to be the turtle island of the Caribbean but over exploitation, as usual, took its toll bringing their numbers to sad proportions. In fact the government still grants licences to harvest even wild turtles. Conditions at the farm also give rise for concern. Filthy tanks were clandestinely sampled by conservationists and the results were horrifying. Essentially they swim in their own waste. Their justification was further seriously undermined by a recent sea water pipe burst which drained a tank. No effort to keep the turtles wet eg by spraying, etc meant that 400 turtles shrivelled up and died in the heat. That's 400: all those turtles in **one** tank. The tourists, of course, have no idea of any of these facts and enjoy the spectacle. You can even swim with them. Rather them than me in that soup. Anxious to be seen to be conservation minded, some of the turtles are supposedly returned to the wild. No figures are quoted. The problem of provenance I have dealt with under the migration chapter.

The farm visitor figures for last year were 250,000. The government says it needs 450,000 to break even. The vast majority of visitors come from the cruise ships and sometimes there are up to seven ships per day, that's 18,000 visitors per DAY. They would have to double that. It seems unthinkable. At the moment there is no cruise ship dock and the passengers are ferried by tender ships to shore. Landing times can be staggered to some extent but at reboarding time in late afternoon it is like herding cattle. They have to form long queues along the quayside and street. One problem is that in the 85° heat, people are melting, so the government has just started to provide free water. That's a holiday?

This is a big problem if they wish more visitors. They will have to build a cruise ship dock and one proposal is to build it south of West Bay at a public beach. This will divide their famous seven mile beach into two, three and a half mile beaches. It doesn't have the same ring.

This could mean bigger environmental problems. I have another story to tell.

The phenomenon of shifting sands in an altered current I have witnessed in another Caribbean island.

In the 1960s the realisation by upcoming nations of the British Commonwealth that they were being fleeced reached its height.

We can do better on our own. If so and so state can do it, then we can do it. There was an overwhelming rush for independence. In the face of an obvious fact that wealth went more one way than the other, you cannot blame the citizens. The difference from the Cuban scenario was that independence meant democracy: ruled by the people for the people. A little fly in the ointment was that no one had done the maths. Also, in the rush of patriotism no one had considered that the skills needed to manage a country had been denied to the native population. The white man had not only ruled but had provided all the necessary skills in management. This is not to say that these skills were not achievable for the indigenous population, just that they had never been available to them. That's oppression. They were an underclass in their own country. It started with Ghandi's India in the late 1940s and as increased communications spread the word around the world, coupled with the near bankruptcy of the UK after the Second World War and its inability to finance the policing of these countries, the floodgates opened. Freedom though, comes at a price. Someone has to know what they are doing. Demonstrations may prove dissatisfaction but do not run an egalitarian country. Bettering one's life depends on trade and produce.

In the Caribbean island states there were some better placed than others.

Comparing Barbados with Dominica (not to be confused with the Dominican Republic, part of Hispaniola, the island which it shares with Haiti) is like comparing chalk with cheese. Dominica is a beautiful island but although it can sustain itself, it seems poorer than it was under British rule. Most life is basic although the saviour of it, as in the case of many other similar islands, is the modern cruise ship docking in Rousseau. So what's the difference? Beaches: Barbados was the island state which led the way. Their tourist infrastructure was already well established, with the Canadian market especially, before independence in 1966. They were on a sure thing. Canadians from Montreal and Quebec jumped on a plane and in a few hours could interrupt their -20° winters with a few days of tropical sun and fun. UK citizens do the same now with package holidays to Spain and the Canaries. We now, also, contribute to the Barbados economy with long haul packages but in the early days of independence there appeared to be problems. To further the development of the infrastructure in order to tap this prosperity the country needed skilled architects, quantity surveyors and engineers to name just a few and no locals were trained in these skills. To give the UK credit, whether it was borne out of a guilty conscience or not, they helped by subsidising the provision of skilled people to not only build the infrastructure but to train the population. In Dominica, there was no point. No beaches, no tourists and the difference, even today, is dramatic. It is the beaches of Barbados which are the cash cow, in particular the west coast ones. They call it their Platinum Coast.

One member of that imported, skilled workforce happened to be a good friend of mine who undertook a three year contract, extended to five as he liked it so much. He moved there with his young family who were the same age as mine and he invited us over. Woohoo! Up until then, Barbados was a stamp in my album along with other treasured ones depicting local life in places like Martinique and Guadeloupe. These were almost mythical places for a child who grew up in the forties and fifties. I only had to raise the air fare, as living there at that time was cheaper than the UK. Working literally night and day, I raised the airfare. That then was my introduction to the Caribbean, and for an energetic young man the beaches of Barbados became my playground. I spent two separate months there in the 1970s. I really felt special, almost a local. With these memories, I just had to go back someday and I did. The beaches in the early 1990s had not changed. They were exactly as I remembered them. Discovery Bay was magical. A long sandy beach and inshore coral dotted around where the children loved to snorkel and identify coral fishes. Six Men's Bay was my favourite: further north and away from the more touristy ones. Wildness and tranquillity took the breath away. The little fishing village at the north end had friendly locals who were a mine of knowledge on the history of this place. Beer in hand, you could talk for hours. They were very knowledgeable although not very productive, but that's the pace of life there. On my return two years later a shock was in store. The excavators were in. They were in the process of carving out a lagoon for a marina and multi-million dollar properties which split Six Men's Bay in two. That's exactly as is proposed for

Seven Mile Beach, Grand Cayman. The excavated rock was dumped in the sea to form a breakwater and large jetty as some of the status symbol yachts were too big to sail in to your back door in the marina. The fishermen were up in arms. The natural beauty of the area was being destroyed for the benefits of the few. That wasn't the most important story they told.

Forgive them for they know not what they do.

'They are playing with fire.' These fishermen knew the ocean currents around these shores. Here we have an island facing the north east trades more than most. The geology of the island is not the same as the rest of the Lesser Antilles. It is not volcanic. It is the tip of an ancient coral reef, exposed in an era when sea levels fell. The thirty metre east coast cliffs expose the coral species right down to their base and they look the very same species as those alive today. That's a lot of coral erosion and, coupled with the ground up shells of molluscs, is what gives Barbados its white sandy beaches so attractive to tourists. The easterly current from the Atlantic carries the sand around the island both north and south and it is caught up in the back eddy to be washed up on the west coast. I created just that scenario in an experiment with two garden hoses. If nothing changes, then the Platinum Coast can continue to be the playground of the rich and famous, but things were going to change as the fishermen pointed out. They knew the currents intimately in their little boats and warned that this very fine sand was finely balanced as well. It might seem a drop in the ocean but it has repercussions in a finely balanced system. Chaos theory came up with the expression *if a butterfly flaps its wings in Japan it affects the weather at the other side of the world.* The fisherman predicted that the sandy beaches would move south and create big problems for the tourist industry. Don't mess with nature if you don't like the consequences. So great was their argument, and so incensed was I on the loss of such natural beauty, that I wrote to the Barbados government to warn them thinking that a tourist would lend extra credence to the argument. Youth thinks it can change the world. I addressed it to Department of the Environment, Government Buildings, Barbados, **WI**. It wasn't like writing to the president of the United States. At that time the population of Barbados was less than my home city. It was like writing to my local council. However, the same result ensued: total disregard. Why would they listen to me, a mere minion?

Six weeks later the letter was returned unopened. It was overwritten: no such address in **W1**. There are obviously postmen in London who don't know there is a world outside that metropolis.

I posted it again spelling out West Indies. I was going to add, between the Atlantic Ocean and the Caribbean Sea. I refrained. The recipient was supposed to take it seriously. As I said, I never got a reply. The outcome of that personal story, however, is that the proof of the pudding is in the eating: that prophesy, on returning today, has been borne out. Many resorts do not have beaches anymore and have closed. Others cling on to what sand is left by putting retaining boulders into the sea to hold the sand. It may work but exacerbates the situation elsewhere. The $10,000 per NIGHT resorts can afford to import sand to heighten their precious beaches: thousands of tons of it and that in turn causes an effect on beaches elsewhere but, with that kind of money at stake, it's 'I'm alright Jack'. Discovery Bay's beautiful beach of my children's day is now referred to as 'The Concrete Walkway'. Not a grain left. That's in a mere twenty years.

Of course politicians come up with many excuses: global warming being the cop out but anyone with half an eye can see that if global warming was the cause then other islands like Grand Cayman and its seven mile beach would be equally affected and it is not. Both it and Grand Anse beach in Grenada have taken batterings from recent hurricanes but they have healed up and, to me, look pretty much the same as they ever did: up until now.

I cannot sit in judgement as I am really not qualified. I only see what I see. The views of 'ignorant' fishermen are to be ignored by 'knowledgeable' politicians. It just so happens that their predictions were correct and the Platinum Coast is slipping through gold and silver and, in some places, tending towards bronze.

Would I dare make a prediction for Seven Mile Beach? Why not? 'Grand Cayman government, be warned.'

There are other environmental issues to consider . . .

The inshore coral on Grand Cayman, which has a tentative hold, is a big snorkelling attraction. A new dock would seriously affect its future. This coast is already heavily developed and new, larger, higher hotels are in the building or planning stages.

I return to the turtles. You are advised that if any turtle nests are evident on the beach you should notify the hotel staff so they can be protected. There are precious few turtles nesting on this beach nowadays and a new cruise ship berth is the last thing that is required.

On the south of the island there is a sound of shallow water behind the reef, and beaches which are seldom used by tourists. It is an area of outstanding wild and natural beauty and the quiet beaches are just what turtles need.

Now here's a surprise. Developers wish to develop this coast by building multi-million dollar houses as they have done in Barbados. Canals are to be gouged out of the shore so that motor boats and yachts can be docked at the back doors (as they have already done in the North Sound). To facilitate access the reef will have to be blasted open: so much for conservation policy. Reef destroyed, turtle nesting beaches dug up, and change in ocean currents with the possible consequences again. There is a worse scenario. Ask the locals, 'What we do when de hurricane come?' Fresh in their minds is hurricane Ivan in 2004

 which devastated the south. That's **with** the protection of the reef. The whole coastline could possibly be swamped much more severely in a future storm but for the reef. There is a campaign to stop this (left), only time will tell.

So why is this island group so attractive to big business? It is well known to be an offshore tax haven. Let's look at the declared selling points.

These are the words I read:

'The Cayman Islands economy is the most stable in the Caribbean and the government, backed by the UK, operates a guaranteed land registry system. This affords you that your purchased property does in fact belong to you and will remain until such times as you may wish to sell. Agency fees are entirely paid for by the seller.

*With no taxes on profits, capital gains, **income** or any withholding taxes charged to foreign investors, the Cayman Islands offer an excellent return on investment along with the stability and security of being a British Commonwealth State. Additionally, there are no estate or death duties payable on assets held in the islands, so this is the ideal place to set up trusts and savings.'*

That's a pretty awesome attraction for big business and money talks. Correction, money shouts and the sound carries a long way. There are innumerable deals in process to carve up Grand Cayman as the local population will readily tell you (well, they told me with one voice.) None of these deals ever mention conservation. It so happens that the subject of deals recently arose in politics and, during my visit, the premier had been deposed awaiting trial on just such corruption charges. A politician on the make: tut, tut, it would never happen in the UK.

Meanwhile, to move on with the conservation policy . . .

Black Coral

It's on the endangered species list as well. This deeper water coral has a great attraction for those making jewellery and it makes very lovely jewellery.

Black coral is the slowest growing of all corals, making growth 200 times slower than your fingernails or the movement of continents. It used to be common in Cayman waters but again, sadly, exploitation has now all but eradicated it. The Caymans have strict laws, in case any remains, to ban its extraction. But with up to 18,000 visitors a day it is a big commodity.

An advert (below) includes their conservation policy which is even used as a selling point. So, apparently, it is OK to plunder Honduras and Belize's reefs for this endangered species: as long as it doesn't come from the Caymans. Hardly a conservation policy and who polices this law and how do you prove provenance?

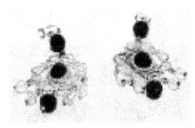

Inexpensive Hand Crafted Trinkets, Paintings, Photos, Carvings and Statues from many of Cayman's most talented artists can be found at Pure Art. Known for their diverse creative selections and many inexpensive items, Pure Art is a favorite among souviner hunters and gift seekers.

Black Coral is not taken from Cayman Islands waters for use in any products sold here; it is imported for crafting from offshre locations including Honduras; harvested by professional divers and taken from depths and locations well beyond recreational dive limitations.

Want your arts and craft products shipped to your home? No problem, all of our recommended galleries ship worldwide and provide online tracking. Duty exemptions for locally produced crafts extend to shipped products so you will not incurr any additional charges beyond shipping costs.

Be sure to check our coupon section for special savings on arts & crafts, jewelry, paintings, souvenirs and much more.

Black coral is black coral, and the country is awash with it. It is also estimated that for every kilo harvested legally under license, at least three times that amount is landed illegally.

Honduras has hardly the reputation of being law compliant but that's another story. You can buy the jewellery everywhere and this **endangered** species is even given away free in a sales pitch (following page).

If you wish to buy some and are worried about customs, the offer to ship worldwide **duty free** for local crafts solves that problem. This means it is imported into countries which ban its sale in that country. This is a UK overseas territory, and the UK government is overseeing these actions, but lobbying is beginning to pay off. The WSPA (World Society for Protection of Animals) has succeeded in getting the subject of the turtle farm before UK parliament and sympathetic MPs are looking for a ban. Can I offer a bit of advice to the Cayman (and UK) governments? There is a way out here (I often wonder if anyone ever takes my advice).

On the previously mentioned idyllic, tiny island of Bequia, part of the island state of St Vincent and the Grenadines, a single road leads from Port Elizabeth to the remote side of the island and a turtle sanctuary. This is supported entirely by donations and one person's love and devotion to these iconic animals. In an effort to restore numbers, nesting turtles are tracked and the eggs dug up. They are hatched in a hatchery and reared past the vulnerable stage where mortality is exceedingly high. They are then released at night on to the same beach on which the eggs were laid. Tagging proves a fantastic return rate as adults. Not only that but, any turtles found injured by outboard motors or caught in fishing nets have their wounds treated and they are safely returned to the sea: strictly no eating.

So Grand Cayman, it seems a good idea to forget the turtle steaks and get with the conservation. Bequia does it with a handful of visitors a day. You have thousands. You will be rewarded by universal support to make up for any shortfall and the tourists will love it. Forget the cruise ship dock. If numbers are kept manageable, with co-operation by the companies, the tourists will love the experience of the shuttle ships rather than walking ashore. In Scotland we built a bridge to the Isle of Skye. The foreign tourists don't want to drive over a bridge: they wish to go 'over the sea to Skye' just the same as Bonnie Prince Charlie did. It's part of the charm. The jobs of the shuttle operators will be saved as well. If you are really serious about conservation, forget South Sound canals and repopulate the turtle beaches. You can afford it. However, developers' money talks and it takes a strong (and corrupt free) government to do this. In the long term you will be rewarded by the benefits of a real eco-friendly island group.

As far as the black coral is concerned, this is a worldwide issue. The first step would be to ban not only its extraction but its sale as well, as many island states and other countries already have. Jewellery made from Caymanite (a local dense rock) is equally charming and could easily be pushed up a level to compensate.

Of course all this is just more of my observations based on experience, and my last experience in this book is the one I will most remember until my dying day.

24

OZ

When Captain James Cook sailed into Botany Bay on 6th May 1770 to claim Eastern Australia for the British, he probably thought it was just another colony to add to the list. If he thought the flora and fauna were just as run of the mill, he would have been even more wrong. Of course it wasn't called Botany Bay then. He had yet to name it. It is said that he called it that after the profusion of plants he saw there when he sailed in. I surmise it may have been slightly less straightforward. On board was a naturalist, one Joseph Banks, a plant collector from the Royal Horticultural Society at Kew. He must have thought all his birthdays had come at once. These plants were unique in every way, many distinct from all the known species and sub species then known to science. He ended up giving his name to the scientific classification of many. I can just imagine Cook trying to drag him away to continue his voyage: such would have been his enthusiasm. He may have even complained about the enormity of the amount of specimens hauled aboard. Botany Bay seemed the perfect name to sarcastically make his point.

Plants were not the only things that were unique. It may have taken some time to realise that most of the indigenous mammals were also unique: different to all known species in the world at that time. Kangaroos were obviously different, on the face of it, but the real difference had yet to be revealed. Present were what looked like ordinary mammals, but not as they knew them. They were mammals ie warm blooded, covered in hair, pentadactyl limbs, suckled their young, all the usual markers except that they were not placental. They all had pouches and gave birth at an early stage in development. Babies were not developed in the womb. More anomalies eventually came to light: a bear that wasn't a bear but a lookalike and mammals that laid eggs, one of which had a beak. Up until then any suggestion would have been laughable fiction. These huge differences must mean that these life forms evolved separately from the rest of the world's flora and fauna. It's easy to understand now but evolution wasn't thrown into the creation argument for another hundred years. Banks must have thought he had landed on another planet.

One more quirk of nature was the strange indigenous human population: proving that the claim by the Dutch, to be the first to discover Australia in the early 1600s, was false. It had been discovered 50,000 years previously. Banks even studied their customs in the relatively short time that he spent there. They may have been strange to him (and he strange to them) but they certainly weren't just ignorant savages. Their culture may have been vastly different but it had to be. They had to be well adapted to live in that different land, as would become obvious once the white man started exploring that sub continent's harsh inner environment.

It didn't take long for the white man to stamp his authority with superior weapons. 'Civilisation' comes at a price. The indigenous animals suffered as well and any that threatened the new influx of settlers were eradicated, but this is a vast land and many species managed to survive. Not so the next species. 'Is it a wolf, is it a tiger?' A simpler way to put it is, 'Is it of the dog or the cat family?' It's none of these apparently. The species is (was) unique. It fitted the description of a wolf but had stripes at its rear quarters and, of course, the young developed in a pouch. It could also hop on its hind legs. It wasn't related to either the wolf or the tiger. The product of convergent evolution: it only looked like a dog and, with the stripes and feline hunting methods, was reminiscent of a tiger. It was the apex predator of Australia and Tasmania, the thylacine or Tasmanian tiger. It clashed with the white man's ideals and threatened the newly introduced livestock. A bounty was put on its head. There is footage on the internet of the last two thylacines that existed in a Hobart zoo. The last one died on 7th September 1936. Previously the animal was in great demand as an oddity and captured specimens were sent to zoos around the world where they languished. Prior to that conservation groups were crying for it to be protected and, true to form, too late as usual. The Australian government granted that protection on 10th July 1936: as you may have worked out, 59 days before the last one died. To hold up that scandal as an example to the rest of the world, conservationists hold a *National Threatened Species Day* in its memory. That title belittles the enormity of the crime. It should read *National Threatened Species, Genus and Family Day*. Species are threatened all the time but never families in terms of taxonomy.

As a respecter of nature I can only feel a sense of loss and shame at what my species has done to that magnificent creature. There are many threatened species today and extinctions happen but there always seems to be another sub species which survives somewhere else in the world. Red kites were threatened with extinction from the UK, pre protection days, but they thrived elsewhere. Even if all red kites in the world were eradicated, there would always be other kite species. The mammoths became extinct 10,000 years ago but there are other related elephant species surviving. Tigers may be persecuted into extinction in the world but other cat members of the taxonomic family *Felidae* will live on, including the moggy lying in front of the hearth. The Pyrennean ibex became extinct as recently as 2000 but there are many other ibex species. A more important (to us) family is *Homininae*. The thylacine extinction is equivalent to the extinction of all chimpanzees and bonobos, all gorillas, all orang-utans, all of us, right down to the very last human being on earth. It may happen, eventually, but is unthinkable in the present era of life on earth. That's what happened to *Thylacinidae*. There are no cousins. The thylacine was the sole surviving member. There used to be other species but they only exist in fossil records from millions of years ago. It was unique in the world. It developed in geographical isolation. When they were declared extinct in 1986, the official time lapse for the classification of 50 years applying, they were extinct, period.

Or were they?

There are many reports of sightings and indeed contact with thylacines. One farmer kept a diary of sightings. Stories abound, one even telling of a life/death struggle when one was wrestled by an individual when attacked. However, you would think a digital camera or mobile phone would come in handy to corroborate these tales. With no such hard evidence, at the moment, they can be consigned to the same fairy tale book as the abominable snowman 'Bigfoot', my country's very own 'Loch

Ness Monster' and extra-terrestrials in flying saucers. Sadly, thylacines are still officially extinct.

Or are they?

Can modern science come to the rescue with cloning? There is plenty of fresh DNA to be had from many well preserved specimens from different locations. It has been done with the aforementioned Pyrennean ibex with limited success. A clone only lived for seven minutes making it the only species to go extinct twice, but science is getting better all the time. If the proposed re-creation of the woolly mammoth is being considered, then surely the thylacine can lay better claim to this Lazarus like miracle. The woolly mammoth died out 10,000 years ago of natural causes such as climate change after the last ice age, albeit some have suggested that primitive human hunting played a part. On the other hand the thylacine died out within some peoples' living memory and it was definitely we humans who wiped it out: although competition from introduced dingoes and disease, due to lack of a remaining genetic diversity, apparently didn't help. Genetic diversity in cloning would be achieved relatively easily because there are many sources from different individual remains. That would be a true breakthrough in modern science. It would also ease my conscience.

It's not going to happen in my lifetime and I'll never see a thylacine apart from those on the film. I can, however, see some of the other strange plants and creatures which fascinated Joseph Banks. I can go to Australia.

The change in my homeland brought about by oil exploration in the North Sea has brought mixed fortunes. Wildlife has had to cope with oil spills and offshore development. Onshore development engulfs more and more countryside with the increasing population requiring housing, storage yards and office blocks. The human population has thrived financially and there seems to be no end to the bonanza. That will surely come as it's not infinite. Personally, I can afford modest travel and some other luxuries due to that boom. I have no personal connection with the oil industry but thrive because of the economic effect, so I would be a hypocrite to knock it completely. Another plus is that, especially in the early days, an influx of specialist staff came from all over the world with their families. Some became great friends and it was very sad to wave goodbye when eventually they were posted back home. It wasn't final though, as we stayed in touch. They could come and stay here to visit friends and we could visit them. I certainly could and Australia was definitely on the list.

Perth, Western Australia is a beautiful city. Many Scottish friends have settled there. Socialising took up much of the short time spent there. Parakeets and kookaburras whetted my appetite but I had a list of other species to see. Where else to see the black swan, symbol of Western Australia, but the Swan River? Brisk six mile walks every morning, as everyone seems to do, keep the population looking fit and healthy. It was a lovely winding river but no black swans. Well, it's a big river. I realised I am not going to have time to do the backwoods thing, venturing into the bush (there's more than one) so the only recourse is the dreaded zoo.

Perth zoo is one of the better ones. It is not cramped and most animals 'appear' happy. The indigenous ones that are not extinct are fascinating. Here was the egg laying echidna but, unfortunately, no platypus which was a disappointment. There is a platypus house in Melbourne but I wasn't going to Melbourne so I never saw the answer to the childhood conundrum, 'What has a body covered in hair, a beak and lays eggs?' I never knew there were so many species of kangaroo and wallaby so I have to admit that zoos are certainly educational. I had to settle for a good day out in civilisation. Perth though, wasn't the end of the trip. I didn't travel all that way just to visit friends and the zoo. The rest of Australia had to be visited as well.

Flying from Perth to Sydney brings home the vastness of the country. That was just the coastal strip down there. Sydney was sightseeing only, crammed into the five days available. The Sydney Harbour Bridge, Bondi Beach, the Darling River and the Opera House: the tiles of which had to be counted to see if the stated two and a half million figure was correct (I made it around about that). The few that were missing I could have offered to fix but I was reminded I was on holiday. A great visit but tiring and I had an even better trip planned to see the real natural attractions in the wild: two weeks in Queensland. An experience with a red back spider in a garage in Perth brought home the natural dangers. The population there accept the danger and have got used to it, but they are wary. It put the wind up me though, so I would have to be careful in Queensland and I did try.

Port Douglas is billed as a reef town 'where the rainforest meets the reef', both fascinating attractions for me and that's why I chose it. It's on many tourists itineraries. Most of it didn't disappoint. The Great Barrier Reef, though, is fifteen miles offshore so the rainforest stops that amount short. I accepted the poetic licence. The trip from Sydney by air further exemplifies this country's size as I travelled from the relatively cool South Australian autumn to the blistering tropics. That was a shock to the system I hadn't allowed for. The date was 1st March and that time of year in Queensland is significant. Landing at Cairns Airport the slatted walkway led to the terminal building. As you walked along every slat let the heat in. It was like walking past a bank of elements from an electric fire. Surely it can't be that hot outside? The terminal is air conditioned, of course, and going outside under cover to the awaiting taxi is bearable. The taxi is also air conditioned. On the thirty mile journey to Port Douglas there is a golf course. It looked so perfectly manicured but no one was playing golf. That doesn't happen in Scotland on a fine day. The reason became clear later. Stepping out into the heat at the apartment took the breath away. The taxi thermometer recorded 37°C. Hot, but not as hot as Perth's 40°C. First things first, let's get some provisions. We weren't slumming it but, hey, no top class hotels on our budget. The girl at the desk advised us that the centre of town was 250 metres away and that there was a bus every twenty minutes. 'A bus for 250 metres? I'll walk thank you.' 'Suit yourself', she said with a shrug of the shoulders. And we walked, but we didn't walk back. A sauna is not for walking in. Hence the reason for no play on the golf course and no play full stop. The Southern US is bad for summer humidity but if you walked with your mouth open here, you could drink it.

Let's get to the beach to cool off. Now I'm still thinking coral sands and reef picturesquely in my mind. This is no coral island. This is a sub-continent with big rivers draining sediments from rainforest to the sea, which is like soup: hot soup at that, 32°C, from the sauna into the Jacuzzi. Prickly heat in the ocean is not keeping cool. Well, only a swimming pool sized part of the ocean within the shark and jellyfish net, and it was rigorously policed by a lifeguard. Sod this we'll go for a walk along the sands instead. With feet paddling in the shallows, away we went. 'Peep, peep' the whistle blew shrilly. 'Get out of the water.' I tried to ignore it, insulted at being treated like a child. 'If you do it, everyone will be doing it.' 'So?' The 'dog eat dog' doctrine of my childhood rising to the surface. Apparently you are not even allowed to paddle outside the netted area.

As the heat intensified to the 40°C mark, a very different 40°C from that of dry Perth, there was nothing else for it. I wasn't going to sit in the small apartment pool for two weeks. If I was going to appreciate Queensland properly I needed air conditioned transport and a small hire car fitted the bill: the hire office entrepreneurially situated across from the apartment block. I wasn't the first to be disappointed with the beach. That really opened the door for adventure. As a free agent I went exploring to try to find the real wildlife of Queensland.

First stop was only a mile away at a small wildlife park on the outskirts of Port Douglas. On the tourist trail, it was a way to see koalas. A great attraction as you could stroke them and feed them. Hardly wild but the only place I saw them, so I cannot complain. What's this? A stone curlew walking around, the same rare bird as the ones I had seen in the East Anglian fens in the UK. It wasn't captive as it flew easily around. They have a large range but I didn't expect this large. When I got home and researched it, it was apparently a bush stone curlew: a sub species, although it looked the same to me. I couldn't possibly be an expert on stone curlews having only seen one or two in my life.

There was a slimy green pool, completely covered in duckweed, with nothing of interest in it according to the baggage. Two funny round thingies sticking out of the water suggested frogs or similar, but they weren't moving. Closer inspection caused a massive swirl. The 'frogs' were its eyes. The baggage screamed embarrassingly as is usual. It became a habit in Australia. A huge crocodile thrashed around in the weed, taking us by surprise. And it was huge, seven or eight metres. I had seen plenty of crocodiles in Borneo at an overcrowded, cruel crocodile farm (where they produced skins to create shoes and handbags for the affluent Asian market) but nothing of that size. Apparently it was not even full size according to the guide, Ozzie crocodiles grow big. My jumping backwards is an innate reaction to quick movement. I am not afraid of mice but they provoke the same instinctive self-preservation movement in an unexpected encounter. I am not particularly afraid of crocodiles either, as long as they are there and I am here. I was to learn more of the Queensland crocodiles later in my travels. 'There and here' are relative.

It was a real first taste of Queensland nature and I relished further experience. That was definitely to follow.

As we drove north towards the town of Mossman there was another surprise. Instead of the much publicised rainforest, there were fields and fields of sugar cane and beautiful specimen plants they were. I hadn't done my homework. Raw sugar is Australia's second biggest export after wheat, forty million tons of it being exported annually. Ninety five percent of that amount is grown in Queensland, contributing $2.5 billion dollars a year to the economy. I am certainly no stranger to sugar cane but associated it with Caribbean islands and the flourishing of the terrible slave trade. That was naïve of me as the required conditions for its healthy growth ie right amount of rainfall, good drainage and fertile soil can be found in many places throughout the tropics and Queensland provides these criteria perfectly. Having a horticultural and botanic curiosity I had to have a closer look. A railway system takes the harvest to the coast and this stands redundant until the harvest from June onwards. This was the growing season and a walk up the track gave an insight into its healthy growth. The fields are planted out with short cuttings of stem and covered with soil. From a single cutting up to a dozen canes can grow with each one full of raw sugar. These ones were far superior in number and health to any I had seen elsewhere.

These fields were once rainforest which was cleared for sugar production and that's a big chunk of rainforest. In the past it was acceptable practice but now the Australian government is wiser. They now realise, as many governments are doing, the value of rainforest to nature and to ourselves. That cannot be undone just like that and humans have to survive, but in future no large scale felling will be taking place in Australia. Unfortunately, it is not so elsewhere.

The cane fields, though, are not devoid of wildlife. Birds of prey patrol them and many animals find food and refuge in the grass forest. A couple of cane toads disappeared off the track into the thickets. They are huge and I followed to try and get a picture. These are non-indigenous, introduced in the 1930s to combat the cane beetle. They had a devastating effect on other wildlife that tried to eat them. They are highly poisonous, especially to snakes. That's rich, considering they are the deadliest snakes on earth but they have a right to be there, unlike the toads. These toads are now spreading way beyond the cane fields and are now threatening wildlife right across tropical Australia despite efforts to control them. Mink and grey squirrels pose the same spreading threat in my home country, along with many other introduced plants and animals. Mess with nature at your peril. For any perceived up side there are always many more down sides.

I didn't get my picture, despite investigating a few rustles in the undergrowth. One movement was the disappearing tail of a dark looking snake, too quick for my camera shot. I'm no Steve Irwin and I was careful, or so I thought. By this time the heat was getting to me and I retreated to the air conditioned car interior to continue my northward journey.

Driving through Mossman there was a fork in the road leading inland so I took it and found myself in the centre of an Aboriginal village. Among these different people I felt uneasy. A fear of the unknown and ageing left me feeling vulnerable. I had landed in ghettos before and didn't like the welcome I received. I drove through and gave the town a miss. There was a local beauty spot to be visited nearby, indicated on the tourist map: the Mossman gorge and falls. The rugged path is well worn and obviously regularly maintained. Spiny vines at each side were pruned back for easy access to the falls although they did reach out their new growth towards the path again. It was a popular spot for gap year students and they were using its waterfall as a chute down to the pools below. I pressed on upstream and the path petered out. Those vines in their profusion blocked the way so I gave up. They were just too sharp. It's a pity because the rainforest higher up looked appealing.

Next day, the first stop was the banks of the Daintree River in the eucalyptus dominated rainforest. A multitude of animal and bird species produced the background cacophony. A visitor centre had an array of early 20th century photographs of the forest and the lumberjacks who were felling it. They were dwarfed by the enormity of just the girth of these logs. The trees were every bit as tall as the Borneo giants. At one time the whole forest consisted of these monsters. Not anymore. These photographs are a sad reminder of the devastation of whole ecosystems, but all is not lost. New growth forest under protection is already an impressive height and future generations will hopefully continue to repair the damage and see the regeneration through to fruition. In fact, most of the rest of Queensland seems to come under headings such as National Forest Reserve, National Park, National Timber Reserve or National State Forest.

Not far after the river crossing there is a walkway through the new forest canopy which is already 70 feet. Below, a cassowary was sifting through the forest floor. Quite rare, because of loss of habitat, it is Queensland's emblem symbolising their excellent regeneration policy. In the canopy many other species kept your eyes busy but it was the spider I remember the most, for a reason. It had spun a web between two branches close to the walkway and it was HUGE, getting near to hand size. There was no point in taking a picture as there was no reference to compare its size with so I asked the baggage to hold her hand next to the web with the motionless spider and I got my picture. When we got home she made up a photo album, as she does, with captions beneath. The spider picture reads 'My hand next to a rainforest spider. Luckily it is dead.' I should have held my tongue but out it came. 'It wasn't dead.' I was lucky. There was no frying pan handy. It became somewhat of a talking point among friends who glowered at me inferring, 'How could you?' In my defence I explained that this was a web spider, not a hunting spider. It wasn't liable to leap off its web and attack her. I think?

That was once we were back at home but meanwhile the trip continued.

Onwards toward Cape Tribulation where the reef is at its nearest point to land, a fact that ancient mariners learned to their cost thus giving it its well-earned name. I spotted the ocean and white sands through the mangrove thicket. Let's have a look.

There was a rough path through the tangle and then a beautiful vista opened up, miles of pristine beach and not a soul in sight, including lifeguards. This was more like it. There was even a breeze, a rarity up until now. We walked and we paddled, watching tiny wading birds dodging the waves and oceanic ones at sea plummeting through the surface. We took photographs of the pure white cockatoos and colourful parrots in the mangroves. The beach seemed to go on forever towards the cape. We had better get back. Where was that path again? We searched the mangroves up one or two blind alleys until we found the right one back to the car.

We then drove to Bloomfield and the road to Cooktown started to get poor. We called it a day, a wonderful day. We must do this again. There is a reason for my describing that day as will be seen later.

Port Douglas is a nice little town in which to spend the day, popular with tourists. If the heat gets too overpowering the little air conditioned shops provide relief. The trees on the central reservation of the main street are festooned with black shapes. There are hundreds of them. Australian fruit bats are big. Gigantic if you compare them with my garden pipistrelles. At dusk they awake from their slumber and the squabbling noise is deafening until all are gone on their nightly foraging and it falls silent. Why don't they roost in the forest? It may be as a refuge from predators such as snakes. They would be easy prey during the day. However, it's an enjoyable sight, seeing them flap away and disappear into the dusk. During the day, it's a nice walk to the end of the pier and just a little cooler. Two young boys are fishing. 'Any luck?' 'Two groupers, just the right size for the frying pan.' Maybe I'll try one for tea at a restaurant and it so happened there was one on the pier, built out over the water. A sign said *George, feeding time 5pm*. How did they know I was here? I couldn't resist it. My namesake apparently was a grouper which came regularly at that time for feeding. I've done the giant tarpon feeding in Cayman and hand fed the wild stingrays in Antigua but this was new. There was also a free glass of prawns with your drink as an enticement to patrons. No second bidding required. At the appointed hour a big bundle of tuna carcasses were tied to a rope and dangled about two metres above the surface. Is he going to drop them in or just dangle them above the surface? After another two rounds of drinks with no more free prawns (I am Scottish), no sign of George. I suggested to the dangler that the two little boys may have caught George. 'Hardly' was the reply, 'unless they had a steel hawser and a 4WD land rover in low ratio.' Who was he kidding? I suggested it was a rip off to sell the beer. 'He'll be here tomorrow, guaranteed, because he'll be really hungry.' 'Oh aye, I'm not falling for it twice.' 'If he doesn't show up you can have your drinks on the house.' I was back next day. The appointed hour came and we waited with prawns and drink in hand. He was late, two whole minutes late. It was the suddenness and the unexpected enormity that was the shock. The waters broke. The baggage screamed (louder than usual). She wasn't the only one. I dropped a prawn. It wasn't a fish, it was a mouth. Somewhere back in the depths was its body. This mouth reared up the two metres and devoured all the tunas in one snap. Two heads only remained and it came up again to polish them off. If I had swung from that rope I could have been accommodated easily in that chasm. The telling of the Christian bible story of Jonah and the whale is a misnomer. That book doesn't mention a whale.

Jonah 1:17 'Now the Lord had prepared a great fish to swallow up Jonah. And Jonah was in the belly of the fish three days and three nights."

Clearly it was a fish. Anyhow, whales may be big but they cannot swallow anything that size as most are krill eaters. Even killer whales would have to rip off bits of him. There are not many fish to fit that bill either but there is one and I can testify. The story should be corrected to read *'Jonah and the grouper'*. Then I might believe it.

Just another of Queensland's surprises of nature, many more to come . . .

The reason I visited the town of Cairns one day was twofold. A really long cable car runway through a section of rainforest takes you up to the small settlement of Kuranda. Although quite tourist orientated, it is exhilarating and well worth a visit. The second reason was to visit the reef. You can see it omnipresent on the horizon, wall to wall. The Great Barrier Reef is the biggest living reef in the world at 1,500 miles long, not to be missed surely. Normally I would ask locals to take me out to a reef but I couldn't find any and at fifteen miles, I would play safe. I went for an organised (and well publicised) excursion. The two unconscious Aboriginal drunks on the pavement gave tourists (that includes me, I have to remind myself) a first impression of native life and it's not a nice impression. We board the ship to discover there are another 250 people on board. This is not good news. Ah well, it is a big reef. Another surprise, the crew come round with jellyfish suits for which you have to **pay**. I wasn't keen and was prepared to chance it but the baggage insisted. Yet another surprise: skin-tight blue Lycra. It's not a pretty picture that the baggage took, with great difficulty, trying to keep the camera steady due to her laughter. As we drew nearer, you could hear the giant Pacific waves crashing in the distance and getting louder and louder. This should be good. The ship stops. There is a platform with a helicopter. We can't stop HERE, the reef is THERE. People are getting into the water. This apparently is it. I follow. There is a lump of rock with fish swimming around. They are not even coral fishes. It looks as if they are fed regularly to keep them there. This is not the reef. My head kept bumping into Japanese female bums. It's difficult to apologise underwater with a snorkel in your mouth. It wasn't intentional, it was inevitable. There were more people in the water than fish. I was back on board within five minutes, totally disillusioned. I should have known. On deck some were being treated for jellyfish stings THROUGH THEIR SUITS. Why were we wearing them then? I asked about the helicopter and was told it was to take people out to see the reef. That might be better but, alas, apparently it wasn't flying today. All in all, big rip-off, and it wasn't cheap. If you hadn't snorkelled before and never seen fish underwater, it may be appealing but to a seasoned campaigner who had been attracted by the thought of a spectacle of world renowned, living, underwater beauty, it sure was a let-down. I disembarked, kicking myself and shaking my head, muttering again, 'I should have known, I should have known.'

There was one other thing I had to do before leaving Queensland. Explore the Daintree River itself. I asked of fishermen on the wharf at Port Douglas and was given the phone number of a local with a boat who fitted the bill. We arranged to meet at, would you believe, the Aboriginal town of Mossman which is where he lived. The result of that meeting was an education in more ways than one. He was a white Australian with a 4x4 and boat in tow. I met his son, a spritely typical twelve year old, and his Aboriginal friend. Black as the ace of spades and a gleaming white smile from ear to ear. 'Pleased to meet you sir' as he shook my hand. It hit hard. Here was a native Australian, intelligent and educated. His smile never faded, so genuine it seemed that he really was pleased to meet me. That smile is still with me. It serves as a reminder to me not to prejudge people. I thought I didn't in general but I just had and that lesson was to be reinforced later that day. 'Would I like to fish for barramundi?' Does Dolly Parton sleep on her back? I had heard tales of the legendary huge barramundi of Australia's great rivers and estuaries. We would cook one for dinner on the riverbank if we got any. Both we and the boys visited a pond and the little black lad netted small fish expertly with a weighted throwing net, that primitive but effective method of fishing. These were the bait. We left the boys and headed for the river, boat in tow. 'Get this on your exposed skin. A tub of lard like substance was given to me. 'I already have on sun cream and insect repellent.' A shake of the head, 'You'll need this. River insects here don't respect high street brands, especially at this time of year.' I had previously got it wrong with my repellent, putting it on in the evening but the Aussie mozzie here is a daytime bloodsucker. I couldn't understand it until I spotted one feeding its face from my leg on the balcony in full sun and it was huge compared to the Caribbean ones. The resultant delayed itch though is the same.

Duly launched we set off up that mysterious watercourse. Crocodiles were sunning themselves on mud banks, watching us go by and clouds of sand-flies rose to attack. The lard stuffie worked, almost, only a few bites. 'Don't sit on the edge of the boat.' 'Why?' 'Crocs.' 'It's OK' I say, 'I'm hardly likely to miss one of them coming towards me'. 'You don't understand George.' We are now on first name terms. 'They stalk the boat from underneath. They can stay under for up to half an hour and when

239

they see any movement, they lunge, faster than you can pull back. It's normally the arm that they catch and they pull you in. It happens all the time. So DON'T sit on the edge of the boat.' Jeez, point taken. 'Have a beer.' He has a crate of Fosters on board, as I have on my apartment balcony, ready to feed the fridge. No better way to avoid dehydration, pleasure wise anyway, maybe not medically. He takes out a box of tissues and wipes the tops. 'What's this for?'

'Leptospirosis, they're antibacterial wipes.' Seeing my puzzlement, he continues, 'Ever heard of Weil's disease?' That rang a bell. It so happens that I had. A friend of mine, in his student gap year travels, had been working on a banana plantation and landed in hospital for six weeks in a critical condition, nearly losing his life. Now where was that again? Oh yes, Queensland, Australia. Gulp!

'But, I thought that was caught from rat urine?' 'Precisely, we have a big rat problem due to the sugar cane.' He went on to explain more. 'They destroy thousands of tons yearly, and that's not all they eat. Their numbers fluctuate but are at a peak at this time of year. They are everywhere.'

'So what has that to do with the beer?' 'You can never tell where these crates have been stored, outside corner shop back doors, in sheds, on balconies (oops), etc. They may be attracted by the smell of the dregs in the empties or just foraging for anything edible, and they urinate everywhere.' He further explained that he had already washed down the bottles before leaving. 'Oh, well' I explained, 'I did see a couple in the cane fields right enough, and a hint of a brown snake fleeing.' He nearly choked on his beer. 'The cane fields, you were in the cane fields?' 'Why yes, but I was careful.' It seemed anything I mentioned was a no, no. 'Queensland' he continued, 'is home to the seven most deadly snakes in the world and they all like to hunt rodents in the cane at this time of year. With the heat they are particularly active and aggressive at this time of year as well. They are not your trivial Pommy adder (I took exception to the Englander reference). They will attack any body heat. It doesn't need a full bite either. Even an abrasion and you are dead. End of story. Nobody in their right minds would go into the cane fields at this time of year.' OMG.

Was this guy a storyteller to be believed? I wasn't going to ask for any proof in this instance, remembering my friend's plight. He sure could tell a lot about that part of the world. Well, it was his homeland. I learned more. Rats and other rodents come in many forms in Australia. There are many indigenous marsupials but they have indigenous placental rats as well. They arrived millions of years ago but long after the development of the marsupials. When the first Europeans arrived the ship rat arrived as well, as in many other pristine parts of the world, with huge consequences for wildlife. Planting sugar cane was a great bonus for them. The snakes were not complaining either, but the ship rat probably also brought the Weil's disease bacterium with them. In the Caribbean, before bacterial knowledge or antibiotic, it was a big killer coming under the name 'Black Jaundice'. Caribbean family history records are immaculately kept and freely available and my research in that field, what with the baggage's ancestry, revealed that a high proportion of deaths of

both sugar cane workers and planter's families were attributed to just that cause.

More information . . . to combat the rat infestation the planters introduced a predator, *Felis catus domestica*, the domestic pussy. Bad news for wildlife, as if that wasn't inevitable. It is estimated that worldwide, domestic cats kill 3.7 billion birds and 20.7 billion animals per year.

With so much rich pickings, the Australian cats went feral and their numbers rocketed. They didn't of course confine their diet to rats. They decimated the more easily caught and unsuspecting indigenous marsupials and birds, rendering many species extinct and pushing others to the brink. There is now a concerted effort to drastically reduce their numbers to save other remaining species. Of course that may irk cat lovers but these wild cats are getting big, so big that they are now attacking small wallabies. Unlike the tale of the survival of the thylacine, there is photographic evidence. The photograph (previous page) is one of many. You wouldn't fancy that purring on your lap.

Other animals catch *Leptospirosis* as well, including domestic dogs which are vulnerable due to their marking and sniffing habits. The feral cats are no exception. If they don't catch it directly from eating their prey, they clean themselves by licking their fur. Apparently, though, they have built up immunity and it hasn't reduced numbers.

Anyone who goes on a tropical holiday and romantically dines Al Fresco under coconut trees may have noticed a ring of sheet aluminium tacked round the trunk. The resort staff won't tell you what it's for and if you don't already know, then be enlightened. Rats don't just eat sugar cane and bananas. They have a particular penchant for coconut and whilst in the process of gnawing through them in the trees, spray the tables below. Thankfully, agile though they are, they can't cross the aluminium sheeting and hopefully you won't get Weil's disease.

And all this before we start fishing . . .

'This seems a likely barramundi layer. Cast under that mangrove over there.' It was my first cast. Here comes dinner, a two foot long specimen but, apparently not according to the rules, TOO SMALL. You can only take them between three and four feet. Smaller and they are juveniles. Larger and they change sex to female for breeding. Strange things exist here. Ah well, we are bound to get another after that quick result. Not another one. No fish dinner playing the wild man on the banks of the Daintree for me. That didn't detract in the slightest from the adventures of that day. We got stuck on a sandbank at the estuary and he got into the water to free the hull. I would help but was quickly told to get back into the boat. He knew the dangers, I didn't.

It was at that point that another conversation started. From the estuary I pointed to Cape Tribulation and recounted the wonderful walk along the beach. His face took on that serious expression again. 'You did what?' 'Yes, I did.' 'Didn't your tour rep warn you what not to do?' 'Sorry, no rep, no tour, I am here under my own steam.' 'Then you listen here, and listen good. Did you ever consider why that wonderful beach was deserted?' 'Hmm, well no.' 'At this time of year the salties are nesting in those mangrove thickets you were poking around in and, if they feel threatened, they most certainly will attack. Then you have two choices. You can either run for it or take to the water. Just to let you know, they can run up to thirty miles an hour for short distances and you can't. That leaves the water option. Now which do you think will win in that medium.' I must have shown a nervous smile at that point because he finished with an emphatic, 'AND I'M NOT EXAGGERATING.'

Then there was the jellyfish. 'You do not paddle in the water at this time of year. These are box jellies and not to be messed with. Best avoid the water altogether.' 'What about the reef trip and the lycra suits?' 'I would advise against it but it is a huge commercial venture and they wouldn't miss the trade. The suits are a must. They lessen the seriousness.' I told him about my disappointment and the helicopter not flying. 'That helicopter is not for sightseeing at this time of year, it's for taking you to hospital if you didn't wear a suit and got stung and, by the way, you wouldn't remember the trip.' 'Oh for . . . sake!' I also asked if there were locals who could have taken me to the main reef. 'Oh yes, I myself could have taken you, but not at this time of year.'

At the end of a wonderful day during which he had pointed out tree, bird and animal species, all new to me, we pulled the boat out of the water and headed back to Mossman. There couldn't be any more dangerous surprises left, surely, but there was. I mentioned the Mossman gorge and my attempt to reach the higher rainforest. Bad news, this is the warning given to visitors (by their tour reps): *'The prickly vines which are cut back on the path are pruned daily as it is a destination on the tourist map. These vines can grow up to a metre a day at this time of year. You can land in hospital in severe pain if they break the skin. Be* *careful when you visit the gorge **but definitely go no further.'** I* might have known.

I was now thinking there can't be any more lessons to learn, surely, but there indeed was one more and one which made the biggest impression of all.

A little insight into my perception of natives in that part of the world is required.

Through the oil industry connection of many of my acquaintances, I envied their opportunities of seeing parts of the world beyond my wildest dreams but it's mostly not as adventurous as it seems. Inviting a friend in for a social evening, he asked if I could make it the following weekend as he was away on business that week. 'Where was it this time?' 'Perth (that's not Perth, Scotland), then KL (Kuala Lumpur), Saigon and home again on Saturday.' It turns out that it's not so exciting. He is met at the airport, driven to the office for a meeting and then to his hotel. Then office, airport and the same again and again, home Saturday. His office is substituted for a first class seat on the plane where he is expected to carry on working on his laptop. It's so whistle stop that he's not even jetlagged at my soiree. As he admits, he could have been anywhere. He saw and experienced nothing about the lands he visited. How awful. Geologists now, they can have more first-hand experiences. They may have to sample in remote places and befriend indigenous peoples. One geologist friend landed up in Irian Jaya. That is the name given to Western New Guinea by the Indonesian government. There is much politics involved here as it was a takeover by Jakarta, occupying the lands of non-Indonesians for the obvious exploitation of New Guinea's massive natural resources. Indigenous peoples are oppressed and regard it as an invading occupation but big western conglomerates have a vested interest, so no liberating forces. Whether it is strictly true I cannot tell but, having seen examples of Indonesian corruption first hand, I can believe it. These New Guinea people (or should I say peoples, for there are many and as many languages and cultural differences) are of Melanesian origin having occupied this part of the world long before any Indonesians arrived. Their cultures are vastly different and my geologist friend was thrown in at the deep end. He had to be accepted by these particular locals and traditionally meet them. The men and women of the village formed separate lines. They were all greeted individually, the men in a reasonably acceptable way but the women a little stranger. The visitor has to crawl through their legs from behind and stand up in front to kiss both nipples, all the way down the line. You have to understand that these people live their lives naked in the first place. Breasts are not considered objects of male sexual desire. They are functional, for feeding babies and piglets. Yes that's piglets. Pigs here are status symbols of wealth and currency, too valuable to let die of starvation if orphaned. They would be shared out to a family pre weaning so that the sow can reproduce as soon as possible again. The geologist contacted his boss to ask whether he knew of this strange welcoming party. 'Well yes, but keep it under your hat.'

I had better do the same.

I have heard of that welcome from two independent sources so it probably is true but the piglet feeding is common knowledge and there are corroborating pictures. These pictures show strange looking people doing strange things and they are akin to, and from, the same Melanesian stock as Australian Aborigines.

Also, I had read about the experience of a Scots girl: on emigrating from my home city to Australia she was shipwrecked, aged thirteen, on Prince of Wales Island in the Torres Straight between New Guinea and Australia's Cape York Peninsula. She was 'rescued' after living for five years with these strange people who were regarded as head-hunters. She lived her teenage years completely naked as they all did. Rescue came when a ship called HMS Rattlesnake called by. The crew were baffled by her language and categorised her as an albino local until someone recognised a Scots word. She spoke her (and my) native Doric with which she was brought up. I learned English at school and have got used to (with difficulty) modifying my dialect in order to be understood abroad (including over the border) but she had not. A Scottish member of the crew was summoned to translate (with difficulty) and the true story unfolded, leading to her being taken to Sydney to meet close relatives. She became a legend and earned the nickname 'Wildflower'. Incidentally, one of her rescuers was one marine biologist, Thomas Henry Huxley.

Yes that's the same one who iterated that famous phrase and became Darwin's bulldog.

That then was my picture of 'Aborigines.' So, in my mind's eye, I went to Australia expecting strange customs. I had an idea of a people with one culture but, in fact, learned that there are over 400 different groups, each with its own culture and independent language. My conception of their culture was like their regarding my culture as European. Along with what I had read, or been told, the underlying mistrust I felt when going there was of their different looks. You don't meet many Aborigines walking down my home city's main street, or indeed London or any other western city. Black Africans, Chinese, Eskimos and Mongolians, Peruvians or Indians and a various mixture of them all are common in the cosmopolitan societies of modern times, but Melanesians? These Aboriginals, Torres Straight Islanders and Papuans are non-existent in my western world experience. It's an inherent fear of the unknown.

With all that at the back of my mind I told my mentor about the drunken Aborigines in Cairns and my shunning the town of Mossman, knowing now that he lived there.

He became indignant and immediately pointed out that most of his close friends were native Australians, rather than white. They were honest, trustworthy and genuine friends, community minded and hardworking. That reminded me of my previously mentioned friend's appreciation of the same virtues in the Baffin Island Eskimo community. 'So, what's your problem? The drunks you saw probably only had a couple of cans of lager to get in that state. They have no tolerance to alcohol in their history.' I thought of the fortune I could have saved if I had had the same weakness. 'Name any city in the world without that problem? And you only saw two.' 'Oh my, he's right.' I thought of my home city and then to Scotland as a whole. With the problems of chronic liver disease the highest in the world due, in no small part, to the consumption of Usque Beatha, the cream of the barley, I realised my hypocrisy. Aborigines are hardly likely to suffer from that affliction with a couple of cans of Fosters. Here was I, categorising a whole multi peopled nation based on my coming across two drunks.

When I think now, in hindsight, about 'Wildflower' she kept her head, literally. She lived as part of the community and apparently was torn between staying and leaving them. The thought of her own family eventually persuaded her to leave but it was a heart rending decision. It doesn't sound so savage a culture after all.

This is all still another lesson in nature, human nature.

We arrived back in Mossman and the son and his friend were there.

'You see that young lad. You could learn more from him about survival here than I can ever tell you. My son owes his life to him.' I am all ears. 'Two years ago they went on a camping and fishing trip upriver, many miles inland.' I immediately empathised, as I had done the same as a boy, and my own son had to be dragged away from that little tent he shared with a friend at the end of the summer break to go back to school. 'They had a brave little fox terrier with them. During the night the black lad woke my son and quickly pushed him out of the tent. Then the terrier started barking, just as a massive crocodile smashed its way through the other end of the tent. The boys escaped but the terrier paid the ultimate price for its bravery: in one mouthful. The poor dog certainly played its part but it was the boy who reacted first and aroused the terrier. Just another reminder, don't mess with crocs in Queensland, anywhere.' 'Goodness, that's some boy.' 'Not really, it's in their genes. They're all the same.' I can't verify that but they have had 50,000 years of a head start on us.

I said goodbye to him, his son and the black lad whose parting words were, 'I hope to see you again someday.' I would love to. My fisherman's parting words to me were, 'Remember, the trick this time of year is to stay alive.'

I wasn't the only one to underestimate and downgrade these native people. Ever since colonisation they have been oppressed and regarded as second class citizens. Not anymore. Coinciding with my visit, there was issued an apology to address a great wrong and it's worth a read:

Apology

At 9:30 am on 13 February 2008, Kevin Rudd presented the apology to Indigenous Australians as a motion to be voted on by the house. The form of the apology was as follows:

Today we honour the Indigenous peoples of this land, the oldest continuing cultures in human history.

We reflect on their past mistreatment.

We reflect in particular on the mistreatment of those who were Stolen Generations – this blemished chapter in our national history.

The time has now come for the nation to turn a new page, a new page in Australia's history by righting the wrongs of the past and so moving forward with confidence to the future.

We apologise for the laws and policies of successive Parliaments and governments that have inflicted profound grief, suffering and loss on these our fellow Australians.

We apologise especially for the removal of Aboriginal and Torres Strait Islander children from their families, their communities and their country.

For the pain, suffering and hurt of these Stolen Generations, their descendants and for their families left behind, we say sorry.

To the mothers and the fathers, the brothers and the sisters, for the breaking up of families and communities, we say sorry.

And for the indignity and degradation thus inflicted on a proud people and a proud culture, we say sorry.

We the Parliament of Australia respectfully request that this apology be received in the spirit in which it is offered as part of the healing of the nation.

For the future we take heart; resolving that this new page in the history of our great continent can now be written.

We today take this first step by acknowledging the past and laying claim to a future that embraces all Australians.

A future where this Parliament resolves that the injustices of the *past must never, never happen again.*

A future where we harness the determination of all Australians, Indigenous and non-Indigenous, to close the gap that lies between us in life expectancy, educational achievement and economic opportunity.

A future where we embrace the possibility of new solutions to enduring problems where old approaches have failed.

A future based on mutual respect, mutual resolve and mutual responsibility

A future where all Australians, whatever their origins, are truly equal partners, with equal opportunities and with an equal stake in shaping the next chapter in the history of this great country, Australia.

It brings a tear to my guilty eye.

Humility is not cowardice. Quite the reverse, it is courageous. How nice would it be for the rest of the world to follow that lead? From Palestine to Northern Ireland, Iraq and Afghanistan and many more: victory only leads to oppression and hatred. Peace only comes with humility. That black boy is not a strange and mysterious person anymore. He is my friend.

Joseph Banks didn't know of any of these dangers as he explored, nor did any other explorer. There must have been many casualties. Perhaps he used aboriginal knowledge to help him. It sounds to me like he was very lucky, as I was told I was. I do know from corroboration that all these dangers do exist but I cannot say to what extent. Were they exaggerated? Should you take the same risks I did?

So, to any other like-minded madman, take advice from someone who knows before you start your exploits. DO visit Queensland. It's fabulous, both the wildlife and its people, but DO take care, especially AT THAT TIME OF YEAR.

EPILOGUE

If you have read this far I am delighted. You either have shared, or been interested in, at least some of my experiences with the natural world. Wildlife is under threat from human activity and greed. I see it from my window in the countryside around me, the UK as a whole and throughout Europe. From my limited experience in travel to the Mediterranean, the United States, the Caribbean, South East Asia and Australia, the picture is the same. However, I still have limited faith in the measures being taken to correct this and the publicity it receives in the media. Kings don't shoot tigers for fun anymore and pressure to stop cruel sports continues. On two major fronts I suspect that humans are more under threat than wildlife. Firstly, global warming may not wipe us out altogether but life will not be the same in the future. Wildlife will adapt faster than we can and may be the eventual winner but there is an even bigger threat.

When starting out in business and facing a bank manager you have to have a business plan. Mine was simple and impressed as a no fail proposition. Take cuttings from plants for free. Grow them on and sell them for money. It seems so easy for anyone to do. Mass production will follow and the money rolls in. It's at that stage that reality sets in. All the cuttings are clones of one another and that means no genetic diversity. Any individual plant prone to a particular pathogen shares that weakness with all the clones and this can lead to devastation on the production line. There is no problem to the customer buying a healthy one as this will be planted and grown in comparative isolation but where there are hundreds growing side by side there is a big risk. Even if the cuttings are taken from a wide range of parent plants growing en masse means that any disease, to which a particular variety or even whole species is prone, can be transmitted very quickly to the whole crop. Moreover, any wholesale use of fungicide or insecticide can induce immunity in offspring very quickly and the problem persists. In human terms the very same problem exists and we are all aware of antibiotic resistant strains of bacteria such as MRSA and *C difficile*.

The reason for the spread of many diseases is crowded and unhygienic conditions. If overpopulation happens in 'wild nature' individual entities just die until numbers are stabilised: resistance and isolation solve the problem to save the species. We humans don't take nature on the chin. We have ways of combating this and treat illnesses and disease in a never ending battle. As long as population is stabilised and comparative isolation is preserved, with effort, the battle can mostly be won. At the moment human overpopulation takes a back seat to climate change but do the maths and visualise a time in the not too distant future. Presently, a population of 6.5 billion is causing problems with the feeding of humans and spread of disease in the world. That's a staggering three times as many as when I was a boy. This is not a problem for most of wildlife although many species will pay the price. It is estimated that by 2050 the figure will be 9 billion. Innovation may stall mass starvation but imagine a little further, to say 18 billion, and on and on. Eventually, surely, it will become unsustainable. Hope springs eternal and it is even suggested that technology will have us colonise other planets by then. For all the advances in technology in my lifetime, I would not bank on it. Our success as a species has come about by vanquishing our natural predators, including micro-organisms causing disease. For all our efforts to create peace and harmony in the world it's not working and surely will get worse as populations explode. Wildlife will be affected most definitely but may be the winner in the end. Their resilience and will to survive with no beliefs to hinder them should see them through our potential Armageddon. The dinosaurs died out but life on earth certainly didn't. We were the winners, eventually, but we may go the same way as them and millions of other life forms in the past: winners only for a very tiny period in the history of life on earth.

Can we reverse all this before it is too late? We surely have to try and, on the face of it, it can be achieved. The obstacles are huge. The pursuit of power, race hatred, greed, beliefs and protection of lavish lifestyles stand in the way as I have experienced. The wildlife of the world sits and waits in the wings, its innovativeness and adaptability much more honed for survival than ours in our present day sheltered lifestyle. At the moment, I can only hope that my future genetic progeny are wiser than myself and my generation. Of course, all that is just another observation.

'The future depends on what we do today.'

Stop Press: that astronomic grandchild of mine is growing up. His choice is not astrophysics but medicine. What a let-down.

Acknowledgements

Mrs Flux, zoology teacher, Aberdeen Academy late 1950s.
She taught me how to think.

Kathleen, my long suffering baggage.

Sheila, the friend who persuaded me to publish.

Jacqui McDonald, a very patient and enthusiastic editor.

Stuart Cheyne, 06media, for all his knowledge and help.

www.ingramcontent.com/pod-product-compliance
Lightning Source LLC
Chambersburg PA
CBHW072245310526
45795CB00011B/88